GENDER IN

Series ed
Pam Sharpe, Patricia Skinner and Penny Summerfield

The expansion of research into the history of women and gender since the 1970s has changed the face of history. Using the insights of feminist theory and of historians of women, gender historians have explored the configuration in the past of gender identities and relations between the sexes. They have also investigated the history of sexuality and family relations, and analysed ideas and ideals of masculinity and femininity. Yet gender history has not abandoned the original, inspirational project of women's history: to recover and reveal the lived experience of women in the past and the present.

The series Gender in History provides a forum for these developments. Its historical coverage extends from the medieval to the modern period, and its geographical scope encompasses not only Europe and North America but all corners of the globe. The series aims to investigate the social and cultural constructions of gender in historical sources, as well as the gendering of historical discourse itself. It embraces both detailed case studies of specific regions or periods, and broader treatments of major themes. Gender in History titles are designed to meet the needs of both scholars and students working in this dynamic area of historical research.

Victorians and the Virgin Mary

MANCHESTER
1824

Manchester University Press

VICTORIANS AND THE VIRGIN MARY

RELIGION AND GENDER IN ENGLAND, 1830–85

Carol Engelhardt Herringer

Manchester University Press

Manchester and New York

distributed exclusively in the USA by Palgrave

Published by Manchester University Press
Oxford Road, Manchester M13 9NR, UK
and Room 400, 175 Fifth Avenue, New York, NY 10010, USA
www.manchesteruniversitypress.co.uk

Distributed in the United States exclusively by
Palgrave Macmillan, 175 Fifth Avenue,
New York, NY 10010, USA

Distributed in Canada exclusively by
UBC Press, University of British Columbia, 2029 West Mall,
Vancouver, BC, Canada V6T 1Z2

British Library Cataloguing-in-Publication Data is available

Library of Congress Cataloging-in-Publication Data is available

ISBN 978 0 7190 9564 1 *paperback*

First published by Manchester University Press in hardback 2008

This paperback edition first published 2014

Printed by Lightning Source

For my parents, with love and gratitude

Contents

Acknowledgements

This book began as a seminar paper and then grew into a dissertation under the able guidance of Jeanne Peterson, whose combination of warmth and intellectual rigour continues to delight and inspire me. While at Indiana University, and in the years since, I have also benefited from the guidance and encouragement of James Eli Adams, Dyan Elliott, Andrew Miller, Robert Orsi, and David Pace; I remain grateful to all of them for their early and continuing support.

During the years in which this project evolved into a book, I received valuable assistance in many forms, including citations, hospitality, and encouragement, from A. M. Allchin, Miriam Bailin, Joep van Beeck, Sarah Boss, Andrew Bradstock, Eamon Carroll, the late Caspar Caulfield, Sally Cunneen, Sheridan Gilley, Helen Hackett, Mary Heimann, Stanley and Mollie Hood, Ian Ker, Gerry Magill, Jeremy Morris, Denis Paz, Geoffrey Rowell, Alison Shell, and Michael Wheeler. I am grateful also to the two anonymous readers from Manchester University Press for their thoughtful comments and useful suggestions for improving the manuscript. The editors at Manchester University Press have made the publication process easier and more rewarding than I ever could have hoped.

I have been blessed with a group of friends and colleagues on both sides of the Atlantic who have provided both the intellectual support without which this book would not have been written and the friendship that makes the research and writing more enjoyable. My deepest thanks to Scott Beasley, Stephen Chapman, John Chappell, Paul Deslandes, Alice Dreger, Michael Drolet, Dan Fenton, Debbie Gershenowitz, Leigh Hayden, Maria LaMonaca, John LaRocca, Patrick Leary, Laura Leming, Scott Lewis, Laura Luehrmann, Joan Milligan, Lydia Murdoch, Paul Murphy, Paul Nagle, Hilary Nightingale, Richard Pierce, Anne Rodrick, Caroline Rose, Michael Suarez, Andrena and Bill Telford, and Liann Tsoukas. Over weekly burritos and margaritas Una Cadegan has encouraged and challenged my ideas on religion and culture, while the most collegial and congenial VICKIs – Rick Incorvati, Barry Milligan, Chris Oldstone-Moore, and Tammy Proctor – have read and commented extensively on drafts of these chapters.

I could not have written this book without the assistance of the archivists and librarians at Indiana University, the British Library, Pusey House, the Bodleian Library, the Birmingham Oratory, the Cambridge University Library, Dr Williams's Library, Lambeth Palace Library, St Deniol's Library, the Vatican archives in Rome, and Wright State University. Among this group, Fr William Davage of Pusey House deserves special mention for his many kindnesses.

Funding for various stages of this book came from Indiana University, in the form of grants and the Victorian Studies Fellowship, Wright State University, in the form of travel grants, and St Deiniol's Library, Hawarden, Wales, which generously offered a scholarship during the final stages of my research. Support in the form of boundless hospitality and a room of my own in London came from two wonderful families, Bobbie Brown's and Carla and Ingo Franke's. Without the conversations, meals, and interest in what I had found in the archives and libraries that both families provided, my trips to London would have been more infrequent, briefer, and far less congenial.

It was at the family dinner table that I first learned to talk about religion, to ask even unanswerable questions, and to debate ideas. My parents, Kath and Tom Engelhardt, are models of commitment, faith, intellectual curiosity, social responsibility, and joy to those around them, while my siblings and their spouses – Marybeth and Mark Lumetta, Christin Engelhardt, Mark Engelhardt, and Moira Konrad – have been the best support network a scholar could want. Michael, Katherine, Stephen, and Clare Lumetta have been, and continue to be, welcome and joyful distractions from the library.

Finally, I am ignoring Tom Herringer's instructions that he not be thanked here, because I know, even if he does not, the role he played in making the final stages of this project easier, by listening to me talk about the most arcane details of nineteenth-century theology, asking insightful questions, and always knowing when to take me out to dinner. I happily look forward to equal amounts of help on the next project, and to a lifetime of shared passions.

As joyfully as I acknowledge the assistance of those above, I must equally firmly claim responsibility for any errors that follow.

1

Religion, gender, and the Virgin Mary

The mother not 'out of sight'

In 1844, John Keble, an Anglican priest and popular poet, was dismayed to find that some of his friends objected to his including a poem about the Virgin Mary, 'Mother out of sight', in his second volume of poems, *Lyra innocentium*. Although Keble defended his poem as being in accordance with both Scripture and 'the doctrinal decisions of the Whole Church',[1] his friends feared that its invocation of the Virgin Mary was evidence that, in the words of one, he 'had advanced considerably in his religious opinions'[2] – in other words, that he was in danger of converting to Roman Catholicism. Even years later, this friend continued to insist that the poem, which was not finally published until 1868, 'might have been harmful originally'.[3]

Several years later, another Anglican's invocation of the Virgin Mary became the topic of a more public debate. In 1849, Priscilla Lydia Sellon, foundress of the Anglican Society of Sisters of Mercy of the Holy Trinity, in Devonport, was forced to reply to anonymous charges published in the *Devonport telegraph* that, in part because of the presence of 'a picture of the Virgin Mary in a gilt frame on the altar' in the chapel of the Sisters' orphanage in Devonport,[4] she and the other sisters were deviating from Anglican practices and leading the children in their care away from the Church of England.[5] In addition to displaying this 'highly Popish print',[6] the sisters were accused of having special devotions to the Virgin Mary and even of being secret Roman Catholics. Sellon herself was alleged to have kept a rosary under her pillow.[7]

In the public inquiry of the charges, convened by Henry Phillpotts, the Bishop of Exeter, Sellon, like Keble, invoked the authority of both Scripture and Anglican teaching in support of the print:

I placed in the oratory, to please the little ones, a print from a picture, which I suppose, may be found in countless drawing rooms in England. But because it represents the Holy Child Jesus in the arms of his mother, it is made a matter of accusation against me. Why did not these cross-questioners ask these unhappy girls *straightforwardly, whether they were taught anything which the Bible and the Church of England do not teach, or whether they ever heard any words or conversation to that tendency?*[8]

Although Sellon was more willing than Keble to acknowledge that the mere invocation of the Virgin Mary was sufficient to generate controversy, several years later she again insisted that the print was an innocent one that 'any person might have in their drawing rooms'.[9] While her attempt to define the print as a marker of bourgeois aesthetics was doomed by its being located in the chapel of her orphanage, she nevertheless rejected any accusations of Marian devotion: 'There are not any prayers addressed to the Blessed Virgin in our services ... I am quite certain that no sister has devotions to the Virgin Mary.'[10]

Keble's and Sellon's experiences were not unusual: a wide range of Victorian sources, both public and private, testifies to the fact that the reactions of Keble's friends and Sellon's foes were typical. The Virgin Mary was a controversial figure in Victorian England, especially between about 1830 and 1885. In sermons, religious tracts, political debates, public lectures, theological treatises, periodicals, and novels, Protestants denounced the Virgin Mary as an interfering mother and a pagan goddess who testified to the links between ancient and modern Rome. Catholics just as energetically rose to defend the Virgin Mary as a loving mother, of all Christians as well as of Jesus, and charged that those who thought otherwise willfully ignored divine truth. The same lines of argument were continued privately, in diaries, personal correspondence, and (no doubt) private conversations. The violence was not always rhetorical: in 1851 Daniel O'Keefe, chaplain of the Benedictine Convent at Hammersmith, complained in a letter to Sir George Grey, the Home Secretary, of hearing that effigies of the Virgin Mary and other saints had been carried in procession and 'burned on Blackheath in the presence ... of 10,000 spectators',[11] and in 1867 the anti-Catholic lectures of William Murphy on topics such as 'Purgatory, the Scapular, and the Blessed Virgin Mary coming down from Heaven to release souls out of Purgatory' inspired riots both inside and outside the lecture halls in which he spoke.[12]

Keble's and Sellon's experiences reveal the multiple, overlapping reasons why the Virgin Mary became a contested figure in Victorian England. Religious causes were, at first glance, paramount: beginning in the 1830s, the growth in the number and prominence of Roman Catholics caused public invocations of the Virgin Mary to become more common. The development, within the Church of England, of the Tractarian and ritualist movements, both of which sought to revive the Church of England's Catholic identity, also encouraged more frequent public references to the Virgin Mary. These two types of Catholicism helped cause a backlash of anti-Catholicism, one aspect of which was a greater willingness to appropriate the Virgin Mary as a symbol of a dangerous and foreign religion. Religious tensions were not, however, the only reason why the Virgin Mary became a controversial figure. Sellon herself hinted at another reason when she attributed the uproar to the age and composition of the figures in the print: 'because it represents the Holy Child Jesus in the arms of his mother, it is made a matter of accusation against me'. In a culture intent on distinguishing the genders, discussions about the Virgin Mary, especially in her role as the mother of Jesus, were a way for Victorians to articulate what characteristics were essentially feminine and which were reserved for the masculine.

Those who engaged in constructing competing images of the Virgin Mary included famous Victorians such as John Henry Newman, William Ewart Gladstone, Henry Edward Manning, Elizabeth Barrett Browning, and George Eliot. Others were once well known but now are barely remembered, including John Cumming, the Presbyterian minister at the Crown Court Church of Scotland in London, famous then as an end-times' prophet with a large congregation but now largely remembered as the subject of George Eliot's diatribe in 'Evangelical teaching: Dr. Cumming'; Catherine Sinclair, a popular anti-Catholic novelist; and Thomas Thelluson Carter, a leading Tractarian and founder of an Anglican sisterhood. Still others were obscure even then: they were rural clergymen, pamphlet authors who hid behind initials and pseudonyms, and anonymous contributors to religious periodicals.

As Sally Cunneen and Jaroslav Pelikan have shown in their surveys of Marian images throughout Christian history, representations were never either fixed or monolithic.[13] Although they are determined somewhat by the biblical evidence and tradition, how people imagine the Virgin Mary changes as the cultural context changes. The early church defined her as the *Theotokos*, or God-bearer, in order to combat heterodoxy by defining Jesus as both fully human and fully divine, while the medievals addressed her with the courtly 'Lady' that reflected chivalric traditions and aspirations. In recent years the rise of feminism has affected representations of the Virgin Mary: feminist theologians have emphasised her maternity, not so much to elevate her motherhood as to argue that, as the person who *first* made the body of Jesus, Mary provides a justification for female priests, while the intense Marian devotion of the late John Paul II may be the result of his conservative views on sexuality and women.[14] In the Victorian era, the competing images of the Virgin Mary allowed Christians to define their religious identities and to establish the essential characteristics of the masculine and the feminine. These discussions were also a way for Victorian Christians to defend a conservative approach to the Bible against new theological developments such as Higher Criticism, Protestant Idealism, and Catholic Modernism. All who contributed to the Marian discussions interpreted Scripture in the traditional way: because they believed that Scripture represented God's word, they were concerned only with how to translate and interpret it. Thus they could enter lengthy discussions about, for example, the significance of the crucifed Jesus assigning Mary to John's care. This is not surprising for, as Peter Hinchliff notes: 'A great many people continued to behave, until well into the last quarter of the nineteenth century, as if biblical scholarship was almost entirely a matter of knowing the *contents* of the Scriptures and the theological meaning which, over the centuries of Christian tradition, had come to be associated with certain books and passages.'[15]

Although Marian representations were shaped by two key debates in Victorian England – those over religion and gender norms – scholars have paid little attention to these evolving and competing representations as sources of information about Victorian culture. Studies of Roman Catholicism and Anglo-Catholicism have not considered them as a way of investigating either devotional practices or how English Catholics shaped their religious and national identities. Mary Heimann's excellent revisionist work *Catholic devotion in Victorian England*[16] gives little attention to the role of Marian devotion in shaping a Roman Catholic identity, even though the Rosary was one of the most popular devotions of the period. In this she follows the precedent set by earlier historians of English Roman Catholicism, including John Bossy, Edward Norman, and Joseph P. Chinnici. Major studies of anti-Roman Catholicism, such as Denis Paz's *Popular anti-Catholicism in mid-Victorian England* and Walter Arnstein's *Protestant versus Catholic in mid-Victorian England: Mr Newdegate and the nuns* pay somewhat more attention to the Marian component of anti-Roman Catholicism, but they do not examine in detail how anti-Catholics used the Virgin Mary to draw a contrast between biblical Christianity and pagan corruptions, between (as they saw it) stalwart, rational, British Protestantism and a weak, effeminate, continental Catholicism. John Wolffe's *The Protestant crusade in Great Britain 1829–1860*[17] contains only a brief reference to the Virgin Mary. Keble and Sellon were only two of the Anglicans who sought a greater recognition of the Virgin Mary in the Church of England, yet neither the role of such Anglicans nor their motivations have been studied in recent works such as Nigel Yates's *Anglican ritualism in Victorian Britain, 1830–1910*[18] or John Shelton Reed's *Glorious battle: the cultural politics of Victorian Anglo-Catholicism*.[19] The first exception to this general trend was John Singleton's article 'The Virgin Mary and religious conflict in Victorian Britain'[20] which examines the polemical uses of Marian devotion by Roman Catholics, Anglo-Catholics, and Protestants. More recently, I have examined primarily Anglican responses to the Virgin Mary.[21] This book expands on those articles by considering dissenting and Roman Catholic representations and so offers a more comprehensive and culturally situated analysis of Victorian representations of the Virgin Mary.

This scant scholarly interest is in sharp contrast to the significant work that has been done on the role of the Virgin Mary in Catholic cultures. Robert A. Orsi's *The Madonna of 115th street: faith and community in Italian Harlem, 1880–1950*, David Blackbourn's *Marpingen: apparitions of the Virgin Mary in nineteenth-century Germany*, Sandra Zimdars-Swartz's *Encountering Mary: from LaSalette to Medjugorge* are among the most significant works that have analysed the different ways in which men and women reacted to the Virgin Mary, and in particular how associating themselves with the Virgin Mary could allow women and girls access to the public sphere, for example through participating in festivals or by claiming to have witnessed Marian apparitions. Perhaps the traditional association of the Virgin Mary with Roman Catholicism has led scholars to assume that there was little to say about her in a predominantly Protestant culture. However, the Victorian debates refute this assumption: where Catholics are a small minority, the Marian images they promote have heightened polemical uses, while Anglican and dissenting rejections of the Virgin Mary described by Catholics reveal that negative representations of the Virgin Mary could be as theologically based and as useful in constructing an identity as were the positive images employed by Catholics.

Catholics and Protestants

Prior to the Henrician Schism, Marian devotion was an integral part of English Roman Catholicism. The Rosary was a popular devotion, Marian shrines and festivals abounded, and Elizabeth of York, the wife of Henry VII, followed the practice of well-born women to wear a girdle, supposedly the Virgin Mary's, during pregnancy. While the sixteenth-century reformers sought to reduce the attention paid to Jesus' mother, they were not hostile to her, especially in comparison to their Victorian successors. They praised her as a model of faith; they wanted merely to lower her status, not denounce her. Their condemnation of Marian shrines and relics differed more in degree than in kind from the critiques of their Roman Catholic contemporaries like Desiderius Erasmus and Thomas More. As England slowly became a (predominantly) Protestant nation during the reign of Elizabeth I (1558–1603), Marian imagery was appropriated to describe the Queen. Scholars disagree about the extent to which the Virgin Mary continued to be invoked or whether Marian icongraphy was subsumed by descriptions of Elizabeth I.[22] However, their agreement that the imagery of the Virgin Mary continued to be used in a positive way suggests a continuation of the pre-Reformation tradition, even if the object of that idealisation may have changed. At the same time, an Anglican tradition of restrained Marian devotion began to develop, beginning with Lancelot Andrewes in Elizabethan England and continuing in the seventeenth century by Andrewes as well as other Caroline divines, including William Laud's protégé Jeremy Taylor, Mark Frank and Herbert Thorndike, and the devotional writer Anthony Stafford, whose *The femall glory* was republished in 1869 by Orby Shipley, an Anglo-Catholic clergyman (and eventually a convert to Roman Catholicism).[23]

At the parish level, after the Restoration Anglican clergymen held up the Virgin Mary as an examplar of adherence to church teachings.[24] This tradition of a restrained Marian devotion was apparent in the poetry of Thomas Ken, Bishop of Bath and Wells and a nonjuror after 1689. Ken praised Mary as 'The true Idea of all Woman-kind'[25] and described her as '*Mary* ever bless'd, whom God decreed,/ Shou'd all in Glory, as in Grace, exceed'.[26] This positive tradition coexisted with one that used the Virgin Mary as shorthand for unorthodox beliefs and practices. Although the complaints could seem trivial – among the charges filed against Archbishop William Laud at his trial in 1644 was that, while he was chancellor of Oxford University, a statue of the Virgin Mary had been erected over the porch of the University Church of St Mary the Virgin – the fact was that even the apparent trivialities showed how widespread was the assumption that invocations of the Virgin Mary were sufficient evidence of deviation from Anglican orthodoxy.

Anti-Marian rhetoric was one component of the anti-Roman Catholicism that characterised England during the reigns of Elizabeth and her successors. The secret Jesuit missions in the sixteenth and seventeenth centuries, the attempted invasion by the Spanish Armada (1588), the Gunpowder Plot (1605), the periodic Jacobite invasions after 1688, and French involvement in the 1798 rebellion in Ireland all contributed to the popular stereotype of English Roman Catholics as actual or potential traitors. Partly because of a perceived link between Roman Catholicism and absolutism, anti-Roman Catholicism was one of the factors that helped incite the English Civil Wars (1642–49) and the 'Glorious Revolution' (1688–89). Even a century later, when religious tensions had somewhat subsided, violent anti-Roman Catholicism briefly reappeared with the Gordon riots in London (1780).

Anti-Roman Catholicism revived in the nineteenth century and was in some ways more significant than earlier manifestations of the prejudice. The vitality of religious conflict in this period has led Arnstein to argue that 'it is more fruitful to look upon the Victorian conflict between Protestantism and Catholicism as a separate chapter rather than as a mere footnote to studies of the Reformation,'[27] while Paz describes anti-Roman Catholicism as 'an integral part of what it meant to be a Victorian.'[28] Many Victorians voiced the standard objections to Roman Catholicism: that the priesthood denied the believer a direct relationship with the Trinity; that Roman Catholics paid more attention to objects and saints than to the Trinity; that Roman Catholicism was not scripturally based; and that Roman Catholics' blind obedience to priest and Pope predisposed them to prefer absolutist governments.

The reinvigoration of anti-Roman Catholicism was partly a response to the increasing numbers of Roman Catholics. The Roman Catholic population multiplied almost ten times, from 80,000 in 1770 to 750,000 in 1850, or to 3.5 per cent of the population, and became more urban and less dependent on the gentry. Much of the increase was due to the immigration of Irish people: by 1851 Irish Roman Catholics outnumbered English Roman Catholics by about three to one.[29] However, anti-Roman Catholicism was so well-established prior to the 1820s that there was no obvious relationship between the number of Irish and the level of anti-Catholicism in any particular area.[30]

Roman Catholics' higher public profile in the nineteenth century also contributed to the inflammation of prejudices against them. Catholic emancipation (by the Catholic Relief Act of 1829) allowed Roman Catholic men who met the property requirements to enter Parliament.[31] In the next decades the prayer campaigns for the conversion of England, which included daily repetitions of the Hail Mary, led by the converts Father Ignatius Spencer (born George Ignatius Spencer, a younger son of the second Earl Spencer) and Ambrose Phillips de Lisle (also Ambrose Lisle Phillips), revived the fear that English Protestantism was under assault, a fear that seemed to be confirmed by the restoration of the Roman Catholic hierarchy in England in 1850. This event, popularly derided as the 'Papal

Aggression', marked the end of the missionary period in England and the regional missionary government, and gave Roman Catholics a leader within their country: Nicholas Wiseman, born a Roman Catholic, who had spent most of his adult life in Rome, first as a student and then as rector at the English College there. His return to London as the new cardinal of Westminster in November 1850, only days before Guy Fawkes' Day, gave an added intensity to the annual anti-Roman Catholic activities and marked the apogee of public anti-Roman Catholicism in the nineteenth century.[32]

Anti-Roman Catholicism was further fuelled by the conversions of prominent Anglicans. A small number of privileged Anglicans, like Phillips de Lisle and Spencer, converted in the 1820s, but the public impact of these early conversions was limited. Anglicans became seriously concerned in the 1840s, when converts became both more numerous and of more prominent position. The most famous and, for Anglicans, unsettling conversion was that of Newman, in 1845. His conversion had been some time in coming: dismayed by the 1841 controversy over his Tract 90, which argued at length that there was no contradiction between Roman Catholic doctrine and the 39 Articles, in 1843 he resigned as vicar of the Church of St Mary the Virgin in Oxford. Even with these warning signs, his late-night, rural conversion in October 1845 sent shock waves throughout the Church of England. Tractarians lost one of their most prominent and articulate spokesmen, while their Anglican opponents seized on it as proof that Tractarianism 'has furnished, and continues to furnish, to Romanism all its most valuable converts'.[33] Newman was followed into the Roman Catholic Church almost immediately by Frederick W. Faber, a flamboyant and emotional man who had been Newman's protégé while a student at Oxford. Both men eventually founded Oratories, Faber's in London and Newman's in Birmingham, but the temperamental differences between the two men saw their relationship deteriorate into an open animosity that extended to relations between the two Oratories. In 1851 the Gorham Judgment precipitated the conversions of other prominent high church Anglicans, including Henry Edward Manning, Robert Isaac Wilberforce, and William Maskell, who were outraged that the lay Privy Council had defined Anglican baptismal doctrine. Manning became, like Newman, one of the most prominent spokesmen for Roman Catholicism, becoming Archbishop of Westminster in 1865 and a cardinal in 1875. Although some converts, like Manning and Wilberforce, were friends, these converts were by no means a coherent group; the relationship between Newman and Manning remained chilly at best. However, many of them did have in common an Oxford education, making them among the most privileged in England and their conversions especially disturbing to Anglicans.

Those conversions brought concern to English Protestants that Roman Catholicism was strengthening itself at the expense of the Established Church: one clergyman fretted that 'At the consecration of Dr. Manning there stood round him not less than one hundred priests who had once held posts – some of them important – in the Anglican church.'[34] The negative reactions to Keble's and Sellon's limited forms of Marian devotions were manifestations of the persistent fear that the English, particularly those of the privileged classes, would convert, not that England would be overwhelmed by Irish immigrants. The Anglican divine Charles Pourtales Golightly, a close friend of Newman's before turning against him and the Oxford Movement, was aghast at the thought that 'no less than 38 members of this University [Oxford] have joined the Romish Communion during the last four years' (1842–46).[35] In particular, Anglicans worried that the material aspects of Roman Catholicism would seduce good Protestants. Sinclair warned: 'Going merely to hear music at the convents and Popish churches often ends in going there to worship ... the excitement of listening to the Stabat Mater and such beautiful music in honour of Mary, is not only profane, but dangerous.'[36] That the prevailing concern was with defections from within rather than assaults from without, when born Roman Catholics far outnumbered converts, suggests that Anglicans perceived weaknesses in their Church. What Jenny Franchot has noted about anti-Roman Catholicism in antebellum America is also true for Victorian anti-Roman Catholicism: 'anti-Catholicism operated as an imaginative category of discourse through which antebellum American writers of popular and elite fictional and historical texts indirectly voiced the tensions and limitations of mainstream Protestant culture.'[37]

Few were as sanguine as William Lockhart's grandfather, who, on hearing that his grandson had converted, said: 'Well, young men take odd courses, now-a-days; he might have taken to the turf.'[38] More typically, these conversions profoundly affected those involved, whether they remained in the Church of England or became Roman Catholic. Those who converted suffered many hardships, including, as David Newsome has noted, 'social ostracism, alienation of friends, loss of money, position, and employment.'[39] For twenty years after his conversion Newman did not see Keble and Edward Bouverie Pusey, two close friends with whom he had shared leadership of the Oxford Movement. The grief felt by those who stayed was expressed by the high churchman and future Prime Minister Gladstone in a letter that in hindsight is doubly sad, given that its receipient, Robert Isaac Wilberforce, was to convert several years later:

I do indeed feel the loss of [Henry Edward] Manning, if and as far as I am capable of feeling anything – It comes to me cumulated, and doubled, with that of James Hope. Nothing like it can ever happen to me again. Arrived now at middle life, I never *can* form I suppose with any other two men the habits of communication ... and dependence, in which I have now for fifteen to eighteen years had with them both.[40]

That Gladstone's sense of loss was not transitory is suggested by a memorandum he wrote in 1876 listing, in chronological order, the names of people who had converted to Roman Catholicism.[41] In the decade after Hope's conversion, Samuel Wilberforce, the Bishop of Oxford and the only one of the Great Emancipator's children not to convert to Roman Catholicism, declared himself 'altogether prostrated by the Sudden (to me) perversion to Rome of my son in law & dearest daughter & can scarcely hold up my head'.[42] Gladstone's and Wilberforce's experiences were not uncommon for men of their class, for as Arnstein has observed: 'Most significant nineteenth-century Englishmen had either a close friend or relative who became a convert to the Roman Catholic faith.'[43]

Many converts were motivated by a search for the authority they believed to be absent from the Church of England. Their pre-conversion attitudes towards the Virgin Mary differed. For some, Marian devotion – or at least the desire for it – preceded conversion. The year before he converted, Faber begged Newman for permission to pray to the Virgin Mary. (Permission was denied, on the grounds that religious practices should remain distinct.[44]) On a trip to Paris in 1845, Sophia (Sargent) Ryder, whose late sister Caroline had been married to Manning, her husband George, and George's sister Sophy purchased rosaries. Sophy was given a book of Marian devotions by Manning, who was in Paris at the time.[45] All three Ryders converted in the spring of 1846. Phillips de Lisle believed that the Virgin Mary encouraged his conversion to Roman Catholicism, which occurred in 1825, when he was 16 years of age. However, Marian devotion was a stumbling-block to others. Newman confessed that even in 1843, when he had essentially given up ministry in the Church of England, 'I could not go to Rome, while I thought what I did of the devotions she sanctioned to the Blessed Virgin and the Saints.'[46] Some converts never did develop a warm Marian devotion. Manning, his gift to Sophy Ryder notwithstanding, was one of them. Nevertheless, the Virgin Mary was blamed for many of those conversions. The Anglo-Catholic bishop Edward Stuart Talbot remembered his mother saying 'that those who went [into the Roman Catholic Church at mid-century] were those who had begun to practise devotions to the Blessed Virgin'.[47] This displacement conveniently allowed Anglicans to ignore the fundamental issues of ecclesiastical authority that troubled the converts and to dismiss them as having an inferior religiosity.

While converts were not necessarily motivated by a desire for more Marian devotion than was allowed in the Church of England, once within the Roman Catholic fold they were likely to practise it. Those converts were a key reason why Marian devotion, which had not been a significant part of recusant Catholicism, revived from the 1830s. However, the converts demonstrated a range of styles of Marian devotion. The baroque extravagance of Faber's prayers was balanced by the restrained warmth typified by Newman and William Bernard Ullathorne, a born Roman Catholic who became Bishop of Birmingham at the restoration of the Roman Catholic hierarchy. Manning's relative lack of interest in Marian devotion did not hinder either his ecclesiastical career or his popularity among English Roman Catholics, suggesting that his devotional style also was representative of English Catholicism. The increase in Marian devotion may have been, as Susan O'Brien argues, attributable in part to the congregations of French and Belgian nuns who began to establish English houses in the 1830s,[48] and it may also have been, as Barbara Corrado Pope has suggested, an expression of anti-modernism.[49] Regardless of their motivations, in practising Marian devotion the converts enacted on a personal level what was occurring on an institutional level. In the Roman Catholic Church the century 1850–1950 is called the Marian age because of the many reported Marian apparitions, the declaration of the Immaculate Conception (1854), and a general increase in Marian devotion.[50]

Marian devotion had polemical as well as religious uses. Unlike their recusant forebears, who were forced by the legal and social situation to suppress public expressions of their faith, Victorian Roman Catholics were emboldened by their civic equality. Their greater confidence led them to invoke the Virgin Mary as a means to assert their identity as Roman Catholics. In England this move was given official sanction by Wiseman, who, when he became Archbishop of Westminster, put an increase in devotion paid to the Virgin at the top of his list of priorities for the Roman Catholic Church in England.[51] Wiseman's formative years were spent in cultures that encouraged Marian devotion: he was born in Seville, into an expatriate Irish Roman Catholic family, moved with his mother and siblings to Ireland after his father's early death, and, following a few years of study in England at St Cuthbert's, Ushaw, embarked on seminary studies in Rome at the age of 16. His years in Rome left him with an enduring sympathy for the Italian styles of worship, as is evident in the Dublin review which he helped to found in 1836, a prominent periodical characterised by an effusive devotional style and a strong defence of the Pope. His support for Marian devotion on becoming Archbishop suggests that he recognised its polemical as well as its personal value.

The Virgin Mary's prominence in nineteenth-century England was not attributable solely to Roman Catholics, either their theology and devotional practices or the animosity these inspired. Keble's and Sellon's desire for limited Marian invocations demonstrates that the development of what came to be called 'Anglo-Catholicism' also played a role in generating those controversies. Anglo-Catholicism grew out of the high-church wing of Anglicanism. High-church Anglicans emphasised ritual, ecclesiastical authority, and the Catholic identity of the Church of England; in politics their interests were often identified with those of the Tory Party. In the middle decades of the nineteenth century, there were three main types of high-church Anglican: traditionalists, Tractarians, and ritualists.

Traditional high church Anglicans defended both the English Reformations and the establishment of the Church of England. They valued the writings of the early church, but they used them conservatively and in conjunction with the reformers, always insisting that Scripture was the basis of belief and that the Established Church had the right to abandon ancient traditions. They (along with many evangelicals) held the mainstream receptionist view of the Eucharist, that is, that Christ was present in the communion elements only to believers rather than to all who partook of the sacrament. Although its fondness for ritual and tradition could lead to accusations that it was too close to Rome, traditional high-church Anglicanism was characterised by a fierce anti-Roman Catholicism, which was pungently expressed by the declaration of the clergyman Walter Farquhar Hook: 'I have always hated the Church of Rome as I would hate the bitterest Enemy of my God.'[52] Other high-church Anglicans declared the Roman Catholic Church to be 'a grossly idolatrous Church, debasing and enslaving her adherents,'[53] as well as being the 'twin sister'[54] of paganism, and they described Roman Catholics as indifferent or irreverent worshippers who had little knowledge of the Bible.[55]

The 'Tractarian' designation derived from the ninety Tracts for the times published between 1833 and 1841. The Tracts, which began as pamphlets and evolved into lengthy treatises, were by various authors associated with Oxford University, some of whom – including Newman, Pusey, Keble, and Isaac Williams – later entered the Marian debates. The Tracts emphasised the Church of England's Catholic identity at the expense of its Protestant identity, and they typically approached religious questions from a doctrinal angle. Like traditional high-church Anglicans, Tractarians valued the writings of the early church. While not denying the primacy of Scripture, Tractarians used Patristic writings more actively and as a more definitive guide to what the beliefs and practices of the Catholic Church should be. One consequence of Tractarians' increasing reliance on Patristic writings was a desire to distance themselves from the English Reformations, one of the forces that propelled Newman's conversion. Some Tractarians (including Keble) proposed the disestablishment of the Church of England to cure what they considered to be its Erastian character. Tractarians extended the traditional high-church view of the Eucharist to the point that their eucharistic beliefs were similar to the Roman Catholic doctrine of transubstantiation or the Lutheran doctrine of consubstantiation. The Tractarian revival of practices associated with the Roman Catholic Church, such as auricular confession, and their establishment of Anglican sisterhoods were protested by other Anglicans as providing a pathway to Rome. Certainly Tractarians had a more sympathetic view of the Roman Catholic Church than did traditional high-church Anglicans. Pusey, for example, hoped for reunion with the Roman Catholic Church, and later in the century a group of Anglo-Catholics worked to attain that goal. This sympathy for Roman Catholicism was seen as treasonous: the Anglo-Irish cleric Michael Hobart Seymour (who spent the last fifty years of his long life as a clergyman in England) attacked Tractarians as 'those modern Churchmen whose bodies, indeed, are in the Church of England, but whose hearts are in the Church of Rome'.[56]

Ritualists, whose appearance as a distinct church party dates from the foundation of the Cambridge Camden Society in 1839, were more concerned with the form of worship, including architecture, vestments, candles, and the like. Their emphasis on the visible practice of religion led Golightly's friend Walter John Trower to complain: 'They value a stole more than doctrine'.[57] Like Tractarians, ritualists disputed the charge that they led people to Rome and argued that the high-church Anglicanism they practised actually prevented Anglicans from converting to Roman Catholicism. Newman and W. G. Ward, an anonymous layman sniffed after their conversions, actually 'were no great sticklers for ritualism. The service at S. Mary's, Oxford, while in Mr. Newman's hands, was generally performed in an unrubrical and slovenly manner, – the most ordinary forms and ceremonies being little heeded. The way to Rome was not paved there by any solemnities of ritualism'.[58] They also denied that they were secret Roman Catholics; the ritualist priest and controversialist Richard Frederick Littledale asserted: 'Ritualism is *not* Romanism in the most essential particulars'.[59] Their impact on the daily life of the Church of England came in the second half of the century, when ritualist priests moved into parishes in significant numbers. Their transformation of the Anglican liturgy led to sometimes violent disruptions of church services beginning in the 1860s. Attempts to repress ritualism through the Purchas Judgment (1871) and the Public Worship Regulation Act (1874; repealed 1963) were largely ineffectual and even counter-productive, but they testify to the controversial status of ritualists.

The concerns of Tractarians and ritualists overlapped to a great extent. Many Tractarians were interested in questions of ritual, and both the Tractarian leader Pusey and John Mason Neale, a founding member of the Cambridge Camden Society, established Anglican sisterhoods. Their opponents within the Church of England frequently treated them as a single adversary. As these two groups moved closer in their concerns after mid-century, they can be subsumed under the general heading 'Anglo-Catholic'. These Anglicans spoke positively of the Virgin Mary. Some of them even went beyond Anglican precedent to describe her as being without sin or to practise limited forms of Marian devotion. As with the Roman Catholics, their purposes were both devotional and polemical. Claiming some Catholic traditions as their own was one way in which these Anglicans implemented their claim that the Church of England was a branch of the universal Catholic Church. A practical consequence of incorporating these traditions, they asserted, was that reviving ritual would make the Anglican Church warmer and thus more appealing to their unchurched or dissenting compatriots. As with Roman Catholics, their Christian practice was more embodied, so that emphasising the Incarnation could lead them to invoke Mary. Finally, Anglo-Catholics were especially interested in encouraging women's spiritual roles within the Established Church – for example by introducing sisterhoods – which makes it unsurprising that they praised the faith they believed Mary had demonstrated as the mother of Jesus. In order to avoid the confusion of evolving group names and in recognition of the fact that their Marian theology did not fundamentally change even as the group names did, I adopt the notion of 'advanced high churchmanship', used by Peter Benedict Nockles and David Newsome[60] and describe these Anglicans as 'advanced Anglicans'. This is not meant to be a positive designation, but rather one that reflects the contemporary sense, voiced by Keble's friend, that they had advanced in their religious beliefs beyond that which the Church of England officially sanctioned.

This delineation of types has its limitations, for it can be difficult to assign high-church Anglicans to one subset or another. For example, some traditional high churchmen contributed to the *Tracts for the times* and many more had an initially positive response to the early *Tracts*. The ambiguity of some high-church Anglicans' positions was exemplified by Henry Phillpotts. A traditional high-churchman, he had been influenced by the Tractarians and was generally supportive of the Anglican Sisters of Mercy in Devonport. However, he also feared that the Tractarians 'sometimes deal with some of the worst corruptions of Rome, in terms not indicating so deep a sense of their pernicious tendency'.[61] Similarly, Samuel Wilberforce supported Anglican sisterhoods, and some of the practices at Cuddesden College, which he founded in 1854, led to charges that he was overly sympathetic to Tractarianism. However, he maintained his strong ties with evangelicals and was notably unsympathetic to the practice of Marian devotion. Hook, one of the Tractarians' strongest critics, had once described himself as 'an Oxford Tract man',[62] although he later ended his friendship with Pusey as a consequence of a dispute over liturgical practices at St Saviour's, Leeds, the church Pusey founded, after his wife's death, as penance for his sins. Golightly had once been a friend of Newman and had subscribed to the *Tracts*, although he later became one of the Tractarians' fiercest critics and headed the subscriptions for Martyrs' Memorial, Oxford. (This tower, located just outside the city centre, memorialises the Marian martyrs Thomas Cranmer, Hugh Latimer, and Nicholas Ridley. Completed in 1843, it was conceived as a direct rebuke to the Tractarians.) Even later, when the divisions between the old high church Anglicans and the Tractarians were deeper, there were many issues that united them, as the Gorham controversy revealed.

In the matter of Marian devotion, the distinctions between Tractarians and high-church Anglicans were much clearer. Traditional high-church Anglicans generally sided with Protestants and against advanced Anglicans and Roman Catholics. Both traditional high churchmen and the members of the Oxford Movement considered themselves the heirs to the seventeenth-century high churchmen, including Andrewes, Laud, and Ken. Nockles argues 'that, in the era of the Oxford Movement, the lineal descendants of pre-Tractarian high churchmanship were those whom Hurrell Froude idiosyncratically labelled the "Zs" [traditional high churchmen] rather than the Tractarians themselves'.[63] At least in the matter of Marian devotion, the Tractarians, and not the traditional high churchmen, were the heirs of the seventeenth-century divines, for they embraced the earlier high-church tradition of Marian devotion that Victorian traditional high churchmen rejected.[64]

Historians usually define Victorian Christianity in terms of a division between the Protestant majority and an occasionally problematical Roman Catholic minority. Advanced Anglicans either are rarely acknowledged or are treated as somewhat annoying exceptions, as in Yates's *Anglican ritualism* and Reed's *Glorious battle*. The alliances formed in the Marian debates, however, upset this schema, as they reveal theological and liturgical commonalities among advanced Anglicans and Roman Catholics. Advanced Anglicans differed from Roman Catholics on a variety of issues, including papal authority and the legitimacy of the Church of England, but they shared a common Catholic theology and culture. Both types of Catholic sought truth in Scripture and tradition, emphasised ritual as part of their spirituality, and believed that the vowed religious life was a viable choice for men and women. Perhaps most importantly, advanced Anglicans described themselves as one branch of the universal Catholic Church. Catholics' common portrait of the Virgin Mary as a woman without sin who was chosen by God to be the virgin mother of the Saviour exemplifies this shared culture. The two groups were further linked by conversions (occasionally back and forth). Some converts, such as Henry Nutcombe Oxenham, believed that their Anglican orders were valid even after converting to Roman Catholicism. Certainly their Protestant opponents thought they had much in common. Mary Heimann argues, in *Catholic devotion in Victorian England*, that English Roman Catholics were more united by religion than divided by class (or, I would add, by gender or geography). In the context of the Marian debates, that assertion can be extended to all Catholics.

In describing Catholics as a group, I am not ignoring the fundamental and intractable differences that separated advanced Anglicans and Roman Catholics, or the fact that these two types of Catholic would have strenuously objected to being classed together. However, their intense investment in constructing unique religious identities for themselves meant that they could not see what they had in common, theologically and liturgically as well as culturally. Because advanced Anglicans could maintain their credibility only by denying that they were secret Roman Catholics, and because in deciding to remain in the Church of England they were rejecting Roman Catholicism as an answer to their complaints about their Church, they could not admit that they had much in common with Roman Catholics. Likewise, Roman Catholics were so invested in asserting that they were members of the true Church and that Anglicans were in error that they could not have admitted that they shared a common theological and cultural identity; otherwise, their calls for reunion between the two Churches or for Anglicans to convert would lose much of their appeal. However, in hindsight and from the vantage point of a more ecumenical time, it is clear that culturally and theologically Catholics had more, and more crucial things, in common. Their broad agreement on the role and nature of the Virgin Mary reflected shared cultural values based on a common theology, one evident in advanced Anglicans' belief that they belonged to the universal Catholic Church. Therefore, in this work the unqualified 'Catholic' refers to both advanced Anglicans and Roman Catholics.

Less surprising to readers will be a common grouping of Protestants, perhaps because of the precedent set by other scholars. Without distinguishing among denominations, Linda Colley argues that 'a common commitment to Protestantism' was a unifying force among Britons. 'To a very limited extent, this had been the case since the Reformation. But throughout the eighteenth and nineteenth centuries, and even after, external pressures and imperatives made the fact that this was an overwhelmingly Protestant culture relevant and compelling in a quite unprecedented way.'[65] This was especially clear in the mid-nineteenth century when the restoration of the Roman Catholic hierarchy and the declaration of the Immaculate Conception made Protestants more inclined to claim a common identity. These Protestants include dissenters such as Baptists, Methodists, Presbyterians, and non-denominational Protestants, in addition to the majority of Anglicans, whether low church, evangelical, or broad church, who described their Church as Protestant and who approved of the Reformation. Traditional high-church Anglicans, who defined the Church of England as both Catholic and Protestant, often allied with Protestants when discussing the Virgin Mary, and so are usually grouped with them here.

The many theological, liturgical, and historical distinctions between Protestants were responsible for their denominational divisions. However, like Catholics, Protestants shared theological beliefs and liturgical practices. Generally, Protestant theology was characterised by a professed reliance on *sola Scriptura*, although in the nineteenth century advances in scholarship led to a focus on the problem of the relationship between the historical Jesus and the Christ. Perhaps the most famous popular expression of this question was Strauss's *Life of Jesus* (the translation of which brought Mary Anne Evans, the future George Eliot, to lose the evangelical faith of her youth). Protestant liturgy was far less elaborate than Catholic liturgy: absent were the ornate vestments, physical gestures like genuflecting to the altar, and decorations like candles and flowers on the altar (all of which provoked displeasure from Protestants when they observed them in Catholic churches). The emphasis was on the word more than the Eucharist (which was celebrated far less frequently than in Anglo-Catholic and especially Roman Catholic churches). Spirituality was more individual and less likely to be mediated, as it was for Catholics, by a priest or a sacrament. Evangelical Protestantism required a conversion experience. The absence of a strong, central authority as in the Roman Catholic Church meant that disputes could be solved by breaking away from a denomination, so that there were, for example, a variety of 'Methodists'.

Protestants were also joined by their willingness to overlook denominational identity to assert a shared Protestant identity. For example, the Congregationalist weekly the *British banner* covered news related to other denominations, including the Baptists and Methodists. Protestants of different denominations regularly collaborated on social and political issues, and evangelicals were found among dissenters as well as within the Church of England. They were also likely to move from one Protestant denomination to another: Thomas Hartwell Horne, for example, worshipped with the Methodists as a young man before deciding that he preferred the episcopacy, a decision that led him to be ordained in the Established Church. Certainly, his decision benefited him materially – he served as Prebendary of St Paul's Cathedral for the final thirty-one years of his life – but even if such conversions were motivated by concerns other than, or in addition to, spiritual ones, it does not change the fact that they were made possible by a shared Protestant identity. That identity characterised even those who were not regular churchgoers: George Eliot, for example, was culturally Protestant even after she abandoned the faith of her youth.

Protestants were further unified when they overlooked denominational divisions to condemn the Catholic Virgin Mary and assert the significance of Protestantism to English national identity. When Cumming, a Presbyterian, worried about retaining 'the disciples of the recent seceders from the Protestant Church',[66] he implicitly acknowledged that the Established Church – the source of most of the converts – must be defended in order to defend Protestantism generally. Discussions about the Virgin Mary reveal a common Protestantism that confirms Colley's assessment: 'These internal [Protestant] rivalries were abundant and serious. But they should not obscure what was still the most striking feature in the religious landscape; the gulf between Protestant and Catholic.'[67] Therefore, while individuals are identified by their denominational affiliation, I am concerned more with their shared identity as Protestants.

The Church of England would seem to present an impediment to this view of Victorian Christians as divided into Catholics and Protestants, because historically that Church had defined itself as both Catholic and Protestant. Some Anglicans asserted that the Church of England actually dated not from the reign of Henry VIII but from 597, when Augustine of Canterbury arrived in England. However, the establishment of the Oxford and ritualist movements made it harder to claim this joint identity, as these Anglicans asserted their membership in the universal Catholic Church and rejected the Reformation along with a Protestant identity. As they made it clear that they also intended to practise devotions more associated with Roman Catholicism, their co-religionists who had defended the Church of England's dual identities found it less appealing to claim that they were Catholic as well as Protestant. The Established Church was not, then, an impediment to this division of Christian culture but an examplar of it. Understanding Victorian culture as divided into distinct cultures, Catholic and Protestant, suggests an additional way of understanding how Victorian culture was organised. As well as being grouped by class, gender, political affiliation, and geography, Victorians grouped themselves by shared affinities based on religious principles that transcended denominations. This schema offers an integrated approach to the Victorian religious landscape. Focusing on what people had in common rather than on what divided them allows the emergence of two competing groups of Christians, which challenges the orthodoxy of a dominant Protestant group in Victorian England.

The feminine ideal

Competing religious traditions were one of the major sources of the Marian debates, but they were not the only source. Indeed, conflicts between Catholics and Protestants had characterised England since the sixteenth century, yet representations of the Virgin Mary were the subject of lengthy and intense public discussions only in the nineteenth century. The peak years for concern over the Catholic Virgin Mary were roughly 1830–85, the same period in which the feminine ideal – that contradictory, ever-evolving image of woman as the embodiment of selfless, sexless love – was ascendant. There was, of course, no single model embodying the feminine ideal, but the repeated descriptions in a variety of genres – including novels, poetry, sermons, parliamentary reports, medical books, and conduct manuals – of women who were characterised primarily as pure and loving shaped an iconic figure. That figure was recognised (and parodied) by Victorians, and has been analysed by scholars of the period, even as the emphasis in the latter decades of the twentieth century has been on deconstructing and destabilising this figure. Not just for simplicity's sake, but also to acknowledge the power of those representations as injunctions, especially over women, the term 'feminine ideal' has utility.

The timing as well as the content of the Marian debates suggests that the other significant factor in inspiring them was the anxious attempt, characteristic of much Victorian discourse, to define woman's nature and duties. One of the main disputes between Catholics and Protestants was whether, and if so to what extent, Mary embodied the three major characteristics most often asserted to be innately feminine: whether she was sinless; whether she remained a virgin; and whether she was a model mother. While the theological, liturgical, and cultural differences between Catholics and Protestants provided the foundation for and one of the sources of the Marian debates, the timing and content of the critique of the Catholic Virgin Mary make it clear that a desire to define woman's nature also was a motivating factor.

I do not posit a crude correlation in which a Victorian concerned to limit or extend the scope of the maternal role would seize on representations of the Virgin Mary as a vehicle to express those concerns, but rather a less conscious relationship in which those who lived in a culture preoccupied with defining woman's nature were drawn to this figure who had traditionally embodied one of the dominant types of the feminine. The opposite also happened, that those drawn to the Virgin Mary for religious reasons viewed her through the prism of their culture's gender norms. Personal motivations played a role for some: those, for example, who idealised their own mothers or who wished they had had an ideal mother may have been drawn to describe the Virgin Mary as the mother they either remembered or wished they had known. Some men whose mothers had died when they were young had a strong Marian devotion, like the Roman Catholic converts Faber and Phillips de Lisle. However, men who had a distant or otherwise unsatisfactory relationship with their mothers – including Newman, Ullathorne, and Williams – also championed Marian devotion. Even men who resisted maternal interference – like Wiseman, who suppressed his mother's written protest to his vicar when he took minor orders at the age of 18 – could imagine that Mary influenced Jesus, even in heaven. Likewise, those who described the Virgin Mary as an ordinary woman could have difficult mothers, as Samuel Wilberforce did, or one like the leading evangelical Edward Bickersteth's, who 'was a woman of uncommon mental strength and energy, too firm and wise to be over-indulgent, and yet so loving that she secured the fondest affections of her children'.[68] Men could also express reservations about Marian devotion while still praising their wives as pious helpmeets.[69] In general there is no overall correlation between the Catholic or Protestant images of the Virgin Mary and individuals' experiences with women, especially their mothers.

In any event, when Victorian Christians praised or condemned how they believed the Virgin Mary had acted, they also revealed what they thought was properly *feminine* or *masculine* behaviour. This use of the Virgin Mary is unsurprising: in his survey *Mary through the centuries: her place in the history of culture*, Pelikan has argued that historically the Virgin Mary 'has provided the content of the definition of the feminine in a way that he [Jesus] has not done for the masculine'.[70] This flexibility is possible because so little is known about this woman who was both physically absent and yet symbolically central to the Christian story of redemption. Except for the narratives of the Annunciation and Nativity in the Gospel of Luke, Mary appears only briefly in the gospels; sometimes she does not even speak. The lack of detailed information about her has allowed Christians to define her in ways that are useful to them. As Cunneen has noted: 'For centuries, ordinary people, as well as theologians and artists, have projected their own needs onto Mary'.[71]

Scholars have usually assumed that nineteenth-century Marian representations merely ratified the rather uninteresting status quo of the docile domestic woman. Cunneen has asserted that 'Mary seemed ... much like the Victorian [feminine] ideal',[72] an equation later repeated by Kimberly van Esveld Adams, who makes 'the Angel in the House' synonymous with 'the domestic Madonna, who is one of the most familiar icons of Victorian womanhood'.[73] Claudia Nelson has argued that in some of her many guises the Angel in the House could 'expand into a semisecular Virgin Mary',[74] and, with Ann Sumner Holmes, refers to the Victorian idealisation of the mother as 'widespread secular mariolatry'.[75] The apparent correlation between the two figures has led Elizabeth Helsinger, Robin Lauterbach, and William Veeder Sheets to conclude that in the Victorian era 'the Anglo-American attitude toward Mary herself is generally positive'[76] and even that '[t]his self-effacing, Mary-like ideal remains a female standard for the rest of the era'.[77]

The equation of the Virgin Mary with the evolving composite known as the feminine ideal is problematical in part because it assumes a single representation of the Virgin Mary. Instead, there were two competing images. The Catholic Virgin Mary was a sinless virgin mother who retained her extraordinary influence with her son throughout eternity and was a model for Christian behaviour. In contrast, the Protestant Virgin had a limited maternal role, bore subsequent children, and shared with all humans the guilt of both original and actual sin. This Virgin was a development of the Protestant reformers' desire to limit the attention the faithful paid to Jesus' mother. Thus they sharply scaled back addresses to her, rejected relics associated with her, and abandoned Marian shrines (including Our Lady of Walsingham in England). The reformers had, however, reduced the emphasis on Jesus' mother while still believing that she was the ever-virgin mother who exemplified Christian virtues. In contrast, Victorian Protestants paid more attention to the Virgin Mary in order to describe her as an ordinary and not particularly admirable woman. Thus a spectrum developed in which the idealised woman was positioned between the two Marys. Although these three types overlapped to some degree, the Victorian ideal was less powerful than the Catholic Virgin but more admirable than the Protestant Virgin. This is not so much a disagreement with as a modification of Singleton's delineation of three Virgin Marys visible in Victorian England: the one loved by Catholics and the two produced by Protestants, 'the mother of Jesus, who was a respected figure from the pages of Scripture, and the Virgin Mary, who was the personification of Irish superstition and Romish idolatry'.[78] Where Singleton sees three Virgins, I apprehend only two, because Catholics and Protestants reacted differently to the Virgin whom Catholics described.

The heroine of George Eliot's novel *Romola* illustrates the relationship between the Catholic Mary and the Victorian model of womanhood. At first Romola seems to confirm Adams's assessment that she is a type of Madonna, for she is a good, beautiful woman who is associated with Marian iconography such as the lily.[79] After her marriage to the selfish, ambitious Tito begins to break down, she is addressed as 'Madonna Romola', mainly by the poorer Florentines. The peasants whom she saves from the plague extend the identification: the teenaged boy who first sees her carrying an orphaned baby thinks she is the original Madonna. All the peasants come to treat her as the Madonna: they bring food offerings to the 'Blessed Lady',[80] and after she returns to Florence they transform her into a mythical creature, 'a woman who had done beautiful loving deeds there, rescuing those who were ready to perish'.[81]

There are, however, several indications that Romola is not the Catholic Madonna. The significance of her title is undermined when her ridiculously vain cousin Monna Brigida is also addressed as 'Madonna',[82] and she leaves behind the orphaned baby, whom she has named and christened, when she returns to Florence. The distinction between the two women is confirmed by the presence in the novel of the Catholic Virgin Mary; the Florentines pray to her and celebrate her feast days. Instead, Romola is a version of the model woman found in many Victorian novels: she is beautiful, intelligent, kind, and dutiful. She helps her father in his work, and then her husband in his, even after she learns to loathe him. She is inferior to her husband in every way but moral power; she cannot stop him from selling her father's beloved library or engaging in political machinations. Her subordinate position to both men is illustrated by her sitting in a chair lower than theirs. Romola is more virtuous and more competent than the Protestant Virgin Mary, but weaker than the Catholic Virgin Mary, for she can never effectively challenge any of the men – her father, her godfather, Savonarola, Tito – who direct her actions. Finally, her goodness is not the result of Christian virtue but her adherence to Duty, the secular religion of Eliot's heroines.

Victorian Protestants viewed the Virgin Mary described by Catholics as a woman who used her motherhood to usurp her son's role. At the forefront of describing the Virgin Mary thus were Protestant clergymen. This was the group most closely associated with defining and deploying the feminine ideal after it had been described by evangelical clergymen in the late eighteenth century; they were crucial in ensuring that it was part of mainstream culture by the 1830s. In this effort they were joined by others who influenced contemporary opinion, including writers and politicians. The Catholic Virgin Mary was the prototype for this figure: both were defined as maternal, non-sexual, and morally superior. One crucial difference between the two women was that the feminine ideal, especially as described in canonical literature after mid-century, often had to develop these characteristics, whereas in Catholic tradition the Virgin Mary had them from the moment of her conception.

Although the Catholic Virgin Mary was the prototype for the feminine ideal, Protestants nevertheless criticised her for possessing those characteristics that they declared were integral to woman's nature. Their choice to critique the Catholic Virgin Mary can be only partially explained by the religious antagonism that characterised Victorian England; their timing and their heated rhetoric suggests that they were actually uneasy with envisioning women as powerful by virtue of their motherhood and moral superiority. I do not suggest that their representations of the Virgin Mary were calculated to limit women's public power, but the effect of their repeatedly describing a woman who overestimated the influence she could have on her son in his work was to define the public sphere as male. Furthermore, they went beyond trying to limit Marian devotion, as their predecessors had, when they described the Virgin as a bad mother. They also declined the obvious opportunity to assert any sort of admirable woman in the place of the Virgin Mary. The result was that the most famous exemplar of feminine virtues in Western Christianity was set aside and not replaced, even with a more ordinary example of praiseworthy female behaviour such as might come from their congregations.

In the late twentieth century, scholarship on the realities and representations of women in Victorian England has been both prolific and profitable, extending and complicating our knowledge of Victorian women of all classes, regions, and occupations. The casual assumption, evident in Walter Houghton's *The Victorian frame of mind*,[83] that the feminine ideal described the reality of most women's experiences began to be challenged in the late 1960s and early 1970s as the influences of social history and the 'second wave' of feminism began to result in investigations of the experiences of ordinary women and groups of women. Scholars came to understand that the ideal was, as Mary Poovey has said of the ideology that produced it, 'both contested and always under construction; because it was always in the making, it was always open to revision, dispute, and the emergence of oppositional formulations.'[84] Nelson, Catherine Robson, and Meredith Veldman have traced back the instability of separate spheres to childhood.[85] Those oppositional formulations included the presence of prostitutes and other 'fallen women', as well as those, like John Stuart Mill and Barbara Leigh Smith Bodichon, who campaigned for more equal treatment for women. A more recent attack on the ideal's relevance comes from those scholars who question whether the Victorian era marked a significant break with earlier ideologies and assumptions.

The ideology of separate spheres, which relied heavily on the construction of a feminine domestic presence to counterbalance a more aggressive masculine presence in the public sphere, has traditionally been interpreted as a response to industrialisation, yet recently some have questioned the degree to which industrialisation removed women from the workforce.[86] Amanda Vickery has argued that Victorian constructions of femininity were not substantially different from those of previous eras. She rejects 'the conceptual vocabulary of "public and private" and "separate spheres" deployed so extensively in women's history ... [because] it has little resonance for the prosperous women' in Georgian England.[87] Her argument in *The gentleman's daughter* is undermined, however, by its definition of 'public' as leisure spectacles rather than the more traditional one of the marketplace or the 'public square'. More recently, Judith S. Lewis has confirmed, in *Sacred to female patriotism: gender, class, and politics in late Georgian Britain*, the traditional view that, by the end of the eighteenth century, political reform movements and the rise of evangelicalism combined to shift women's activities from political and public ones to more private endeavours such as philanthropy and religion.

The deconstructions of both the feminine ideal and the ideology that produced it are useful reminders that this composite iconographic figure was not monolithic and could never be fully implemented. However, we risk going too far and relegating it to the margins when in fact its psychological power enabled it to play a significant part in the lives of many Victorians. This image of womanhood was associated most with the middle classes, but it touched all levels of Victorian society. Working-class movements like Chartism adopted it as proof of their respectability, while its intimate affiliation with organised religion ensured that it had a wide influence.[88]

The feminine ideal, in spite of its necessarily imperfect implementation, was one of the defining characteristics of Victorian culture. The many Victorians who criticised the Catholic Virgin Mary for precisely those ways in which she conformed to and extended the ideal, and their positing a less attractive version of this woman, suggest that those most closely associated with promoting the ideal had doubts about its effects on society or its attainability. Protestant Victorians' new interest in defining the Virgin Mary as a woman of limited power and virtue coincided with the period when women were urged to model themselves after this complicated and contradictory image of womanhood. This timing, as well as the often harsh rhetoric, suggests that they were responding to factors besides religious differences. The Catholic Virgin Mary demonstrated that the very virtues that were intended to restrict women to the domestic sphere were in fact means by which to access the public sphere. Roman Catholics addressed prayers to her, exhibited and paraded statues of her, and believed she could intercede with Jesus on their behalf. The hostile reactions to this woman suggest that the feminine ideal failed not merely because it was internally contradictory and therefore unstable, nor because it was difficult if not impossible for women to incorporate its precepts into their private lives. A third reason for the ideal's collapse was that those who promulgated it realised, when confronted with the Catholic Virgin Mary, that an exceptionally virtuous woman could access a great deal of power. The Catholic Virgin Mary thwarted the purpose of the ideal, which was designed to prevent women from competing with men in the public sphere.

Because the Marian debates were part of a diffused cultural dynamic, no evidence exists of an absolute connection between hostile reactions to the Catholic Virgin Mary and anxiety about the power implicit in representations of woman as morally superior and self-sacrificing. The absence of absolute evidence does not undermine my argument, however. That argument is made by the preponderance of evidence that the Protestant hostility to the Catholic Virgin Mary, which differed in quality and quantity from that of the Reformation and post-Reformation critiques, was encouraged by something other than theological or liturgical differences. The Marian controversies became most heated during the decades in which the feminine ideal was dominant, and they focused on the three characteristics alleged to be essentially feminine: virginity, maternity, and moral superiority.

The Marian debates were dominated by men, especially the clergy. Few women wrote publicly and extensively on the Virgin Mary, partly because they were less likely than men (especially clerics) to have either the training or the outlet for such writing. More significantly, neither Virgin Mary was a viable role model for Protestant women: the Catholic Mary was culturally too foreign, while the Protestant one was too docile. The Virgin Mary was not so obviously a role model for men, but they had a specific motivation that women lacked: by defining the Virgin Mary, they could define their own masculine identity. Catholic men generally described a woman who ultimately ratified masculine authority, either because she was so exceptional that her power and prestige could not be accessed by other women or because she was a loving mother who ultimately submitted to divine authority, which was understood to be masculine. Protestant men used harsher language to achieve the same goal of strengthening masculine authority. The degree of animosity they expressed suggests that they perceived masculine authority as being threatened by the figure of a strong mother. Their willingness to denounce the Catholic Virgin Mary, the woman who exemplified the virtues said to be innately feminine, and to replace her with a more ordinary woman indicates that the potential challenge to masculine prerogatives was most apparent to the Protestant clergy who were, ironically, closely identified with the promulgation of the ideal. Peter Gay, James Eli Adams, Sean Gill, Nelson, and Veldman[89] have described how the feminisation of religion in the nineteenth century, coupled with the ungendered virtues promoted by Christianity– including charity, chastity, and humility – made it difficult for Christian men, and especially the clergy, to defend the ideology of separate spheres on which the masculine ideal was premised. One solution to that quandary was to reject a woman whose virtues and power made her preeminent among humans in order to reclaim religion as a masculine enterprise, thus justifying the clerical monopoly on the pulpit, and by extension male control of the public sphere. An analysis of the Marian debates therefore addresses what Michael Roper and John Tosh call the 'crucial problem' of analyses of masculinity, that 'women are almost entirely absent from these accounts, seemingly on the assumption that masculinity takes on a sharper focus when women are removed from the scene'.[90] On the contrary, those debates reveal that masculinity is shaped with an awareness of, and often in response to, femininity.

Although the clergy were a minority numerically, they were among the most influential groups in the largely Christian culture of Victorian

England. Their monopoly on the pulpit gave them regular access to the, roughly, 50 per cent of Victorians who attended church or chapel weekly. They reached a wider audience by publishing their sermons in periodicals such as the *Pulpit* or the *Penny pulpit*, or in pamphlet form. The Victorian reading public's 'seemingly insatiable appetite for reading, particularly devotional works'[91] ensured that more sermons and other religious works were published than were other titles, including novels.[92] While circulating libraries may have given novels a wider readership, the availability of sermons in pamphlet form might have given them a longer shelf life in individual homes. Clerics also gave public speeches, participated in public disputes, and wrote fiction and essays. *Cartes des visites* with clergymen's photos, which were traded and collected, further testify to clerical influence and popularity by giving them a 'star' quality akin to that of the stage actors and actresses more commonly associated with such keepsakes.[93]

The Marian debates were not confined to sermons, theological works, polemical tracts, prayer books, and religious periodicals. The continuation of these debates in novels, plays, and poems, as well as in letters and diaries, suggests that arguments that were first expressed in the pulpit were also adopted by those who entered church or chapel infrequently or not at all. I focus on the public debates rather than private devotional practices because I am interested in the broader cultural discussions rather than private patterns of devotion, although certainly there was at least some, and probably often a significant, overlap between public and private expressions of religious belief. One indication of this overlap is that few in England publicly defended Catholics' belief that the Virgin Mary was the sinless and ever-virgin Mother of God. Given the regularity with which religious debates gripped English society and the number and ferocity of attacks on the Virgin Mary, we can be confident that had either the Protestant image of the Virgin Mary or the Protestant denunciations of the Catholic Virgin Mary proved uncongenial to many Victorian Protestants we would have heard about it. This lack of opposition indicates not indifference, but assent.

Book outline

Neither Protestant nor Catholic representations of the Virgin Mary changed significantly during the period covered, partly because the Roman Catholic version was well-established before 1830. Even the declaration of the Immaculate Conception in 1854 largely confirmed popular Roman Catholic opinion. Likewise, the feminine ideal was modified but not fundamentally changed until the 1880s, when it was challenged by the 'New Woman'. Because the arguments over the Virgin Mary's role and nature were rehearsed over and over during the nineteenth century, a thematic rather than a chronological approach to the debate is more useful.

Chapter 2 describes the Catholic portrait of the Virgin Mary as the sinless Mother of God who participated in her son's work. This traditional portrait of the Virgin Mary re-entered public discourse in England beginning in the 1830s as a result of the growing public presence of Roman Catholics and the development of Tractarianism and ritualism. This Virgin Mary was an important part of the devotional life of Catholics; invoking her also allowed Catholics to shape an identity based in part on a rejection of Protestantism. This image of the Virgin Mary showed Catholics' receptivity to the figure of an idealised woman, as well as their reluctance to allow her power, prerogatives, or prominence to be accessed by other women.

Chapter 3 describes the contrasting portrait of the Protestant Virgin Mary, an ordinary and even erring woman whose maternal role was very limited. This woman, who was a more negative figure than the woman envisioned by the reformers, also emerged beginning in the 1830s, partly as a response to the Catholic Virgin Mary. This Virgin Mary was an expression of Protestants' religious beliefs, particularly the emphasis on *sola Scriptura* and a direct relationship between the divine and the devout, yet it also had a polemical purpose. In promoting this figure and denouncing the Catholic Virgin Mary, Protestants could argue that Catholicism was a corrupt form of Christianity and that Protestantism was the biblical religion. In addition, by describing a woman whose motherhood gave her no special prerogatives, Protestants could counteract the popular perception that women were innately maternal and that this characteristic gave them an influence over the public sphere.

Chapters 2 and 3 demonstrate the coherence of Catholics and Protestants respectively. The Catholic unity was challenged, however, by the declaration of the Immaculate Conception in 1854. Chapter 4 examines the English reception of the Immaculate Conception, which was the only new Marian dogma in this period. This key moment in Victorian religious history, which has been largely overlooked, shows how English Christians reacted to a religious dogma with no direct scriptural evidence. This controversial topic was the one most likely to encourage broad participation from non-Anglican Protestants. As we might expect, Roman Catholics had a generally positive response, especially after some initial hesitation, but Protestants resoundingly rejected it. Advanced Anglicans were ambivalent: many believed the Virgin Mary to be without sin but were hesitant to declare dogmatic a belief with no scriptural basis. This debate also helps illuminate attitudes of Victorian Christians about the relationship between sexual intercourse, the body, and sin.

Chapter 5 describes how four men of different religious views and temperaments – Charles Kingsley, Edward Bouverie Pusey, Frederick W. Faber, and John Henry Newman – could define the Virgin Mary in such a way that they could construct a masculine self-identity in opposition to, or in conjunction with, the woman they envisioned. Individually these men offer proof that, while religious differences allowed the Marian debates to occur, the debates would not have been possible without the Victorian preoccupation with defining either gender as distinct from the other. They and the other Victorians whose voices are heard in the following pages show us that a Virgin Mary who was a source of controversy reveals far more about Victorian culture than does the passive model of domesticity scholars have assumed her to be.

Notes

1   John Keble, letter to J. T. Coleridge, 18 June 1845; reprinted in J. T. Coleridge, *A memoir of the Rev. John Keble, M.A., late vicar of Hursley*, 2nd edn (Oxford and London: James Parker & Co., 1869), pp. 290–1.

2   Coleridge, *A memoir of the Rev. John Keble*, p. 289.

3   Coleridge, *A memoir of the Rev. John Keble*, p. 290; the complete poem is printed in ibid., pp. 314–16.

4   *Report of the inquiry instituted by the Right Reverend the Lord Bishop of Exeter, as Visitor of the Orphans' Home, established by the Sisters of Mercy, at Morice Town, Devonport, into the truth of certain statements published in the 'Devonport telegraph', February 10th, 1849* (Plymouth: Roger Lidstone, London: J. Masters, and Exeter: H. J. Wallis, 1849), p. 64.

5   *Report of the inquiry*, p. 5; for more information on the Marian controversies involving Sellon, see Michael Hill, *The religious order: a study of virtuoso religion and its legitimation in the nineteenth-century Church of England* (London: Heinemann Educational Books, 1973), p. 216.

6   *Report of the inquiry*, p. 64.

7   *Report of the inquiry*, p. 5; this charge, which Sellon denied, was never addressed, as Bishop Phillpotts insisted that he would not 'pursue a lady into her bed-chamber, and enquire what she had there.'

8   *Report of the inquiry*, p. 75, emphasis in original.

9   The superior of the Society (Lydia Sellon), *Reply to a tract by the Rev. J. Spurrell, vicar of Great Shelford, containing certain charges concerning the Society of the Sisters of Mercy of Devonport and Plymouth* (London: Joseph Masters, 1852), p. 11.

10 (Sellon), *Reply to a tract by the Rev. J. Spurrell*, p. 12.

11 The National Archives, London (hereafter NA), HO45 3783l, letter from Daniel

O'Keefe to Sir George Grey, 8 December 1851; Grey's office found the complaint to be unsubstantiated.

12 NA, HO45 7991, printed notice of William Murphy's lectures to be delivered at the Agricultural Hall, Snow Hill, Wolverhampton, 18–22 February 1867, fol. 9. For an account of Murphy's activities in the 1860s, see Walter Arnstein, *Protestant versus Catholic in mid-Victorian England: Mr. Newdegate and the nuns* (Columbia and London: University of Missouri Press, 1982), chapter 7.

13 Sally Cunneen, *In search of Mary: the woman and the symbol* (New York: Ballantine, 1996); Jaroslav Pelikan, *Mary through the centuries: her place in the history of culture* (New Haven, CT, and London: Yale University Press, 1996).

14 Barbara Corrado Pope, 'Immaculate and powerful: the Marian revival in the nineteenth century', in Clarissa W. Atkinson, Constance H. Buchanan, and Margaret R. Miles (eds), *Immaculate and powerful: the female in sacred image and social reality* (Boston, MA: Beacon Press, 1985), p. 196.

15 Peter Hinchliff, *God and history: aspects of British theology, 1875–1914* (Oxford: Clarendon Press, Oxford and New York: Oxford University Press, 1992), p. 25; emphasis in original.

16 Mary Heimann, *Catholic devotion in Victorian England* (Oxford: Clarendon Press, 1995).

17 John Wolffe, *The Protestant crusade in Great Britain* (Oxford: Clarendon Press, 1991).

18 Nigel Yates, *Anglican ritualism in Victorian Britain, 1830–1910* (Oxford and New York: Clarendon Press, 1999).

19 John Shelton Reed, *Glorious battle: the cultural politics of Victorian Anglo-Catholicism* (Nashville, TN, and London: Vanderbilt University Press, 1996).

20 *Journal of ecclesiastical history*, 43 (1992), 16–34.

21 Carol Marie Engelhardt, 'Mother Mary and Victorian Protestants', *Studies in church history*, 39 (2002), 298–307; 'The Virgin Mary and Victorian masculinity', in Andrew Bradstock, Sean Gill, and Anne Hogan (eds), *Masculinity and spirituality in Victorian culture* (London: Macmillan, 2000), pp. 44–57; 'The paradigmatic Angel in the House: Victorian Anglicans and the Virgin Mary', in Anne Hogan and Andrew Bradstock (eds), *Women of faith in Victorian culture: reassessing 'The Angel in the House'* (London: Macmillan, 1998), pp. 159–71.

22 E. C. Wilson, Frances A. Yates, Roy Strong, Jean Wilson, Stephen Greenblatt, and Lisa Jardine are among those who argue that Marian imagery was subsumed by Elizabeth I. See E. C. Wilson, *England's Eliza* (New York: Octagon, 1966 [1939]); Frances A. Yates, 'Queen Elizabeth as Astraea', *Journal of the Warburg and Courtauld Institutes*, 10 (1947), 27–82 and *Astraea: the imperial theme in the sixteenth century* (London: Routledge, 1975); Roy Strong and Jean Wilson, *Entertainments for Elizabeth I* (Woodbridge: D. S. Brewer, 1980); Stephen Greenblatt, *Renaissance self-fashioning from More to Shakespeare* (Chicago, IL: University of Chicago Press, 1980); and Lisa Jardine, *Still harping on daughters: women and drama in the age of Shakespeare* (Hemel Hempstead: Harvester, 1983). Helen Hackett's revisionist *Virgin mother, maiden queen: Elizabeth I and the cult of the Virgin Mary* (London: Macmillan, 1995) holds that Marian imagery coexisted with the cult of Elizabeth I.

23 For more information on the early Anglican tradition of Marian devotion, see A. M. Allchin, *The joy of all creation: an Anglican meditation on the place of Mary*, rev. edn (London: New City, 1993), chapters 2–5.

24 David Cressy, *Birth, marriage and death: ritual, religion and the life-cycle in Tudor and Stuart England* (Oxford: Oxford University Press, 1997), p. 226.

25 Thomas Ken, D.D., 'Sion: or, Philothea', *The works of the Right Reverend, learned and pious Thomas Ken, D.D.*, 4 vols (London: John Wyat, 1721), vol. 4, p. 365.

26 Thomas Ken, 'The Annunciation', *The works of the Right Reverend, learned and pious Thomas Ken, D.D.*, 4 vols (London: John Wyat, 1721), vol. 1, p. 22, emphasis in original; see also Anthony Stafford, *The femall glory: or, the life and death of our Blessed Lady, the Holy Virgin* (London: Thomas Harper, 1635); reprinted as *Life of the Blessed Virgin, together with the apology of the author, and an essay on the cultus of the Blessed Virgin Mary*, ed. Orby Shipley, 4th edn (London: Longmans, Green, Reader, and Dyer, 1869).

27 Arnstein, *Protestant versus Catholic in mid-Victorian England*, p. 3.

28 D. G. Paz, *Popular anti-Catholicism in mid-Victorian England* (Stanford, CA: Stanford University Press, 1992), p. 300.

29 John Bossy, *The English Catholic community 1570–1850* (New York: Oxford University Press, 1976), p. 308. Although Irish immigrants comprised a significant percentage of the Roman Catholic Church in England by 1850, they never exercised leadership in proportion to their numbers.

30 Paz, *Popular anti-Catholicism in mid-Victorian England*, p. 51; Edward Norman, *The English Catholic Church in the nineteenth century* (Oxford: Clarendon, 1984), p. 21.

31 The text of the Act is found Norman, *The English Catholic Church in the nineteenth century*, pp. 131–9. The Act did not give full civic equality, however, for it prevented Roman Catholics from holding certain offices, banned religious orders, and prohibited their priests from wearing clerical garb in public.

32 Arnstein, *Protestant versus Catholic in mid-Victorian England*, p. 7.

33 William Palmer, *A statement of circumstances connected with the proposal of resolutions at a special general meeting of the Bristol Church Union, October 1, 1850* (London: Francis & John Rivington, 1850), p. 15.

34 'Romish ritualism: an ecclesiastical death-bed', *Wesleyan–Methodist magazine* (5th series), 11: 11 (November 1865), 1000.

35 Pusey House, Oxford, LBV 37, letter from Charles Pourtales Golightly to the vice-chancellor of Oxford, 5 January 1846.

36 Catherine Sinclair, *Popish legends, or Bible truths* (London: Longman, Brown, Green, and Longmans, 1852), p. xxv.

37 Jenny Franchot, *Roads to Rome: the antebellum Protestant encounter with Catholicism* (Berkeley: University of California Press, 1994), p. xvii.

38 (William Lockhart), *Biography of Father Lockhart: reprinted, with additions, from the autumn number of 'The Ratcliffian'* (Leicester: Ratcliffe College, and Market Weighton: St William's Press, 1893), p. 13n. In contrast, Lockhart's great-aunts 'were much alarmed, and said the lad had best not come to see them, as they supposed, from their recollections of monks and friars abroad, he would now go barefooted, and with a shaved crown' (p. 13n).

39 David Newsome, *The parting of friends: the Wilberforces and Henry Manning* (Grand Rapids, MI: William B. Eerdmans, 1993), p. 312.

40 Bodleian Library, Oxford, MSS Wilberforce, c. 67, letter from W. E. Gladstone to Archdeacon Robert Wilberforce, 11 April 1851, fol. 26, emphasis in original.

41 British Library, London, ADD MS 44452, memorandum by W. E. Gladstone, undated (?1876), fols 243–4.

42 Bodleian Library, Oxford, MSS Wilberforce, c. 20, letter from Samuel Wilberforce, 24 October (1868), fol. 114.

43 Arnstein, *Protestant versus Catholic in mid-Victorian England*, p. 42.

44 Ronald Chapman, *Father Faber* (Westminster, MD: Newman Press, 1961), pp. 99, 101.

45 Newsome, *The parting of friends*, pp. 310–11.

46 John Henry Newman, *Apologia pro vitâ suâ*, Introduction by Philip Hughes (New York: Doubleday, 1956 [1864]), p. 147.

47 Edward Stuart Talbot, *Memories of early life* (London: A. R. Mowbray, 1924), p. 10.

48 Susan O'Brien, 'French nuns in nineteenth-century England', *Past and present*, 154 (1997), 171–2.

49 See Pope, 'Immaculate and powerful', p. 181.

50 For a fuller description of the apparitions and their cultural significance, see Sandra L. Zimdars-Swartz, *Encountering Mary: from LaSalette to Medjugorge* (Princeton, NJ: Princeton University Press, 1991), and Pope, 'Immaculate and powerful.'

51 Norman, *The English Catholic Church in the nineteenth century*, p. 146.

52 Bodleian Library, Oxford, MSS Wilberforce, d. 38, letter from W. F. Hook to Samuel Wilberforce, 12 September 1858, fol. 176; see also Peter Benedict Nockles, *The Oxford Movement in context: Anglican High Churchmanship, 1760–1857* (Cambridge: Cambridge University Press, 1994), p. 164.

53 G. Poynder, Preface to John Poynder, *Extracts from three speeches delivered by the late John Poynder, Esq., at the East India House, in the years 1830, 1836, and 1839: demonstrating the direct support and encouragement given by the company to idolatry; together with extracts from other sources on the subject of idolatry, and the Indian Mutinies, with remarks by the editor* (London: Wertheim & Macintosh, 1857), pp. 3–4; see also Palmer, *A statement of circumstances connected with the proposal of resolutions*, p. 52; Seymour, *Pilgrimage*, p. 368.

54 John Poynder, *Popery in alliance with heathenism: letters proving that where the Bible is wholly unknown, as in the heathen world, or only partially known, as in the Romish Church, idolatry and superstition are inevitable*, 2nd edn (London: J. Hatchard & Son, 1835), pp. 113–14.

55 (Augustin Gaspard Edouart), *An address to the parishioners of Leominster upon the worship of the Virgin Mary* (London: John F. Shaw & Co., 1866), p. 4; M. Hobart Seymour, *A pilgrimage to Rome* (London: Seeleys, 1848), p. 1.

56 M. Hobart Seymour, *A lecture, delivered at the Guildhall Bath, on Monday, Dec. 2, 1850, on the recent Papal Aggression* (Bath: M. A. Pocock, n.d. [?1850]), p. 12.

57 Lambeth Palace Library, London, Golightly Papers, MS 1810, letter from Walter John Trower to Charles Pourtales Golightly, n.d. (?1869), fol. 214.

58 (A Layman), *The solemnity of our Anglo-Catholic ritualism defended: a letter to the Lord Bishop of London in reply to certain censures in his recent Charge to the Clergy* (London: W. J. Cleaver, 1850), p. 31.

59 Richard Frederick Littledale, *Ritualists not Romanists* (n.d.), p. 2, emphasis in original; see also William Gresley, *A word of remonstrance with the evangelicals* (London: Joseph Masters, and Lichfield: Thomas George Lomax, 1850), p. 11; (A Layman), *The solemnity of our Anglo-Catholic ritualism defended*, pp. 31–2.

60 Nockles, *The Oxford Movement in context*, pp. 38–9; Newsome, *The parting of friends*, p. 318.

61 Henry (Phillpotts), Lord Bishop of Exeter, *Charge delivered to the clergy of the diocese*

of Exeter (London: John Murray, 1839), p. 77.

62 Paz, *Popular anti-Catholicism in mid-Victorian England*, p. 135.

63 Nockles, *The Oxford Movement in context*, p. 20.

64 For an analysis of the seventeenth-century Anglican tradition of Marian devotion, see Allchin, *The joy of all creation*, chapters 2–6; Hilda Graef, *Mary: a history of doctrine and devotion* (London and New York: Sheed & Ward, 1965), vol. 2, pp. 63–7.

65 Linda Colley, *Britons: forging the nation 1707–1837* (New Haven, CT, and London: Yale University Press, 1992), p. 18.

66 Rev. Dr (John) Cumming, *The Immaculate Conception: its antecedents and consequences; taken from the 'Times', and corrected by the author* (London: published for the Protestant Reformation Society by James Miller, n.d. [?c. 1855]), p. 6.

67 Colley, *Britons*, pp. 18–19.

68 T. R. Birks, *Memoir of the Rev. Edward Bickersteth, late rector of Watton, Herts*, 2 vols (London: Seeleys, 1851), p. 2.

69 (Thomas Hartwell Horne), *Reminiscences personal and bibliographical of Thomas Hartwell Horne, B.D. F.S.A., with notes by his daughter, Sarah Anne Cheyne, and a short introduction by the Rev. Joseph B. M'Caul* (London: Longman, Green, Longman, & Roberts, 1862), p. 27.

70 Pelikan, *Mary through the centuries*, p. 1.

71 Cunneen, *In search of Mary*, p. 13.

72 Cunneen, *In search of Mary*, p. 256.

73 Kimberly van Esveld Adams, *Our Lady of Victorian feminism: the Madonna in the works of Anna Jameson, Margaret Fuller, and George Eliot* (Athens, OH: Ohio University Press, 2001), p. 89.

74 Claudia Nelson, *Boys will be girls: the feminine ethic and British children's fiction, 1857–1917* (New Brunswick, NJ, and London: Rutgers University Press), p. 4.

75 Claudia Nelson and Ann Sumner Holmes, 'Introduction', in Ann Sumner Holmes and Claudia Nelson (eds), *Maternal instincts: visions of motherhood and sexuality in Britain, 1875–1925* (Houndsmills and London: Macmillan, and New York: St. Martin's, 1997), p. 2.

76 Elizabeth Helsinger, Robin Lauder Sheets, and William Veeder, *The woman question: society and literature in Britain and America, 1837–1883*, 3 vols (New York: Garland, 1983), vol. 2, p. 195.

77 Helsinger et al., *The woman question*, vol. 2, p. 196.

78 Singleton, 'The Virgin Mary and religious conflict', p. 34.

79 George Eliot, *Romola* (London: Penguin, 1996 [1862–63]), p. 197.

80 Eliot, *Romola*, 558.

81 Eliot, *Romola*, p. 559.

82 Eliot, *Romola*, pp. 436–48.

83 Walter Houghton, *The Victorian frame of mind* (New Haven, CT: Yale University Press, 1957).

84 Mary Poovey, *Uneven developments: the ideological work of gender in mid-Victorian England* (Chicago, IL: University of Chicago Press, 1988), p. 3.

85 Meredith Veldman, 'Dutiful daughter versus all-boy: Jesus, gender, and the secularization of Victorian society', *Nineteenth-Century Studies*, 11 (1997), 1–24; Nelson, *Boys will be girls*; Catherine Robson, *Men in Wonderland: the lost girlhood of the Victorian gentleman* (Princeton, NJ, and Oxford: Princeton University Press, 2001).

86 See, for example, Pat Hudson, 'Women and industrialization', in June Purvis (ed.), *Women's history: Britain, 1850–1945. An introduction* (New York: St. Martin's, 1995), pp. 27–8.

87 Amanda Vickery, *The gentleman's daughter: women's lives in Georgian England* (New Haven, CT, and London: Yale University Press, 1998), p. 10.

88 See Sean Gill, *Women and the Church of England: from the eighteenth century to the present* (London: SPCK, 1994), chapter 3; Anna Clark, *The struggle for the breeches: gender and the making of the British working class* (Berkeley: University of California Press, 1995), especially part III.

89 Peter Gay, 'The manliness of Christ', in R. W. Davis and R. J. Helmstader (eds), *Religion and irreligion in Victorian society* (London and New York: Routledge, 1992), pp. 102–16; James Eli Adams, *Dandies and desert saints: styles of Victorian masculinity* (Ithaca, NY, and London: Cornell University Press, 1995); Nelson, *Boys will be girls*; Gill, *Women and the Church of England*, pp. 83–7; Veldman, 'Dutiful daughter versus all-boy', pp. 1–24.

90 Michael Roper and John Tosh, 'Historians and the politics of masculinity', in Michael Roper and John Tosh (eds), *Manful assertions: masculinities in Britain since 1800* (London: Routledge, 1991), p. 3.

91 Ian Bradley, *Abide with me: the world of Victorian hymns* (London: SCM Press, 1997), p. 57.

92 Webb notes that 'of the roughly 45,000 books published in England between 1816 and 1851, well over 10,000 were religious works, far outdistancing the next largest category – history and geography – with 4,900, and fiction with 3,500': R. K. Webb, 'The Victorian reading public', in Boris Ford (ed.), *The new Pelican guide to English literature* (London: Harmondsworth, 1982 [1958]), vol. 6, p. 199. This trend continued well into the second half of the nineteenth century: Veldman, 'Dutiful daughter versus all-boy', p. 3.

93 I am grateful to M. Jeanne Peterson for this information. In the 1860s the *Church times* advertised cards with images of leading Anglo-Catholics: Reed, *Glorious battle*, p. 215.

2

The Catholic Virgin Mary

The Virgin Mary described by Victorian Catholics is a familiar figure. She is the default image most have of the Virgin Mary: the young woman who is a fixture in crèche scenes, who lovingly cradles her divine son in Renaissance and Baroque images, and who later in life stands stalwartly and sorrowfully at the foot of the cross. She is the woman to whom Roman Catholics have traditionally turned for intercession, aid, and comfort. This image was developed by medieval Christians and elaborated on by their successors, so that by the nineteenth century her virtues, achievements, and powers had been described repeatedly in sermons, theological treatises, and devotional manuals. Churches, chapels, and shrines testified to and reinforced her prominent place in the Catholic tradition.

This Catholic Virgin had no significant public role in England in the seventeenth and eighteenth centuries, because recusants were by necessity and choice generally restrained in their public devotions.[1] By the 1830s, however, Roman Catholics and advanced Anglicans began publicly to invoke her as a model of Christian fidelity and an intercessor for sinners. The standard explanation for the increased Marian devotion in the Victorian era is the 'second spring' thesis. First voiced by John Henry Newman in 1852, this view holds that a wan, defensive, and dull Catholicism gave way to a vital, expressive faith after 1829. That thesis has been persuasively challenged by Mary Heimann's demonstration, in *Catholic devotion in Victorian England*, according to which recusant devotions continued to be popular in Victorian England. Given that there was no sharp break in the devotional tradition and that the recusant Church was more vibrant than previously imagined, the monocausal 'second spring' thesis is inadequate to explain the new public role accorded the Catholic Virgin Mary. The increased prominence of the Catholic Virgin is more satisfactorily explained by a nexus of religious and cultural factors.

Catholics most often defended Marian devotion on religious grounds: they argued that, sanctioned by Scripture and tradition, it promoted a close relationship with God. That belief, long held by Roman Catholics, found support among the ritualists and Tractarians who revived limited forms of Marian devotion within the Church of England. The international context encouraged those domestic developments, for the resurgence of Marian devotion in England occurred in the context of an increase in Marian devotions throughout the Roman Catholic Church in this period. In addition, invoking the Virgin Mary allowed both Roman Catholics and advanced Anglicans to distinguish themselves sharply from Protestants as they claimed that they were the more faithful Christians. Finally, Marian devotion became more popular at the same time as the idealisation of women as both virginal and maternal and as morally superior to men was widespread, at least in public discourse. The public acceptance of that image of feminine virtue may have encouraged Catholics to invoke her prototype more frequently.

Victorian Catholics promulgated their image of the Virgin Mary through devotional manuals, sermons, visual images, public controversies, and religious periodicals. This Virgin Mary was, in her broad outlines, essentially similar to the traditional Roman Catholic depictions of the Virgin. However, she had not had a significant public presence in England since the sixteenth century, so in one sense this was a new image in the nineteenth century. (However, references to her abounded in England, in that many Anglican churches were dedicated to St Mary the Virgin.[2] One of the most prominent of these was the University Church at Oxford, where Newman served as vicar from 1828 to 1843.) As with medieval and early modern representations of the Virgin, there were variations, from the slight to the significant, in Victorian Catholic representations. Certainly Roman Catholics tended to be more effusive than advanced Anglicans in describing the Virgin Mary's role and merits. There were also variations within each denomination. Some Roman Catholics were more fervent than others and delineated an extensive sphere of maternal authority for Mary. Some Anglicans were less hesitant than others to embrace forms of Marian devotion more associated with Rome than with Canterbury. The sharpest debate discussed in this chapter was among advanced Anglicans over whether prayer to the Virgin was allowed. (The most controversial question, the Immaculate Conception, is discussed in chapter 5.) The Catholic portrait of the Virgin Mary was never uniform, but was rather an evolving composite created by a variety of believers, not all of whom agreed with or even liked each other. However, the striking coherence of the overall portrait testifies to shared values, both cultural and theological, among Catholics.

Mary's intimate relationship with God

Catholics described Mary as being uniquely close to God, both as a faithful worshipper and as the mother of Jesus. In fact, her fidelity and her motherhood were inextricably intertwined in their representations: they believed that she was chosen to be Jesus' mother because of her faith, and that as Jesus' mother her faith both increased and was increasingly demonstrated. The linkage of these two characteristics was clear in Catholic interpretations of her first gospel appearance, when the angel Gabriel announced that she would bear the Saviour. His words and her response were evidence of her zeal for God, the Roman Catholic writer Michael Henry Dziewicki assured his readers: 'none did the will of the Father so perfectly as Mary did, nor so constantly; so that the Lord chose her for His Mother according to the flesh, because she was His Mother according to the spirit.'[3] Both Anglicans and Roman Catholics would have been reminded of Mary's role in the Incarnation when they celebrated the Feast of the Annunciation on 25 March and recited the *Magnificat*,[4] Mary's song commemorating the event, in their daily services.

When the Catholic Mary agreed to the Incarnation, she entered into a uniquely close physical relationship with the divine. Catholics frequently referred to 'the womb of the pure and ever-virgin mother',[5] which, in a sermon preached two-and-a-half years after his conversion, Newman elevated to 'that tabernacle from which He took flesh'.[6] Although Scripture says little about Mary's pregnancy beyond her post-Annunciation visit to her pregnant cousin Elizabeth,[7] Catholics pondered the reality that the embroyonic Jesus was physically dependent on his mother. The advanced Anglican Charles Lindley Wood (later Viscount Halifax) posited, in a debate with the first Earl of Redesdale (the former John Thomas Freeman Mitford), that the 'Blessed Virgin bore within herself for nine months God the Word, while he was taking to Himself of her substance, our nature from its very first beginning',[8] while Edward Bouverie Pusey rejoiced in a sermon that 'Almighty God took our poor human flesh to be united co-eternally with His Godhead ... in the humility of the Virgin's womb'.[9]

That this physical relationship demonstrated a mutual dependence between Creator and created was clear in William Bernard Ullathorne's meditation on Mary's pregnancy, which was filled with images of the physical connection between mother and child.

> And whilst the Godhead dwelt bodily in Him, He, for nine months, dwelt bodily in her. And all that time He breathed of her breath and lived of her life. All that time, the stream which nourished the growth of life in Jesus flowed from the heart of Mary, and, at each pulsation,

flowed back again, and re-entered His Mother's heart, enriching her with His divinest spirit.[10]

Ullathorne, whose Marian theology resembled the restrained warmth of Newman's, described mother and son's heartbeats in rhythmic diction that echoed the pulses themselves. That comforting rhythm underscored the interdependence of Mary and her son, which was key to Catholic images of the Virgin, as it disguised the radical nature of the relationship, that God was dependent on a woman's assent and on her body.

The Catholic willingness to discuss Mary's pregnancy was congruent with the realities of nineteenth-century life, for pregnant women were not uncommon sights in Victorian England: Judith Schneid Lewis notes that 'at no time during the century 1760 to 1860 does there seem to have been any social taboo against appearing visibly pregnant in public, contrary to popular myth'.[11] Working-class women did not have the luxury of being sequestered during pregnancy, while elite women went for drives, to the opera, to weddings, to the Continent, and even to court while nine months' pregnant.[12] Queen Victoria seems not to have allowed her many pregnancies to have limited her public appearances: the 1840 attempt on her life was made when, while four months pregnant, she was out for a drive with Prince Albert;[13] the following year, when she was seven months pregnant, she attended a council at which new ministers were appointed.[14] In Mrs Gaskell's novel *North and south*, Edith Lennox is unable to go to Milton to help her cousin Margaret after Mr Hale's death, not because she is pregnant, but because she is approaching her confinement, suggesting that there was no need for her to remain at home merely because she was pregnant. Perhaps the most striking image of a pregnant Victorian woman is that of Charles Kingsley's mother, Mary, who walked the moors, hoping to communicate her love of nature to her unborn child. Restrictions on a pregnant woman's appearing in public would have been inconvenient, if not impracticable, for in the nineteenth century women were likely to spend much of their married lives pregnant. They tended to have babies two years apart (sooner if the earlier baby died), so that they were pregnant or nursing for 13–18 years of their adult lives.[15]

Catholics believed that the bond formed between Jesus and Mary during those nine months continued after his birth. Going beyond static crèche scenes while ignoring the less pleasant realities of soiled diapers and maternal sleep deprivation, they imagined that the baby once 'hidden within the womb of Mary'[16] now 'play[ed] with Mary's hair'[17] with 'those tiny hands'[18] and 'clasp[ed] Mary's neck/ In timid tight embrace'.[19] Although there is no scriptural discussion of Mary's care for her infant, Catholics assumed that Jesus 'was nursed and tended by her; He was suckled by her; He lay in her arms'.[20] Drawing on their tradition of depicting a lactating Mary, Catholics frequently drew attention to Mary's nourishing breasts and the intimacy of the relationship they mediated when they identified Mary as the one 'who nursed and fed and cherished Him at her breasts'.[21] The Anglo-Catholic poet Christina Rossetti, who twice served as the model for the Virgin Mary for her brother Dante Gabriel,[22] reduced her to a 'breastful of milk'[23] in her poem 'A Christmas carol'.[24] The references to Mary breastfeeding Jesus are at odds with popular stereotypes of Victorian prudery, though they were congruent with a long-term shift, beginning in the seventeenth century, that urged women to nurse their own babies.[25] To encourage breastfeeding, mothers were told that nursing was a means by which to influence their children's moral development: as one Anglican priest reminded his parishioners, 'the Infant Jesus was nourished from the breasts of His Mother; and ... the office of a mother is carried on beyond the birth of a child, not only in the matter of food, but also in the secret transmission of energy and character, which are apparently as indelible as the germ of life itself'.[26] Sharing this assumption, 'S.B.H.', a 'British mother' distressed by Queen Victoria's decision not to breastfeed her first child, urged the royal mother: '*Thyself* a nursing-mother to thy royal infant be.'[27]

The close physical and spiritual relationship Catholics believed existed between Jesus and Mary was expressed by the title by which they, especially Roman Catholics, referred to Mary: Mother of God. To combat the Nestorian heresy that Jesus' human and divine natures were separate, the Council of Ephesus had declared in 431 that Mary was the *Theotokos*, or God-bearer, which in the Western tradition was rendered 'Mother of God.' This doctrine was fundamentally concerned with affirming that Jesus' nature was both human and divine, as Pusey, quoting Article 2, explained:

> Inseparable is His Godhead from His Body, in any way of Being, Natural or Supernatural. This follows from the doctrine of the Incarnation; that God the Son 'took man's nature in the womb of the Blessed Virgin of her substance; so that two whole and perfect natures, that is to say, the Godhead and Manhood, were joined together in One Person, never to be divided'.[28]

Ullathorne agreed that the title was concerned primarily with Jesus rather than his mother, arguing: 'if you deny that Mary is the Mother of God, you separate Jesus from Himself; you separate his divinity from His humanity, and thus you deny that He is the God–man'.[29] However, those unfamiliar with the theology and history behind the title might well have concluded that Catholics considered Mary, as the parent, to be superior to God in the person of her son, Jesus. Pusey, who preferred the untranslated *Theotokos*, was especially vigilant in guarding against any prayers, such as the Litany of Loretto, that he thought implied Mary's superiority to God by virtue of her role as Mother of God.[30] That Pusey's discomfort with the Litany of Loretto was cultural as well as theological is suggested by the recusant priest and historian John Lingard according to whom that Litany was a 'jargon of mysterious, unintelligible, aye even "portentous sounds."'[31] These variations are reminders that the Catholic portrait of the Virgin Mary was never entirely stable; advanced Anglicans and recusants were less likely to accord her titles or credit her with characteristics that expanded her power. The variations, however, were less important than a broad agreement to describe an idyllic relationship between mother and child, one that domesticated the Christian story of salvation and highlighted the woman's role in it.

Catholics believed that the close relationship between mother and son continued beyond Jesus' infancy. They were confident that Jesus loved and respected the woman who was, as Newman several times asserted prior to his conversion, 'the only one whom Christ revered on earth' and 'His only natural superior.'[32] Therefore, they often ignored Joseph, either by imagining 'years of holy happy intercourse'[33] between mother and son on the divine plan for salvation[34] or by depicting the adolescent Jesus as subject only to Mary's authority.[35] John Keble pointed to Joseph's redundancy when he noted, in his controversial poem 'Mother out of sight', that Jesus must look like Mary: 'Angel nor Saint His face may see/ Apart from what He took of thee.'[36] Some Roman Catholics went so far as to shift the emphasis from his obedience to her control, as the *Dublin review* did when it informed its readers: 'During far the greater portion of God's Human Life upon earth, she exercised over Him the authority of a mother.'[37] This meant, according to Ullathorne, that during the first thirty years of Jesus' life, 'Mary guided the ways of Jesus. She was the minister of the Father's will to His incarnate Son ... During all that time, she not only studied the life of Jesus, but she commanded His will, and guided His actions; and those actions were each of them contributing to the glory of God and the salvation of the world.'[38] Catholics' emphasis on the importance of Mary's role in the Incarnation and the necessary redundancy of Joseph could lead to their crediting her with more authority even than that allowed by the most effusive Victorian paeans to maternal influence. Victorian mothers were supposed to guide but not command, and even that influence was rarely extended so far into their children's lives.

Catholics generally described Mary's maternal authority as lasting for only the first thirty years of Jesus' life, that is, until he entered the public sphere when he performed his first miracle at the wedding at Cana. While they believed that Jesus performed this miracle at her instigation,[39] they usually identified this episode as marking the conclusion of her direct influence. According to Newman, 'that subjection, that familiar family life, was not to last to the end',[40] even if, as the advanced Anglican clergyman Freeman Wills believed, it was 'with unwillingness and lingering that He began His ministry and left His mother's side'.[41] Wills's somewhat maudlin image notwithstanding, advanced Anglicans were usually more careful than Roman Catholics to delineate an end to Mary's maternal authority. Richard William Church, the Anglo-Catholic chronicler of the Oxford Movement and Dean of St Paul's Cathedral, in London, believed that, at the wedding at Cana, 'He stopped His mother, when she seemed to interfere; He would not be brought into public, as a worker of miracles'.[42] While a few Roman Catholics assumed that Mary participated in her son's public life, for example by asking him to perform other miracles after the wedding at Cana,[43] most Catholics believed that her restriction to the private sphere was one of her virtues. As the advanced Anglican priest Montague Henry Noel declared, 'her very obscurity and humility fill us with admiration'.[44]

Although the Catholic Mary's authority ended when her son began his ministry, their unique intimacy did not necessarily, for some Catholics imagined that she followed her son until his earthly ministry ended at the cross. Here again Catholics' willingness to fill in scriptural silences enabled them to produce a portrait of Mary more sympathetic than the one offered by the gospels. Although Scripture records only that 'there stood by the cross of Jesus his mother, and his mother's sister, Mary the wife of Cleophas, and Mary Magdalene',[45] Catholics assumed that, as his mother, Mary suffered with her son. The advanced Anglican clergyman Alfred Lush assured his congregation: 'The dreadful agonies, the excruciating pains which her Son was then undergoing, were all seen, were all felt by His mother. For He was her Son. And did ever [a] mother see her son suffer, without suffering also?'.[46] Yet her suffering 'more than any martyr's agony'[47] was also a sign of her fidelity, William Towry Law (a younger son of Edward, first Baron Ellenborough) argued in a work defending his recent conversion to Roman Catholicism. Father Sebastian of the Blessed Sacrament (Sebastian Keens), a priest in the Congregation of the Cross and Passion of Our Lord Jesus Christ, agreed, imagining that she 'endured all her sufferings without murmuring, nor did she seek vengeance on those who afflicted Jesus'.[48]

Catholics may have drawn a contrast between her stoical support and Peter's impetuously striking off the soldier's ear in the Garden of

Gethsemane. While Jesus rebuked Peter's act of retribution, Mary was rewarded with a final sign of her son's love for her. Jesus loved Mary so much that, Keble said, he was concerned with her welfare even in the midst of his greatest suffering: 'E'en from the tree He deign'd to bow/ For her His agonisèd brow,/ Her, His sole earthly care.'[49] The *Stabat Mater*, a medieval meditation on Mary's sorrows at the crucifixion that was available in Roman Catholic devotional works such as the *Raccolta: or, collection of indulgenced prayers*[50] and Father Sebastian's *Manual of devotions*,[51] as well as in the Anglican *Hymns ancient & modern*,[52] encouraged Catholics to ponder Mary's loss. The *Lyra Catholica* of the Roman Catholic convert and priest of the Birmingham Oratory Edward Caswall was used also by Victorian Anglicans and included what Ian Bradley has termed 'a particularly fine translation of the *Stabat Mater*'.[53] These meditations, which were the sorrowful counterparts to the joyful Catholic meditations on the intimacy between Mary and Jesus at the Nativity, developed the theme that the Virgin Mary was closer to God than was any other human being. Cooperating with God in the salvation of the world, she shared God's suffering as well as God's joy.

Some Roman Catholics radically extended Mary's maternal influence to the point of her consenting to Jesus' death on the cross. This was the corollary to their belief that she had freely chosen to bear him, Nicholas Wiseman explained: 'As she accepted Him at His Incarnation, she yielded Him at His death.'[54] She accepted his death shortly after he was born, according to Father Sebastian, when she heard Simeon's prophecy that 'a sword shall pierce through thy own soul also'.[55] A few even went so far as to assert, as Wiseman did in a lecture delivered in London in 1865, that 'she became a co-operator, as far as possible, with God in His great work; she became the priestess on the part of mankind'.[56] This meant only, the *Dublin review* explained, 'that, having been redeemed herself, she co-operated most closely and intimately with our Lord, by sympathy, by congruous merit, by impetration by suffering, in redeeming others'.[57] However, even those who extended Mary's role did not insist on it. In a rare moment of restraint, the normally effusive *Dublin review* admitted: 'If to any Catholic such expressions appear strained and far-fetched, he is in no way called on to adopt or even think of them.'[58] Because these beliefs were not dogmatic, most Catholics must have agreed with Pusey in rejecting the notion 'that the Blessed Virgin had authority over our Blessed Lord in regard to this His Divine work, and that it was accomplished, in part, in obedience to her maternal authority'.[59]

If the Catholic Mary's maternal authority was generally limited, her maternal identity continued into eternity. 'He calls thee Mother evermore',[60] Keble assured the Virgin. This was only natural, according to the Roman Catholic convert and priest William Lockhart (who identified himself as one of Newman's 'oldest living disciples'[61]): 'The relation of mother and son can never be dissolved; once a mother always a mother, – she can never cease to be what she is.' Therefore, he continued, Jesus 'still owns her as His Mother before the angels of God – still pays her all the duty and the love which the most dutiful of sons can pay to the holiest of mothers'.[62] Some Roman Catholics went further, imagining that Mary actively cooperated with her son in heaven. Daniel French, a lay Roman Catholic barrister who in 1851 engaged in public disputes with the Presbyterian controversialist John Cumming, was confident that 'she who obtained the working of the first glorious miracle at the marriage-feast of Cana, before his day for working miracles was come, can still obtain, by her holy influence, the working of yet more miraculous conversions'.[63] Lockhart took the assumption that the Virgin Mary could sway her son one step further, arguing that she continued to exert her maternal authority even in heaven: 'On earth He obeyed her in all that was the will of God: is it unreasonable to suppose that He may still in some way submit His will to Mary?'[64] The image of a divine being who was eternally subject to his human mother must have been startling, especially in a culture that promoted maternal influence rather than maternal authority. However, Lockhart attributed unlimited power to Mary only because he believed 'that, as Mary's will is always in accordance with the will of God, the assent of Jesus follows *in order* the will of Mary, and that Jesus pours forth His graces upon God's elect at the intercession of Mary'.[65] With this shift, Lockhart both limited Mary's authority and reinforced the Catholic belief that she was exceptionally good. Almost two decades later, the *Dublin review* likewise simultaneously expanded and limited Mary's power, arguing: 'God will never refuse her anything she asks', because 'she will never ask anything inconsistent with His Providence'.[66]

The Catholic portrait of the Virgin Mary as a loving mother who was deserving of the highest devotion paid to mortals was a traditional one, albeit one that had on the Continent increased in fervency in the eighteenth century. Henry Edward Manning even insisted that such veneration had begun during her lifetime, when the devotion of the apostles outstripped even that of well-known devotees such as St Bernard, St Bonaventure, and St Alphonsus Liguori,[67] although he acknowledged that his assertion was 'without proofs in words'.[68] The claim of tradition was one of the strongest justifications Catholics had for promoting this view of the Virgin. However, the emergence of several specific factors, beginning in the 1830s, encouraged Catholics to promote the image. Catholic emancipation, the restoration of the hierarchy, and the influx of well-educated, confident converts made Roman Catholics more willing to publicise practices, such as Marian devotion, that marked their confessional identity. Likewise, Tractarians and ritualists embraced this image of the Virgin Mary as they recovered beliefs and practices long absent from, or never practised by, the Church of England. While Catholics justified their view of the Virgin Mary on theological and historical grounds, in the polemical atmosphere that characterised Victorian religion they also had strategic motives for promulgating their portrait of the Virgin Mary. Invoking the most familiar symbol of Catholicism served to sharpen a distinct Catholic identity, especially as English Protestants became publicly hostile to the Catholic Mary in a way that they had not been previously.

Vowed virginity and independence

The Catholic Mary was, as a mother, defined as being in relationship with the divine, whether with Jesus her son, God the Father or the Holy Ghost who had been the means of her conceiving. She was, as the painter and poet Dante Gabriel Rossetti described her, 'a Daughter born to God,/ Mother of Christ from stall to rood,/ and Wife unto the Holy Ghost'.[69] At the same time, her actions and relationships made her a singular figure: her role as the Mother of God and an exemplar of Christian faith made her an object of devotion for Catholics who sought her assistance and saw in her a model for their own behaviour.

Catholics believed that Mary's ability to act independently was apparent at the Annunciation. According to the Gospel of Luke, when Gabriel announced to Mary, 'And, behold, thou shalt conceive in thy womb, and bring forth a son, and shalt call his name Jesus', Mary replied, 'How shall this be, seeing I know not a man?'[70] Catholics interpreted this question as evidence that she was not, Newman declared, 'merely ... the physical instrument of our Lord's taking flesh, but ... an intelligent, responsible cause of it; her faith and obedience being accessories to the Incarnation'.[71] God approved her desire for knowledge, Wiseman believed: God 'gives her time to deliberate; He accords her permission to suggest difficulties, to make her own terms'.[72] Not only did God wait for Mary's agreement before proceeding with his plan but, according to some, he was required to do so. John Jerome, a lawyer and Roman Catholic convert who eagerly defended his new church, stated this plainly: 'It was only necessary that the consent of Mary should be freely given' for the Incarnation to occur.[73]

The Anglo-Catholic priest Orby Shipley made plain the implication that she had the power to thwart God's plan when he stated that

> the Incarnation could not have taken place without S. Mary's consent. Had she refused to listen to the Angel, the HOLY GHOST would never have over-shadowed her, nor would there have been born of her that HOLY THING, Which is called the SON of GOD; and if the SON could not have become incarnate without her consent, neither could the Atonement for sin have taken place.[74]

Shipley's seems like an extreme position, for it gave a human the power to thwart the divine will. However, he could posit that Mary's 'No' would have blocked the salvation of the world only because he believed that she never erred. This restriction on her ability to make some choices does not, however, undo the fact that the Catholic Mary was an extraordinarily powerful woman. Imagining, as the Tractarian poet and clergyman Isaac Williams did, 'how awful was that moment when God had made known His will to the Blessed Virgin before she had given the answer',[75] Catholics described a woman with the power to deny, or at least delay, salvation to all humans. Believing that she had not refused the angel's invitation, Catholics created a scenario in which she could have done so. Like thrill-seekers at an amusement park, they allowed themselves to be temporarily frightened, certain that they had nothing to fear. This scenario underscored the power with which they believed the Virgin Mary to be invested. It was because Catholics believed that the Virgin Mary was uniquely close to God that they could also trust that she would always act rightly: her freedom was limited by her fidelity to God. The restriction meant that she was doubly powerful; she was both unable to err and able to make God wait upon her.

The angel Gabriel responded to Mary's question about how she would bear a child by saying, 'The Holy Ghost shall come upon thee, and the power of the Highest shall overshadow thee: therefore also that holy thing which shall be born of thee shall be called the Son of God.'[76] Historically Christians had believed that his words showed that Mary had conceived as a virgin, in fulfilment of the prophecy of Isaiah 7:14: 'Behold, a virgin shall conceive, and bear a son, and shall call his name Immanuel.'[77] Catholics held as well that Mary had remained a 'pure and ever-virgin mother'[78] after the birth of Jesus. Although some in the early church supposed that Mary had borne other children, belief in her eternal virginity became generally accepted by the late second or the early third century.[79] In Catholic tradition Mary and Joseph had a celibate marriage because she was, as Keble described her in 'Mother out of sight', 'th'

Enthroned Spouse'[80] of the Holy Ghost. In the mid-1870s R. J. Wilson, an advanced Anglican priest, distributed prayer cards invoking 'Mary, ever a Virgin, Mother of our God and Lord Jesus Christ' and 'Blessed Mary, Ever Virgin Mother of God'[81] (although he was later forced to defend them in *A letter to the Archbishop of Canterbury*), while by 1880 the Sisterhood of St Margaret's, using the Sarum Breviary, chanted at Sext, 'In the burning bush which Moses saw unconsumed: we recognise the preservation of thy glorious virginity, O Mother of God.'[82] Some Catholics even believed the ancient legends, held by many of the Church Fathers, that Mary had remained intact during the birth of Jesus.[83] Her eternal virginity highlighted her independence from Joseph. The absence of an earthly father, while theologically necessary, was a reminder that, as Janice Capel Anderson has noted, 'it is not the husband that [*sic*] ultimately controls the woman's reproductive powers.'[84]

Because they believed that Mary was ever-virgin, Catholics insisted that gospel references to Jesus' 'brethren' were to his 'cousins'[85] or to Joseph's sons from an earlier marriage.[86] References to Jesus as Mary's 'first-born' child did not necessarily imply that other children followed, argued Williams. After noting that this term was used in the Old Testament with reference to the Passover, he continued: 'when it is said that she brought forth her Son, the First-born, Scripture speaks of things infinitely vast and Divine, and not as indicating other subsequent children, as some would extract from the expression.'[87] Catholics also appealed to the Church Fathers to support their position that Mary was ever-virgin: Newman devoted a section of his *Selected treatises of St Athanasius in controversy with the Arians* to Athanasius's defence of Mary's eternal virginity.[88] A less authoritative source was the legend, which first appeared in the mid-second century *Protoevangelum* of James, that Mary had vowed virginity as a child. Although such a vow would have been unthinkable in Mary's Jewish culture,[89] the basis for it was her question to the angel, 'How shall this be since I know not a man?'[90]

The medievals believed that Mary's alleged vow had been conditional. They thought that Mary would have consummated her marriage if God had so desired, and that only after the birth of Jesus did she inform Joseph of her vow, at which point he agreed to it.[91] By the nineteenth century, however, Catholics described a woman who was more assertive in guarding her virginity. Newman (who, immediately after his conversion, believed the legends that Mary had vowed virginity for a brief time) several times declared that Mary had initially hesitated to assent to the angel's words because she wanted to preserve her virginity,[92] while Ullathorne described her at the Annunciation as 'solicitous for that virginity which she had vowed and given unto God'.[93] Victorians could find this interpretation in Dziewicki's *Legend of the Blessed Virgin Mary, Mother of Christ our Lord*, in which Mary informed the high priest that she could not marry, for she had 'vowed a vow unto God, that I shall remain ever a virgin. And I know that my vow is acceptable unto Him, for He moved me to make it, and He delighteth in purity'.[94] This vow was further evidence of Mary's fidelity to God, according to Catholics who subscribed to this apocryphal belief. Some Roman Catholics went further and argued that Mary understood her virginity as an even higher virtue than bearing the Saviour. Wiseman believed that Mary had hesitated to assent to the angel's message at the Annunciation because she was reluctant 'to surrender the precious gift which she values higher than the highest imaginable honours'.[95] The Roman Catholic priest Frederick Charles Husenbeth, a prolific writer and editor, introduced Victorians to eighteenth-century and continental works that portrayed Mary as not consenting to the Incarnation until she was convinced that motherhood would 'not entrench in the least upon her virginal purity'.[96]

Catholics defended Mary's eternal virginity as being, as Newman argued, 'the legitimate development *of* that doctrine', that is, the Incarnation.[97] The eternal virginity of Mary was held not just by priests and nuns, who could find it a validation of their choice of celibacy, but also by married Catholics. Williams, who had seven children, thought that Mary was ever-virgin, as did Ambrose Phillips de Lisle, the father of sixteen; Wood, the father of six, shocked Lady Frederick Cavendish by declaring, 'If I had to choose between an immoral celibate clergy and a moral married clergy, I would choose the former'.[98] Some seemed repelled by the idea that Mary may have had sexual intercourse. Like a knight defending a lady's honour, Williams declared that saying Mary had other children was 'derogatory to our Lord's mother, and His reputed father or natural guardian'.[99] Even as an Anglican Newman had believed that Mary was perpetually a virgin.[100] However, conversion encouraged Newman to elaborate on his Marian beliefs. Shortly after his conversion to Roman Catholicism, he argued that belief in Mary's eternal virginity was predicated on her bearing Jesus: 'The notion of St. Mary having children after our Lord is horrible, when the doctrine of the Incarnation is once understood';[101] and some time later he reiterated his belief that 'the idea was monstrous'.[102] The words 'horrible' and 'monstrous' are startling, especially for a man like Newman who delighted in children. The violence of this language suggests that the notion of Mary's having sexual intercourse – and presumably experiencing sexual passion – following the birth of Jesus prompted Catholics, whether married like Williams or celibate like Newman, to reject the suggestion that Mary and Joseph had consummated their marriage. It would have been difficult for Catholics to reconcile a sexually experienced Mary with their image of the saintly mother. The deep identification of Mary as a virgin-mother means that there is considerably less about her as a wife in Catholic tradition.

Catholics' belief that Mary was ever-virgin was also consistent with their belief that she had a uniquely close relationship with Jesus. Envisioning her as an eternal virgin excluded the possibility that she would be distracted by other children. It was also consistent with their view that she was a formidable woman. A Mary who chose to remain a virgin was an actor, a distinction that was increased by the fact that Jewish culture did not value life-long virginity. Besides not needing a man to fulfill her childbearing duty, the Catholic Mary was independent in other ways. In Western societies, marriage made a woman dependent on her husband for her legal, social, and economic identity. The Virgin Mary, however, had only the façade of a married woman, for in the Catholic tradition she was a more powerful and more prominent figure than Joseph, whose role was to protect her from the consequences of out-of-wedlock motherhood by contracting a marriage that would not be consummated. It was not simply her virginity in itself, but her choice to remain a virgin even within marriage that made her independent.

The Catholic portrait of the Virgin Mary, while derived from Scripture and tradition and inspired by religious feelings, was also motivated by the need to defend aspects of Catholicism, especially those opposed to Protestant beliefs and practices. An ever-virgin Mary validated Catholics' traditional certainty that vowed virginity was a legitimate and even holy choice. They were not among those whom the poet Lewis Morris derided as 'Rude souls and coarse, to whom virginity/ Seems a dead thing and cold'.[103] Newman defended vowed virginity as being 'higher than the marriage-state, not in itself, viewed from any mere natural respect, but as being the free act of self-consecration to God, and from the personal religious purpose which it involves'.[104] Catholics showed the value they placed on virginity by founding sisterhoods and encouraging women in their vocations. Pusey, John Mason Neale, and Thomas Thelluson Carter, all married men, founded Anglican sisterhoods; Pusey even encouraged his daughter in her desire to become an Anglican sister, although her wish was thwarted by her early death. (Pusey, who found the Church Fathers' defence of vowed virginity especially convincing,[105] further endorsed celibacy by restricting membership, in the highest 'rule' of the Society of the Holy Cross, to celibates.) Frederick W. Faber assured a woman who wanted to take a private vow of virginity that 'the supernatural destiny of virgins' was to follow '[a]ll His ways, His turns, His retreats, His hidings of Himself, His compassionate unbendings of His glory, His unspeakable familiarities of love'.[106] Neale agreed, promising the sisters at St Margaret's, East Grinstead, that, having 'chosen the higher and holier estate of chastity',[107] they were able to imitate Jesus, their bridegroom,[108] more closely, and even that they would achieve a higher place in heaven than that given to 'any ordinary Christian'.[109]

Historians often follow the lead of Victorian Protestants in regarding Victorian Catholics as counter-cultural or culturally marginal. However, the Catholic belief that Mary was ever-virgin was congruent in some ways with their temporal culture's high valuation of female virginity. Although Western culture had traditionally constructed women as more carnal than men, one result of the evangelical assertion that women were less carnal than men was the high value that mainstream Victorian culture placed on female virginity. Most heroines of Victorian literature were virgins (although matrimony was ratified by their being generally married or engaged just before the novel ended), and the ideal male–female relationship was frequently represented as that of brother and sister or father and daughter in prescriptive manuals, such as Sarah Ellis's well-known works, as well as in novels and paintings. (Maggie Tulliver's rejection of two suitors in George Eliot's The mill on the Floss in an attempt to salvage her relationship with her brother is an extreme example of the privileging of the sibling relationship.) Lewis has concluded that the elaborate weddings of the Victorian elite were a result of their sentimentalising of virginity.[110]

Victorian property-owning classes valued virginity for marriageable women in part because they assumed it would ensure that another man's children would not inherit the husband's money. The writer Caroline Norton, whose unhappy marriage transformed her into a crusader for the reform of divorce and custody laws, noted sardonically that 'property, not morality, being the thing held sacred' by her countrymen, their great horror was that 'the wife's adultery may give the husband a spurious son to inherit!'[111] It was also important symbolically: in an age of commercial competition, female virginity functioned as a promise of innocence, purity, and passivity to offset masculine aggression. Dinah Morris, Stephen Blackpool's friend Rachael, Agnes Wickfield, and numerous other maiden heroines in Victorian literature serve as the guiding moral lights to the men who struggle with their passions and to make a place for themselves in the world.

The Catholic Virgin Mary was nevertheless an anomaly in Victorian culture, as most women preferred to be married. Although a married woman was legally oppressed and could face other potential disadvantages – either the extreme ones experienced by Norton or the more common ones of boredom or incompatibility – she had more independence than did her spinster sisters. She ran a household, managed a social life, and faced fewer restrictions on her activities outside the home. However, the Virgin Mary was congruent with mainstream Victorian culture inasmuch as female sexuality was rarely discussed, even when women were married. As Dr William Acton famously pronounced, 'the majority of women (happily for them) are not very much troubled with sexual feeling of any kind'.[112] Acton's view was not representative of Victorians generally or of Catholics specifically, insofar as we can discern what their private lives were like.[113] M. Jeanne Peterson argues[114] that forms of premarital sexual activity were common among intended couples of the privileged classes. Noteworthy Victorians who enjoyed the physical as well as the emotional side of marriage include the Kingsleys, the Patmores, and of course the Queen and Prince Consort; Kingsley hoped that married bliss would continue in what John Maynard has termed 'his oddly sexual heaven'.[115] Public discourse, however, was characterised by a marked reluctance to talk about sexuality, marital or otherwise. Discussion of sexual intercourse and its consequences is not found even where we would expect to find it, in advice literature.[116] This silence marks Victorian novels also, which generally avoid describing the first year or so of the heroine's marriage. They frequently conclude with the engagement or marriage, then provide a coda in which the hero and heroine appear with at least one child. Thus could the image of 'passionlessness', to use Nancy Cott's term,[117] if not virginity, be promulgated. Edith Lennox's two pregnancies, in *North and south*, are the exceptions that prove this rule. Her first pregnancy is the more remarkable, because we have a fairly clear idea of when conception occurs: we hear of Edith's marriage to Captain Lennox, their honeymoon in Scotland, the progress of her pregnancy, and finally the birth of her child.

Although lifelong virginity was not a Victorian value, 10–20 per cent of all Victorian women remained single.[118] Furthermore, the growing number of both Anglo-Catholic and Roman Catholic convents in Victorian England, especially in the second half of the nineteenth century, meant that more women could choose to imitate the Catholic Mary's religiously motivated virginity. The handful of Roman Catholic convents in 1840 had grown to over 300 by 1880, thanks to the arrival of continental orders as well as the establishment of a dozen new English orders, largely by female converts.[119] Susan Mumm estimates that approximately 10,000 women had spent at least some time in an Anglican convent between 1845, when the first sisterhood was established, and 1900.[120]

Many who supported sisterhoods, whether Anglican or Roman Catholic, saw them as a more palatable option than poverty-stricken spinsterhood.[121] More positively, convents offered women the opportunity to do useful work, including nursing, teaching, and charity work, in addition to the usual household duties. Because of the work they performed, Mumm argues, 'sisterhoods were undoubtedly the most attractive channel of full-time work for women within the Church of England'.[122] Furthermore, vowed virginity offered women a further option to marriage and spinsterhood, one that gave them some advantages lay women did not enjoy. In addition to escaping the dangers associated with pregnancy and childbirth, vowed religious women in positions of authority within their congregations wielded financial, spiritual, and social power. Anglican sisters generally had less autonomy than their Roman Catholic counterparts partly because the Anglican hierarchy's considerable opposition to those orders meant a greater – and more hostile – degree of supervision by bishops. Moreover, the sisterhoods were often founded by men who retained a measure of control by supervising their activities, preaching in their chapels, and hearing their confessions. Nevertheless, both Michael Hill and A. M. Allchin have argued that these institutions laid the foundation for eventual female emancipation.[123]

The convents offered thousands of women the opportunity to achieve some of the independence represented by the Catholic Virgin Mary. Generally the Catholic Virgin Mary did not offer other women access to the expansive power she wielded. However, as a virgin she did provide a model of female autonomy, as Ullathorne explained: 'Mary has delivered woman in a yet more striking way. She has given honour to the state of virginity. She has established it is [sic] a state of life by her example and her influence. Woman is made free, because she has a choice of states. She may keep her freedom to the Lord her God, or she may give it to a husband.'[124] Ullathorne, and the thousands of women who joined Roman Catholic and Angican orders, thus contradicted Theodora Jankowski's conclusion that 'virgins lost real power once the mother of Christ became the desired examplar of virginal behavior'.[125]

Mary as the model Christian

Because she was defined as being uniquely close to God and one who had shown herself capable of freely choosing to do God's will, the Catholic Mary was held up as the prime exemplar of Christian faith. Catholics believed that Mary's faith was evident throughout the gospels. They were sure that her mere presence at the wedding at Cana was due to her faithfulness to her son's mission,[126] and when the hosts ran out of wine her faith was displayed in her 'humble yet fearless confidence in the power and readiness of Jesus to supply the lack'.[127] Catholics found contemporary praise for Mary in the unnamed woman who called out to Jesus, 'Blessed is the womb that bore thee, and the paps that gave thee suck.' Jesus deflected the praise, saying, 'Yea rather, blessed are they that hear the word of God, and keep it.'[128] However, Catholics turned Jesus' apparent rebuke to Mary's advantage, arguing that Jesus had not denied the worth of Mary's motherhood, but had only praised her faith more than her maternity. Jesus had acknowledged, Williams contended, only that 'it was by the faith of the Blessed Virgin that our Incarnate Lord was to be born of her'.[129] Roman Catholics even transformed that praise into a prayer: 'Blessed is the womb of the Virgin Mary, that bore the Son of the eternal Father. And blessed are the paps that gave suck to Christ our Lord.'[130]

A key component of the feminine ideal was the belief that women were more spiritual than men. The Virgin Mary, already the exemplar of female piety in Catholic discourse, was enlisted to serve as a model of female behaviour. Jane Eliza Leeson, a hymn-writer, author of children's books, and later Roman Catholic convert, urged the girls who read her conduct manual masquerading as a meditation on Mary's life, *The wreath of lilies: a gift for the young* – which was popular enough to go through a second edition in 1849 – to think about the Virgin Mary in Nazareth as a humble girl distinguished by her 'cheerful diligence about her work, and a holy simplicity in her manner, and a look of quiet happiness, such as they only know who walk with God'.[131] The Catholic Mary also modelled the gracious domestic helper when, at the wedding at Cana, her discreet resolution of the problem of a lack of wine demonstrated, Husenbeth believed, 'a certain eagerness for a good deed, and out of a motive of charity'.[132] Perhaps because her actions were within the domestic sphere, some Catholics believed that she was a member of the household rather than a guest. Williams, who lauded Mary's 'watchful consideration and contemplativeness'[133] when the wine was exhausted, concluded that 'the blessed Virgin's giving directions to the servants has the appearance of one thus at home in that family, rather than if she were a mere guest or stranger there'.[134] Leeson agreed with this hypothesis, insisting that Mary behaved 'as though she were one of the household, rather than as a guest invited for a day; we may suppose her to have found a home there for a season, with some of her kindred'.[135] Whether a thoughtful outsider or a member of the household obliged to look after the comfort of her guests, the Catholic Mary modelled the sort of behaviour that conduct manuals constantly urged on Victorian girls and women. She could also serve as a model of maternal religious behaviour. Scandalised by the 'extremely negligent'[136] mothers who allowed their children 'to wander from home without necessity, to amuse themselves in public streets, to play in bye-ways and roads, in a word, to do just as their whims suggest',[137] Father Sebastian urged the women who read his *Manual of devotions in honour of the seven dolours of the Blessed Virgin Mary*: 'Imitate the example of the Blessed Virgin; she, like a prudent and virtuous parent, took to the Temple whilst very young her Divine Son Jesus; she did so, as you have seen, for your particular instruction.'[138]

In these ways the Catholic Virgin Mary could seem like the type of woman who was frequently praised by Victorian commentators: she was a cheerful helper whose responsibilities were domestic and religious. However, a woman's sphere of action was usually limited to her own family or, at most, her own community. This was generally true even after the 1860s, when women were urged, in exhortations such as John Ruskin's popular lecture 'Of Queens' Gardens', to apply their domestic virtues to the outside world. Even in those representations of female influence, women were never envisioned as competitors to men. The Catholic Virgin Mary, however, was given no such limitations, for her sphere became the entire world when Catholics described her as being the mother of all believers.[139] The scriptural basis for that belief was Jesus' assigning his mother and his favourite disciple into each other's care just before he died.[140] Phillips de Lisle explained that 'by bearing him she became entitled spiritually to be the mother of all the elect; for they are the *mystical members* of Christ, and they are also called in scripture *his brethren*: so that the church interprets our Lord's words on the cross, wherein he commanded St John to look upon Mary as his mother, as addressed to all the elect.'[141]

This traditional belief had been maintained by recusants, but in the Victorian era it became more popular and was even adopted by some advanced Anglicans. In 'Mother out of sight', Keble urged Christians to turn to Mary, '[o]ur own, our only Mother',[142] while Shipley found evidence for this trope in the traditional parallel between Mary and Eve: 'If we say that the latter is the Mother of all sinners, because of her consent to sin, so we must say that our Lady is the Mother of the righteous, through her consent to the Incarnation.'[143] Lay orders such as the Confraternity of the Scapular of Mount Carmel and sodalities like the Children of Mary encouraged Roman Catholics to think of Mary as a protective mother.[144] Those whose mothers had died young were perhaps particularly open to viewing Mary as a second mother. After his mother's death, Faber became one of the most ardent advocates of Mary's spiritual motherhood. Following his conversion, he invited his new co-religionists to join him in addressing Mary as 'Dear Mama' or even 'Dearest Mama'. Few Catholics accepted Faber's invitation, being more likely to agree with Noel that this was 'sickly sentimentality'.[145] More restrained, and more typical, was Herbert Vaughan, the future Cardinal of Westminster. After his mother, Eliza, died in childbirth in 1853, Vaughan assured his father: 'The Blessed Virgin will now more than ever be to us a mother.'[146] Perhaps John Vaughan accepted his son's reassurance, for he had been praying to the Virgin since he was in school.[147] What is recorded, however, is that he adopted another ideal: he thought of his dead wife as 'the sweet guardian spirit, the beauteous angel'.[148] Both Vaughans prayed to Eliza as they would to the Virgin: shortly after his mother's death, Vaughan told his father, 'I invoke her as a saint; whenever I call upon one Mother, I call upon the other.'[149]

Catholics further expanded Mary's sphere of action when they posited her as a model for male as well as female behaviour. Although Protestants frequently complained that the Catholic Virgin Mary stood between the divine and the devout, there was a strain of Catholic thinking which said that believers who imaginatively experienced what Mary experienced would become closer to God. Thus Catholic men as well as women were told to imagine Mary's experiences in their prayers. This was one aspect of the late medieval practice, popularised by St Ignatius Loyola, that urged believers to place themselves imaginatively in biblical episodes. One of the most beautiful Victorian expressions of this idea was in the 1883 poem 'The Blessed Virgin compared to the air we breathe' by the convert and Jesuit priest Gerard Manley Hopkins. First Hopkins reminded believers of the physicality of the Incarnation, then shifted to a spiritual reconception of the Incarnation.

> Of her flesh he took flesh:
> He does take fresh and fresh,
> Though much the mystery how,
> Not flesh but spirit now
> And makes, O marvellous!
> New Nazareths in us,
> Where she shall yet conceive
> Him, morning, noon, and eve.[150]

Hopkins's dwelling on the physicality of the Incarnation – 'Of her flesh he took flesh' – was consistent with the Catholic tradition of materiality in religion, often expressed in Catholics' use of tangible objects, such as images and candles, to represent spiritual beliefs. He then moves beyond the historical moment to imagine that the Holy Spirit now 'makes, O marvellous!/ New Nazareths in us,/ Where she shall yet conceive/ Him, morning, noon, and eve'. While Mary still conceives Jesus, each Christian imaginatively conceives Nazareth, thus allowing a useful prayer experience without challenging Mary's unique role. Fusing the physical and the imaginative in order to promote spiritual growth, Hopkins urged all Christians to bring Jesus to bear in the world.

Hopkins's suggestion that men as well as women imagine the experience of pregnancy or, at least, of something growing in them is a reminder that the Catholic Mary did not merely uphold existing gender boundaries: she also undermined those boundaries, which many Victorians struggled so hard to maintain, when she was enlisted in the project to urge men to imagine the experience of pregnancy. Furthermore, the celebration of her pregnancy as a creative endeavour that all Christians should imagine for their spiritual profit severed pregnancy from its traditional associations with nature and in opposition to masculine reason. Instead, pregnancy was re-imagined in this case as something creative and desirable. The Catholic Virgin Mary was never merely a promoter of those feminine virtues that restricted women to the domestic sphere: she could also undermine the theory of separate spheres that supported the feminine ideal.

The two moments in Mary's life that were most significant to Catholics were her experience of becoming a mother – beginning with the Annunciation and concluding at the Nativity – and Jesus' Passion. Therefore, Catholics also believed that imagining Mary's experience at the crucifixion would bring them closer to God. Catholics who prayed the Rosary were probably most accustomed to this concept, for the medieval prayer follows the main events of Jesus' life, including his Passion, as experienced by Mary. Richard Challoner's *The garden of the soul* – a recusant devotional manual that remained popular in the Victorian era – drew on this approach when it advocated to the faithful:

> In your way to the Church or chapel, put yourself in the company of the blessed Virgin, and the other pious women going to Mount *Calvary*, to be present at the passion and death of our Lord. Represent your Saviour as carrying his cross before you, to be immolated thereon for your sins, and bewail these sins of yours, as the causes of all his sufferings.[151]

In 'Mother out of sight', Keble eliminated the bodily separation of the worshipper from the Virgin Mary when, referring to Simeon's prophecy,[152] he proclaimed that all Christians shared her sorrow at the crucifixion: 'Feel we the sword that pierc'd Thy side.'[153] Newman combined those approaches when he asked Catholics first to imagine they were at Calvary with Mary, and then to be absorbed by her in order to understand the meaning of Jesus' sacrifice.

Depend on it, the way to enter into the sufferings of the Son, is to enter into the sufferings of the Mother. Place yourself at the foot of the Cross, see Mary standing there, looking up and pierced with the sword. Imagine her feelings, make them your own. Let her be your great pattern. Feel what she felt and you will worthily mourn over the death and passion of your and her Saviour.[154]

Newman's instruction to the worshipper to imagine himself or herself as Mary was, like Keble's briefer exhortation, consistent with the Catholic tradition of ignoring gender boundaries. Such suggestions were, nevertheless, somewhat surprising, for they identified Catholics with two marginalised groups: women and unmanly men. Victorian Protestants frequently stereotyped Catholicism as a feminine religion, one that was irrational and superstitious, in contrast to a masculine, rational Protestantism. Italy, the country associated more than any other with Roman Catholicism, was designated a feminine country while England was gendered masculine.[155] Because women were generally believed to be less rational than men, they were considered to be especially susceptible to Catholicism. The anti-Catholic writer Catherine Sinclair warned that the Roman Catholic Church worked 'chiefly through female influence, to gain in this country supreme power, as well as unlimited wealth'.[156] Even sympathetic portraits of Catholic men speak of them in feminine terms. Wiseman, who had known Lingard as a schoolboy, later recalled him in almost womanly terms, noting his 'specific acts of thoughtful and delicate kindness, which showed a tender heart mindful of its duties'.[157] The alleged attractiveness of Catholicism to effeminate men was incorporated into popular novels such as those by Kingsley. Lancelot, the semi-autobiographical Protestant hero of Kingsley's *Yeast*,[158] warns his cousin, a Tractarian curate (and eventual Roman Catholic convert), that Catholics are doing religion a disservice: 'Be sure, that as long as you and yours make piety a synonym for unmanliness, you will never convert either me or any other good sportsman.'[159] Sean Gill acknowledges the 'association of celibacy and Anglo-Catholic ritual with "effeminacy"',[160] while John Shelton Reed argues that many who opposed Anglo-Catholicism sensed 'that there was something not quite *right* about some young Anglo-Catholics. They believed that the movement often attracted and nourished young men who were indifferent to or repelled by the Victorians' rigorous standards of manliness.'[161] While Reed concludes that the critics were on to something, Gill argues that attempts to label individual Catholics as homosexuals 'inevitably lead to verdicts of not proven for lack of evidence'.[162]

Catholics were further considered of dubious masculinity because they were deemed untrustworthy. One of the most famous charges of Tractarian dishonesty was Thomas Arnold's diatribe against the 'Oxford malignants', those 'conspirators [who] commenced one of the most extraordinary courses of agitation ever yet witnessed'.[163] Since the sixteenth century, Roman Catholics had been stereotyped as potential or actual traitors, a view continued in the nineteenth century in novels such as Sinclair's *Beatrice*, which portrayed them as the sneaky antithesis of the upright and honest members of the Established Church, and in Kingsley's infamous charge: 'Truth, for its own sake, has never been a virtue with the Roman clergy'.[164] Catholic men, however, demonstrated a careless disdain for the charges that they were effeminate or otherwise unmanly when they insisted that the Virgin Mary was an aide to their spirituality. In fact, they went their critics one better, for their praise of the Virgin Mary could be used to solidify masculine, especially priestly, authority, for they never suggested that the individual women they knew could fulfill the same role. The Virgin Mary whom Catholics described was a singular woman whose power and prerogatives could not be accessed by other women.

Mary as an object of devotion

Traditionally, Roman Catholics' praise for the Virgin Mary's virtues culminated in their asking her to intercede, or even to act, on their behalf. One of the most popular intercessory prayers was the Hail Mary. The traditional Catholic interpretation of the angelic salutation formed the first part of the familiar prayer: 'Hail Mary, full of grace, the Lord is with thee; blessed art thou among women'.[165] This refrain would have been familiar to English Roman Catholics, for the Hail Mary was typically included in their devotional manuals,[166] and the Public Rosary[167] (a recusant devotion) was one of the two most popular church-based devotions throughout the nineteenth century.[168] They may also have known of Father Ignatius Spencer's mid-century prayer campaign, which urged all in England to say one Hail Mary every day for conversions in England.[169] The prayer was central to their devotions: Phillips de Lisle believed it to 'rank next to the Lord's Prayer',[170] while French defended it as having been approved 'by the holiest men that ever breathed upon this earth – the holiest fathers of the Church, and the holiest women that ever adorned Christendom'.[171] For their private prayers, Roman Catholics could find the Rosary and other traditional Marian prayers such as the Hail Mary, the Litany of Loretto, the *Ave Maris Stella*, and the *Stabat Mater* in recusant works that remained popular in the nineteenth century, such as Challoner's *The garden of the soul* and *The key of heaven*, in more recent works like *The golden manual* and *The Rosary*, and in translations of continental works, such as the *Raccolta*. Roman Catholics also said novenas, nine days of prayers for specific intentions. These were widely available in works such as Faber's *The devout child of Mary*; *A novena in honour of the Most Blessed Virgin Mary of Mount Carmel, Mother of God, and our Dear Lady*; and the *Raccolta*.

Marian prayers praised attributes Catholics ascribed to the Virgin, not only the obvious one of virginity, but also her sanctity and divine maternity.[172] These prayers begged 'our tender Mother, our loving Mediatrix, the Stewardess of God's graces, the Queen of the Universe, and Mother of God'[173] for her intercession: she was asked to 'recommend them [their prayers] to the mercy of thy Son'[174] or to 'obtain for me, from thy blessed Son, true humility and perfect resignation'[175], and 'the virtue of temperance and the gift of counsel'.[176] They could also address Jesus through her: 'O Sacred Heart of Jesus! through the Immaculate Heart of Mary, I offer Thee all the prayers, labours, and crosses of this day.'[177] Sometimes they expanded her role from messenger to actor, asking her to 'defend me from my enemies in my last hour, and present me to thy divine Son.'[178]

Roman Catholics prayed to the Virgin or, through her, to Jesus because they believed that, as Newman informed Pusey, 'her office above is one of perpetual intercession for the faithful militant',[179] as it had been since the early church.[180] They also believed that her intercession was effective. Drawing on the medieval belief that Christ always obeyed Mary,[181] the Carmelite novena assured the faithful that 'the intercession of the Most Holy Virgin Mary is a most powerful method of obtaining benefits and favours from the Majesty of God; since, as this Holy Queen is really and truly the Mother of God, Her dear Son will not deny Her any thing which She asks of Him'.[182] Faber, always eager to offer testimonials to her intercessions, assured his friend and fellow-convert John Brande Morris that he had 'asked a great thing of our dear Lady in the Santa Casa and she got it for me in ten minutes.'[183] Morris must have found nothing surprising in this statement, because in his dramatic poem *Taleetha koomee*, when Salome, the mother of St John and St James, describes Mary's intercessory powers, St John the Evangelist responds: 'be it as she [the Virgin Mary] wills!'[184] Phillips de Lisle was convinced that her intercession had improved his relationship with his father, who had opposed his conversion to Roman Catholicism;[185] while, more broadly, Manning asserted: 'The answers to prayer through her intercession, in every age of the Church, and in every State of life, and in all manner of trials, public and private, have taught the faithful that she bears an office of power and patronage over us.'[186]

The Marian devotion of English Roman Catholics was part of a devotion to Christ, rather than an attempt to replace the son with the mother. As Wiseman argued, 'the devotion to the Blessed Mother of God must not be considered as a detached practice, but as part of a system'.[187] Therefore, whatever its practical effects in the realm of personal piety may have been (a topic that deserves further treatment), Marian devotion would, Roman Catholics said, increase their love for God. A Tractarian convert to Roman Catholicism insisted: 'No man can love and honour Mary the mother of Jesus as we love and honour her, without feeling that the more he loves her the more he loves her Son and her Lord'.[188] Roman Catholics also defended the corollary that, as an English Redemptorist priest argued, 'the further a Catholic is from sanctity, the further is he from devotion to Mary'.[189] Catholics believed that in praising Mary they were merely following the lead of Jesus, who had, French argued, performed the miracle at Cana in order to 'show the eminent dignity of the blessed woman'.[190]

Thus Roman Catholics denied Protestants' accusations that they worshipped the Virgin Mary or indeed anyone other than the Trinity.[191] As Lingard insisted, Roman Catholics 'no more pray to them [the saints] than we pray to our fellow men upon earth'.[192] A Roman Catholic convert accused his former co-religionists of bad faith in making these charges: 'Protestants of ordinary sense and charity ... are aware that the Catholic does not positively worship the blessed Virgin Mary as God, and that we depend on her prayers, and on those of other Saints, simply *as* prayers offered up for us by our fellow-creatures now in glory'.[193] Roman Catholic apologists explained the distinctions between *dulia* (devotion to the saints), *hyperdulia* (devotion due to Mary), and *latria* (the worship reserved for the Trinity).[194] Further evidence against these charges was the fact that Roman Catholics did not believe that Marian devotion was required for salvation. Even in 1877, after several decades of increasing Marian devotion, *The garden of the soul*'s list of 'What every Christian must believe' included only Christological beliefs. While the virginal conception and birth were among those beliefs,[195] they were clearly defined as Christological and did not imply the need for Marian devotion. In fact, only a minority of prayers in devotional manuals referred to the Virgin Mary. Slightly over one-quarter of the *Raccolta*, for example, was dedicated to Marian prayers; an even smaller percentage of the 1877 edition of *The garden of the soul*. Besides the Public Rosary, the other most popular church-based devotion was the Benediction of the Blessed Sacrament, a recusant devotion that focused on Jesus.[196]

Unlike Roman Catholics, Anglicans could find no consensus, in either their tradition or their practice, on prayer to the saints. Article 22 condemned the 'Romish doctrine concerning purgatory, pardons, worshipping and adoration, as well of images as of relics, and also invocation of saints' as 'a fond thing vainly invented, and ground upon no warranty of Scripture, but rather repugnant to the Word of God'. The Church of England observed saints' days, but because some traditional high churchmen (who generally resisted devotion to the saints) as well as advanced Anglicans dated their writings by saints' days, this suggests that the acknowledging of saints was not to be confused with devotion.[197] The confusion over whether prayer to the saints was allowed resulted in the Rev. T. E. Morris, student and tutor of Christ Church, Oxford, having to explain to Philip Wynter, the vice-chancellor of the University, that when he referred in an 1843 sermon to 'Laud the martyred archbishop, who, let us trust, still intercedes for this Church', he had not violated Article 22.[198] In 1850 William Maskell, domestic chaplain to Bishop Henry Philpotts, asked plaintively, 'what does the church of England now teach us respecting the blessed virgin Mary? Is it wrong – I do not ask, is it *right*, but is it *wrong* – especially to invoke her, or is it not wrong?'[199]

Some advanced Anglicans were confident that prayers to the saints were allowed. As an Anglican, Newman defended prayer to the dead on the basis of Jewish law, its ability to comfort the living, and its potential to assist the dead.[200] Others appealed to the English divines to support their argument that Article 22 (of the 39 *Articles of Religion*, 1562) did not condemn the invocation of saints, but merely the 'Romish' practice of idolatry and superstition.[201] Pusey's Scottish colleague and friend Alexander Penrose Forbes, bishop of Brechin, found prayer to the saints to be acceptable because he found it to be similar to asking for the prayers of the living.[202] Declaring that the appearances of saints in dreams proved the existence of communication between heaven and earth,[203] Robert Owen, a Tractarian and fellow of Jesus College, Oxford, was certain that the saints could pray for the Church on earth because they continued to help Christ in heaven.[204] 'H.N.T.' answered the question he posed as a pamphlet title – *May we ask the saints to pray for us?* – in the affirmative: he defended the practice of asking saints for their intercession on the grounds that the scriptural evidence for life after death assumes that the saints are conscious, and that 'if the Saints are conscious they must pray. Prayer is part of the very existence of one who loves God.'[205]

The question of Marian devotion was a major, and especially contentious, part of the discussion of praying to the saints. In his poem 'The Annunciation', Keble seemed to imply that a limited form of Marian devotion was acceptable when he said that Mary 'all but adoring love may claim'.[206] His controversial poem 'Mother out of sight' advocated repeating the *Magnificat*,[207] while both poems recommended reciting the scriptural first half of the Hail Mary.[208] Believing that Marian devotion would complement, rather than distract from, devotion to God, Keble urged Anglicans to repeat the angelic salutation after they had prayed to God:

> Therefore, as kneeling day by day,
> We to Our Father duteous pray;
> So unforbidden we may speak,
> An Ave to Christ's Mother meek.'[209]

The same pattern of praying, first, the Lord's Prayer and then the Hail Mary was found in nineteenth-century Roman Catholic prayerbooks.[210] Perhaps the anxiety his friends had felt in 1845 was not entirely unwarranted.

Other advanced Anglicans agreed with Keble. The *Monthly packet*, a periodical for Anglican girls published by Keble's 'daughter-like neighbor Charlotte Yonge',[211] advocated repeating the scriptural first half on the grounds that it 'was an anthem, not a prayer, and was to be taken as ascribing glory to Him who took our flesh upon Him, and did not abhor the Virgin's womb'.[212] While still an Anglican, Shipley argued that because it was 'never prohibited in any of our own authorised documents, the Cultus [of the Virgin Mary] is left to the devout feeling of each individual Anglican'.[213] In 1854, a few years before he left the Church of England for the Roman Catholic Church, Henry Nutcombe Oxenham repeatedly used the refrain 'Hail, Mary, Full of grace' in his poem, 'Three peals of the Angelus'.[214] Although at mid-century the suggestion that Lydia Sellon (as she was known; she did not use her first name) owned a rosary was a matter of scandal,[215] by the early 1880s the Society of the Holy and Undivided Trinity, an Anglican sisterhood based in Oxford, was giving each sister a rosary as part of the limited personal possessions she was allowed[216] and the sisters at St Margaret's, East Grinstead, were chanting the angelic salutation during Advent, using a prayerbook based on the medieval *Sarum Missal*.[217]

Other advanced Anglicans were, however, uneasy about Marian devotion. As an Anglican Newman had rejected the Hail Mary as encouraging 'that direct worship of the Blessed Virgin and the Saints, which is the great practical offence of the Latin Church'.[218] In 1859, Neale worried that 'within the last thirty or forty years the Roman attitude to S. Mary has become more than startling – really awful'.[219] Fifteen years later William Ewart Gladstone, who sympathised with both traditional high churchmen and advanced Anglicans, voiced similar sentiments when he warned: 'The growth of what is often termed among Protestants Mariolatry ... was notoriously advancing, but it seems not fast enough to satisfy the dominant party'.[220] Advanced Anglicans rejected 'the adoration and invocation of the blessed Virgin'[221] when it seemed to supersede the worship of Jesus. Noel agreed: 'The more I have seen of Roman Catholics the more I fear that many of them worship the Blessed Virgin Mary, and practically put her before Christ.'[222]

As Anglicans who rejected the Reformation and claimed that they belonged to the universal Catholic Church, advanced Anglicans were in a liminal position. Thus it is fitting that ambivalence was possibly the position most typical of them. Carter, for example, was uneasy with asking the saints for their prayers, on the grounds that one should not pray to creatures.[223] He was nonetheless convinced that the saints in heaven prayed for those on earth: 'As they have been raised nearer to God, and are more intensely filled with the life of God, so we cannot but suppose that their prayers for us have become more fervent, and the efficacy of their prayers more sure.'[224] Pusey dedicated a substantial portion of his *Eirenicon* and an even greater portion of his *First letter to Newman* to condemning the popular continental system of Marian devotion and reported: 'I have myself been asked by Roman Catholics to pray for my conversion: once only I was asked to pray [to] our Lord. On the other occasions, I was exclusively asked to pray [to] the Blessed Virgin for it.'[225] However, his sermons and other writings evidence a profound reverence for Mary as both a model of faith and the *Theotokos*. His ambivalence led the high church traditionalist George Miller to accuse him of 'self-contradiction'.[226] The – by this point – strongly Protestant Anglican divine Charles Pourtales Golightly was less forgiving, warning Wynter that even Pusey's equivocations regarding prayer to the saints put him in violation of Article 22 and insisting that Pusey be required to resubscribe to that article before being allowed to preach at the University.[227]

Advanced Anglicans' esteem for Mary and the desire expressed by some for limited forms of Marian devotion reinforced their Catholic identity, an identity that was cultural as well as theological. This common identity was stronger than their disagreements over the forms of Marian devotion. Because Marian devotion had polemical as well as spiritual uses, Catholics championed the practice to strengthen their claim that theirs was the warmer, truer faith. As Law argued: 'Catholics give not a cold, hesitating, reluctant assent to the truth – *the reality* of the Incarnation of God the Son. They dwell, they meditate deeply in their hearts upon the truth that the Infant Jesus, in the crib at Bethlehem, was "The Word made Flesh", "was God", and that "all things were made by Him" (St John i).'[228] Thus Catholics could argue that their practice of Christianity was not only more appealing to those who found Protestantism too cold but was the true form of Christianity. The angel Gabriel's greeting to Mary – 'Hail Mary, full of grace, the Lord is with thee' – provided irrefutable evidence, the Roman Catholic priest Stephen Keenan argued, that those who dismissed Mary as an ordinary woman were 'blasphemers' who 'utter a falsehood in the face of that exalted creature, – a falsehood in the face of the Angel; nay, a falsehood in the very face of God himself'.[229] Manning reversed the familiar Protestant charge that Marian devotion was evidence of heresy when he questioned the faith of those who did not venerate the Virgin: 'The devotion we bear to the Blessed Mother, is a sign of the true Church of Jesus Christ. The absence of it is a sign fatal to those who have it not'.[230] Catholics said that their use of the title 'Mother of God' proved that they practised the pure and ancient form of Christianity.[231] Shipley despaired of 'the fatal heresy [which] has been distinctly and positively enunciated that Mary is *not* the Mother of GOD',[232] which he could attribute only to 'the wide-spread Nestorianism of the present day'.[233] It is no coincidence that Marian devotion was revived in England as Roman Catholics were gaining in numbers and privileges and as Anglo-Catholicism began to develop. For polemical as well as pious reasons, Catholics joined to describe the Virgin Mary as a woman uniquely pure and uniquely blessed who was deserving of praise.

Conclusion

Victorian culture is replete with images of women who, because of their maternal nature (even if not fulfilled in childbearing), could influence a small part of the world for good. The Virgin Mary described by Catholics was in some ways an extension of that type of woman: her cooperation was essential for human salvation, and it was at her urging that Jesus performed his first public miracle. The Catholic Mary can also be read as an expression of the popular notion that women were more spiritual than men. She was also a particularly intimate role model, for Catholics were urged to meditate on her experiences and even to imagine themselves as sharing them. Given the many ways in which the Catholic Mary embodied the qualities Victorian women were often urged to exhibit, it is not surprising that scholars have assumed that she was a widely accepted figure in Victorian England. In fact, however, it was only the Catholic minority who viewed her as an admirable woman. England's long tradition of anti-Catholicism, which increased sharply in the nineteenth century, alone was probably sufficient to ensure that a figure so associated with Roman Catholicism would find few Protestant admirers. However, it was not just the culture of anti-Catholicism that prevented the Virgin Mary from being widely admired. That culture had existed at the popular level since the seventeenth century, and it was not until the 1830s that Protestants marked out the Virgin Mary for special condemnation. Two factors help to explain this change.

As a powerful woman with an extensive sphere of action, the Catholic Virgin Mary challenged the ideology that described women as morally superior but actually made them subordinate to men by locating them in the domestic sphere. The rhetoric of the feminine ideal notwithstanding, women occupied an inferior position in Victorian England. They were disadvantaged politically, legally, economically, and socially; their educational and work opportunities were limited in comparison to men's. Yet the Catholic Mary defied these restrictions as she moved beyond the limits of the domestic sphere to command the attention of men as well as women.

In addition, the Catholic Mary blurred the gender boundaries Victorian discourse worked so hard to separate when she was held up as a model for men as well as women. Certainly Victorian culture produced other models of behaviour that ignored gender boundaries. Purity crusaders such as Josephine Butler, famous for her campaigns against the Contagious Diseases Acts in the 1870s, and Ellice Hopkins, the Anglican social reformer who founded the White Cross Army, sought to apply female standards of chastity to men, while children of both sexes were taught feminine standards of behaviour. In those cases, however, the application of the feminine model was limited, either to one aspect or to one period of a person's life. The commission to bring Jesus to bear in the world would, in contrast, affect every aspect of the believer's behaviour. The Catholic Mary, as a model for life-long behaviour, obviated gender boundaries. Michael Roper and John Tosh have argued that in nineteenth-century England 'the achievement of manhood depended on a disparagement of the feminine without and within'.[234] Yet the Catholic Mary encouraged men to embrace the feminine without and within.

Catholics described Mary as the Virgin–Mother who assisted and even guided Jesus throughout his life. However, while Catholic devotions that urged worshippers to imagine themselves as Mary temporarily feminised male worshippers, they did not make women equal to men. Rather, they reinforced Mary's singularity, as worshippers were urged, not to become feminine, but to become Mary. In this way, the Victorian Catholic Virgin Mary played the same role that she did in other cultures. She was not, generally, a model of female autonomy – even vowed religious women who patterned their virginity after hers were answerable to priests and bishops – but she was nevertheless a potentially subversive figure, for she demonstrated that describing women as innately good and maternal could give them influence beyond the domestic sphere. The difficulties this recognition posed for those who were in the Protestant majority are explored in chapter 3.

Notes

1 This is not to say that the Virgin Mary was never privately invoked, especially in the chapels of the Roman Catholic Queen Henrietta Maria and Queen Catherine of Braganza and of the convert James II and his second wife, Mary of Modena. An amusing example comes from the reign of Charles II, who preferred Roman Catholic mistresses: when his favourite, Louise, Duchess of Portland, recovered from an illness in 1677, her confessor credited the Virgin Mary: Ronald Hutton, *Charles II* (Oxford: Clarendon, 1989), p. 336.

2 A survey of *Crockford's clerical directory* (1892) indicates that, of those churches for whom dedications are given, the most popular was the Virgin Mary.

3 Michael Henry Dziewicki, *Legend of the Blessed Virgin Mary, mother of Christ Our Lord* (London and Derby: Thomas Richardson & Son, 1882), pp. 57–8.

4 Lk 1:46–55.

5 Frederick George Lee, *The truth as it is in Jesus: a sermon preached at the Church of S. Martin, Leicester, on Monday, March 2, 1868, at the opening of the Lent assizes* (London: Joseph Masters, 1868), p. 3.

6 John Henry Newman, 'Our Lady in the gospel', *Faith and prejudice, and other unpublished sermons of Cardinal Newman*, ed. Birmingham Oratory (New York: Sheed & Ward, 1956), pp. 88–9.

7 Lk 1:39–56.

8 Earl of Redesdale and Charles L. Wood, *The doctrine of the Real Presence: correspondence between the Earl of Redesdale and the Honourable Charles L. Wood* (London: John Murray, 1879), p. 23.

9 E. B. Pusey, 'Eve: the course of temptation', *Lenten sermons, preached chiefly to young men at the universities, between A.D. 1858–1874* (Oxford: James B. Parker & Co. and London: Rivingtons, 1874), p. 118.

10 William Bernard Ullathorne, *The Immaculate Conception of the Mother of God: an exposition* (Baltimore, MD: John Murphy & Co. and Pittsburgh, PA: George Quigley, 1855), p. 12.

11 Judith Schneid Lewis, *In the family way: childbearing in the British aristocracy, 1760–1860* (New Brunswick, NJ: Rutgers University Press, 1986), p. 124.

12 Lewis, *In the family way*, pp. 124–7.

13 Cecil Woodham-Smith, *Queen Victoria: from her birth to the death of the Prince Consort* (New York: Alfred A. Knopf, 1972), pp. 212–13.

14 Woodham-Smith, *Queen Victoria*, p. 223.

15 Leonore Davidoff and Catherine Hall, *Family fortunes: men and women of the English middle class, 1780–1850* (Chicago, IL: University of Chicago Press, 1987), pp. 335–8; Lewis, *In the family way*, pp. 122–3.

16 William Lockhart, *The communion of saints; or the Catholic doctrine concerning our relation to the Blessed Virgin, the angels, and the saints*, 2nd edn (London: Burns, Oates, & Co., n.d.), p. 51.

17 Frederick W. Faber, 'The infant Jesus', in Frederick W. Faber, *Jesus and Mary: or, Catholic hymns* (London: James Burns, 1849), p. 21, line 26.

18 Faber, 'The infant Jesus', p. 21, line 25.

19 Faber, 'The infant Jesus', p. 21, lines 29–30.

20 John Henry Newman, 'On the fitness of the glories of Mary', in John Henry Newman, *Discourses addressed to mixed congregations* (London: Longmans, Green, & Co., 1897 [1849]), p. 362.

21 William Towry Law, *Unity, and faithful adherence to the Word of God, are only to be found in the Catholic Church: a letter to his late parishioners* (London: Burns & Lambert, 1852), p. 44.

22 The paintings were *Ecce Ancilla Domini* and *The girlhood of Mary Virgin* (1847–49).

23 Christina Rossetti, 'A Christmas carol', *The complete poems of Christina Rossetti*, ed. R. W. Crump (Baton Rouge and London: Louisiana State University Press, 1979), p. 217, line 19.

24 This poem was published posthumously, in Christina Rossetti, *The poetical works of Christina Georgina Rossetti* (London: Macmillan, 1904). When set to music by Gustav Holst for *The English hymnal* (1906), it became the popular Christmas hymn 'In the bleak midwinter'.

25 Vickery, *The gentleman's daughter*, p. 107.

26 A Parish Priest, *Concerning the honour due to Our Lady* (Holborn: W. Knott, 1885), p. 4.

27 'S.B.H.', 'A British mother's address to Queen Victoria', *Christian lady's magazine*, 15 (January–June 1841), p. 128, line 7, emphasis in original.

28 E. B. Pusey, *The Real Presence of the body and blood of our Lord Jesus Christ the doctrine of the English Church, with a vindication of the reception by the wicked and of the adoration of our Lord Jesus Christ truly present* (Oxford: John Henry Parker, 1857), p. 330.

29 Ullathorne, *The Immaculate Conception*, p. 7.

30 E. B. Pusey, *The Church of England a portion of Christ's one holy Catholic Church, and a means of restoring visible unity: an Eirenicon in a letter to the author of* The Christian year (Oxford: John Henry & James Parker; London: Rivingtons, 1865), p. 160; E. B. Pusey, *First letter to the Very Rev. J. H. Newman, D.D., in explanation chiefly in regard to the reverential love due to the ever-blessed Theotokos, and the doctrine of her Immaculate Conception* (Oxford: James Parker and London: Rivingtons, 1869), p. 36.

31 Quoted in Joseph P. Chinnici, *The English Catholic enlightenment: John Lingard and the Cisalpine Movement, 1780–1850* (Shepherdstown, WV: Patmos Press, 1980), p. 141.

32 John Henry Newman, 'The Annunciation of the Blessed Virgin Mary – on the honour due to her', Course of sermons and lectures on Saints days & holidays, No. 291, archived at Birmingham Oratory, Newman Papers, fol. 15; see also Richard R. Richards, *The birth, life, and death of the Blessed Virgin Mary: also, the birth, life, sufferings, and death of Our Lord and Saviour Jesus Christ; to which are added retaliations of divine providence* (St Day: Richard Skinner, 1861), p. 12.

33 John Edwards, 'The purification of the Virgin–Mother', in Frederick George Lee (ed.), *Miscellaneous sermons by clergymen of the Church of England* (London: Joseph Masters and Aberdeen: A. Brown & Co., 1860), p. 55.

34 Ambrose Lisle Phillips, *Manual of devotion for the use of the Brethren and Sisters of the Confraternity of the Living Rosary of the Blessed Virgin Mary, established in the parishes of Grace Dieu and Whitwick* (Derby: Printed by Richardson & Son for the Catholic Book Society, 1843), pp. 8–9.

35 (William Lockhart) *The Rosary of the Most Blessed Virgin Mary: with the Litany of Loretto, and other devotions* (London: James Burns, n.d. [1849]), p. 13.

36 Keble, 'Mother out of sight', p. 317, lines 75–6.

37 'Mary in the gospels', *Dublin review* (new ser.), 8: 16 (April 1867), 441; see also Newman, 'On the fitness of the glories of Mary', p. 362; Newman, 'A letter addressed to the Rev. E. B. Pusey, D.D., on occasion of his Eirenicon', in *Certain difficulties felt by Anglicans in Catholic teaching considered* (1865; London: Burns, Oates, & Co., 1875), p. 444.

38 Ullathorne, *The Immaculate Conception*, pp. 13–14.

39 (John Cumming and Daniel French) *The Hammersmith Protestant discussion; being an authenticated report of the controversial discussion between the Rev. John Cumming, D.D., of the Scottish National Church, Crown Court, Covent Garden, and Daniel French, Esq., barrister-at-law, on the differences between Protestantism and Popery; held at Hammersmith, during the months of April and May, MDCCCXXXIX*, new edn (London: Arthur Hall & Co., 1851), p. 248; Law, *Unity, and faithful adherence*, p. 44; John Brande Morris, *Talectha koomee: or the gospel prophecy of Our Blessed Lady's Assumption: a drama in four acts* (London: Burns & Lambert, 1858), p. 159; Nicholas Wiseman, 'Extracts from lecture by Cardinal Wiseman', in J. Shaw Mulholland (ed.), *The world's Madonna: a history of the Blessed Virgin Mary* (London: Burns & Oates and New York, Cincinnati, OH, Chicago, IL: Benziger Brothers, 1909), p. 24; M. Scally, *A sermon on the most ancient and venerable Order of the Ever Blessed Virgin Mary of Mount Carmel: in which is clearly explained, the devotion peculiar to that same; the duties to be performed by the members of the confraternity correctly expounded; the errors of many uninformed on these duties corrected; and by which all who desire in sincerity the conversion of England are invited to become the Advocates of Devotion to Mary* (London: Henry Lucas, 1849), p. 5; Isaac Williams, *Devotional commentary on the gospel narratives*, new edn, 8 vols (London, Oxford, Cambridge: Rivingtons, 1869), vol. 3, pp. 294–5.

40 Newman, 'Our Lady in the gospel', p. 92.

41 Freeman Wills, *Seven last words from the cross* (London: R. Clay, Sons, & Taylor, 1876), p. 17.

42 R. W. Church, *Village sermons preached at Whatley* (1892; London: Macmillan, 1897), p. 41.

43 Morris, *Talectha Koomee*, 159; Dziewicki, *Legend of the Blessed Virgin Mary*, p. 56.

44 M. H. Noel, *Do Roman Catholics worship the Virgin Mary? A sermon preached at S. Barnabas', Oxford, on the twelfth Sunday after Trinity, 1872* (Oxford: A. R. Mowbray & Co. and London: Simpkin, Marshall, & Co., n.d), p. 17.

45 Jn 19:25.

46 Lush, *A sermon, preached in the Church of Saint Mary, Greywell, on Good-Friday, 1853: being also the Festival of the Annunciation of the Blessed Virgin Mary* (London: John & Charles Mozley, 1853), p. 12; see also William Chatterton Dix, 'The embracing of the body of Christ by his Virgin–Mother', in Orby Shipley (ed.), *Lyra mystica: hymns and verses on sacred subjects, ancient and modern* (London: Longman, Green, Longman, Roberts, & Green, 1865), p. 38; Wiseman, 'Extracts from lecture', p. 7; Wills, *Seven last words*, p. 15.

47 Law, *Unity, and faithful adherence*, p. 44.

48 Father Sebastian of the Blessed Sacrament (Sebastian Keens), *Manual of devotions in honour of the seven dolours of the Blessed Virgin Mary*, 2nd edn (London: Denis Lane, 1868), p. 81.

49 J. Keble, 'The Annunciation of the Blessed Virgin Mary', *The Christian year* (1827; New York: Thomas Y. Cromwell, 1890), p. 232, lines 34–6; see also Charles Thomas (Longley), *Christ's dying hours: a sermon preached on the occasion of the re-opening of St Margaret's Church, Hilston, Holderness, on Thursday, July 31, 1862* (private circulation; London: n.p., 1862), pp. 15–17.

50 *Raccolta: or, collection of indulgenced prayers*, trans. Ambrose St John (London: Burns & Lambert, 1857), pp. 204–8.

51 *Raccolta*, pp. 204–8; Father Sebastian, *Manual of devotions*, pp. 230–5.

52 *Hymns ancient and modern, for use in the services of the Church* (London: Novello & Co., n.d. [1865]), p. 94.

53 Bradley, *Abide with me*, p. 23.

54 Wiseman, 'Extracts from lecture', p. 8.

55 Lk 2:35; Father Sebastian, *Manual of devotions*, p. 17.

56 Wiseman, 'Extracts from lecture', p. 8.

57 'Dr Pusey on Marian doctrine: Peace through the truth', *Dublin review* (new ser.), 7: 14 (October 1866), 460.

58 'Dr Pusey on Marian devotion', *Dublin review* (new ser.), 7: 13 (July 1866), 186–7.

59 Pusey, *Eirenicon*, p. 160.

60 Keble, 'Mother out of sight', p. 317, line 74.

61 St Deiniol's Library, Hawarden, Wales, 63/F/15.

62 (Lockhart) *The Rosary of the Most Blessed Virgin Mary*, p. 13.

63 (Cumming and French) *The Hammersmith Protestant discussion*, p. 248.

64 (Lockhart) *The Rosary of the Most Blessed Virgin Mary*, p. 13.

65 (Lockhart) *The Rosary of the Most Blessed Virgin Mary*, p. 13, emphasis in original.

66 'Lecky's "History of rationalism"', *Dublin review* (new ser.), 7: 13 (July 1866), 58.

67 Manning, Preface to *Meditations on the life of the Blessed Virgin*, pp. viii–ix.

68 Manning, Preface to *Meditations on the life of the Blessed Virgin*, p. ix.

69 Dante Gabriel Rossetti, 'Ave', in Orby Shipley (ed.), *Carmina Mariana: an English anthology in verse in honour of or in relation to the Blessed Virgin Mary* (London: Spottiswoode & Co., 1893), p. 334, lines 5–7.

70 Lk 1:31, 34.

71 Newman, 'Letter to Pusey', pp. 386–7.

72 Wiseman, 'Extracts from lecture', p. 3.

73 John Jerome, *Cuddesden versus Vatican, or, a lawyer's demurrer to the Oxford theology concerning the Immaculate Conception and worship of the Blessed Virgin Mary* (Paris: J. Lerous & Jouby, Tours: Jules Bouserez, London: Burns & Lambert, London: Richardson & Son, 1855), p. 22.

74 Orby Shipley, 'On the cultus of the Blessed Virgin Mary', in Anthony Stafford, *Life of the Blessed Virgin, together with the apology of the author, and an essay on the cultus of the Blessed Virgin Mary*, ed. Orby Shipley (London: Longmans, Green, Reader, & Dyer, 1869), pp. xxx–xxxi.

75 Isaac Williams, *Female characters of Holy Scripture*, new edn (London, Oxford, Cambridge: Rivingtons, 1869), p. 325.

76 Lk 1:35.

77 The correct translation of the crucial word is 'maid', not the traditional 'virgin.' In this context, however, the two words were virtually interchangeable, for Judaic Law made it clear that maids – i.e. unmarried women – were to be virgins.

78 Lee, *The truth as it is in Jesus*, p. 3; see also Edwards, 'The purification of the Virgin-Mother', p. 52.

79 Tertullian (c. 160–after 220) was the last Church Father to hold that Mary and Joseph eventually consummated their marriage, but this was an unorthodox opinion even when he asserted it. Those who followed him – including Clement of Alexandria (d. 215), Origen (d. 253), Athanasius (c. 296–373), Basil of Caesarea (d. 379), Gregory of Nyssa (d. 394), Epiphanius (d. 403), St John Chrysostom (c. 347–407), Ambrose (339–397), Jerome (c. 342–420), and Augustine (354–430) – believed that Mary was perpetually a virgin, and many added as well that she remained a virgin *in partu*. For further discussion of patristic beliefs, see Graef, *Mary*, vol. 1, pp. 13, 41–5, 51–2, 54–6, 63, 65–7, 70–1, 74, 79–81, 89–92, 95–6, 154.

80 Keble, 'Mother out of sight', p. 318, line 90.

81 R. J. Wilson, *Our relation to the saints: some notes gathered from English divines* (Privately printed: n.d. [?1874]), p. 3.

82 Sisterhood of St Margaret's, East Grinstead, *Breviary offices from Lauds to Compline inclusive, translated and arranged for use from the Sarum Book*, 2nd edn (London: J. T. Hayes, 1880), p. 211.

83 E. B. Pusey, *The Presence of Christ in the Holy Eucharist: a sermon, preached before the University, in the Cathedral Church of Christ, in Oxford, on the second Sunday after Epiphany, 1853* (Oxford and London: John Henry Parker, London: Francis & John Rivington, 1853), p. 23; E. B. Pusey, *The doctrine of the Real Presence, as contained in the Fathers from the death of S. John the Evangelist to the fourth General Council, vindicated, in notes on a sermon, 'The Presence of Christ in the Holy Eucharist', preached A.D. 1853, before the University of Oxford* (Oxford: John Henry Parker, London: F. & J. Rivington, 1855), pp. 58–9; Orby Shipley (ed.), *Invocation of saints and angels: compiled from Greek, English, and Latin sources, for the use of members of the Church of England* (London: Longmans, Green, Reader, & Dyer, 1869), p. 188.

84 Janice Capel Anderson, 'Mary's difference: gender and patriarchy in the birth narratives', *Journal of Religion*, 67 (1987), 195–6.

85 Ullathorne, *The Immaculate Conception*, p. 96.

86 *The views of Bishop Pearson and the fathers of the English Reformation on the subject of the ever-virginity of Saint Mary the Virgin* (London: J. H. Parker & Co. and Brighton: H. & C. Treacher, 1889), pp. 15–16.

87 Williams, *Devotional commentary on the gospel narratives*, p. 80.

88 John Henry Newman, *Selected treatises of St Athanasius in controversy with the Arians* (London: Longmans, Green, & Co., 1903), vol. 2, pp. 204–10.

89 Raymond E. Brown, Karl P. Donfried, Joseph A. Fitzmyer, and John Reumann (eds), *Mary in the New Testament* (New York and Mahwah, NJ: Paulist Press, 1978), pp. 114–15.

90 Phillips, *Manual of devotion*, pp. 44–5.

91 Dyan Elliott, *Spiritual marriage: sexual abstinence in medieval wedlock* (Princeton, NJ: Princeton University Press, 1993), pp. 144n, 178.

92 John Henry Newman, 'The glories of Mary for the sake of her son', in *Discourses addressed to mixed congregations*, p. 352; Newman, 'Our Lady in the gospel', pp. 87, 91.

93 Ullathorne, *The Immaculate Conception*, p. 6.

94 Dziewicki, *Legend of the Blessed Virgin Mary*, p. 22.

95 Wiseman, 'Extracts from lecture', p. 3.

96 Alban Butler, *The lives of the Fathers, martyrs, and other principal saints, compiled from original documents and other authentic records*, ed. F. C. Husenbeth, 2 vols (London and Dublin: Henry & Co., n.d. [?1857–60; first publ. 1756–59]), p. 380; see also Abbé Orsini, 'The history of the Blessed Virgin Mary, Mother of God, completed by the traditions of the East, the writings of the Holy Fathers, and the private history of the Hebrews', trans. F. C. Husenbeth, in Butler, *The lives of the Fathers*, p. lv.

97 Birmingham Oratory, Birmingham, Newman Papers, private diary of John Henry Newman, memorandum dated May 1846, emphasis in original.

98 Quoted. in J. G. Lockhart, *Charles Lindley Viscount Halifax*, part I: *1830–1885* (London: Geoffrey Bles, Centenary Press, 1935), p. 255.

99 Williams, *Devotional commentary on the gospel narratives*, p. 80.

100 Newman, *Selected treatises of St Athanasius*, vol. 2, pp. 208–10.

101 Newman papers, private diary, memorandum dated May 1846.

102 Newman, *Selected treatises of St Athanasius*, p. 206.

103 Lewis Morris, 'Motherhood: an ode', in Shipley (ed.), *Carmina Mariana*, p. 250.

104 Newman, 'Letter to Pusey', p. 392.

105 Hill, *The religious order*, p. 151.

106 F. W. Faber, letter to Lady Minna Fitzalan Howard, December 12, 1862, reprinted in Frederick W. Faber, *Faber: poet and priest*, ed. Raleigh Addington (Glamorgan, Wales: D. Brown & Sons, 1974), p. 337, emphasis in original.

107 J. M. Neale, *Sermons on the Blessed Sacrament: preached in the Oratory of S. Margaret's, East Grinstead*, 7th edn (London: J. T. Hayes, n.d. [?1871; first publ. 1870;]), p. 42.

108 Neale, *Sermons on the Blessed Sacrament*, p. 82.

109 Neale, *Sermons for some feast days in the Christian year, as preached in the Oratory of S. Margaret's, East Grinstead* (London: J. T. Hayes, n.d.), p. 69.

110 Lewis, *In the family way*, pp. 226–7.

111 Caroline Norton, *English laws for women in the nineteenth century* (London, 1854; republished as *Caroline Norton's defense* [Chicago: Academy Chicago, 1982]), p. 152.

112 William Acton, *The functions and disorders of the reproductive organs* (Philadelphia, PA: Lindsay & Blakiston, 1867), p. 144.

113 John Maynard, *Victorian discourses on sexuality and religion* (Cambridge: Cambridge University Press, 1993), p. 43; Peter Gay, *The bourgeois experience: Victoria to Freud*, 5 vols (New York: Oxford University Press, 1984, 1993, 1995, 1998), especially vol. 2; Carol Z. and Peter N. Stearns, 'Victorian sexuality: can historians do it better?', *Journal of Social History*, 18 (1985), 625–34.

114 M. Jeanne Peterson, *Family, love, and work in the lives of Victorian gentlewomen* (Bloomington and Indianapolis: Indiana University Press, 1989).

115 Maynard, *Victorian discourses*, p. 120.

116 Lewis, *In the family way*, p. 73.

117 Nancy F. Cott, 'Passionlessness: an interpretation of Victorian sexual ideology, 1790–1850', *Signs*, 4 (1978), 219–36

118 Sheila Ryan Johansson, 'Demographic contributions to the history of Victorian women', in Barbara Kanner (ed.), *The women of England: from Anglo-Saxon times to the present* (Hamden, CT: Archon Books, 1979), p. 277.

119 For a more detailed history of Roman Catholic orders for women in England at this time, see Susan O'Brien, 'Religious life for women', in V. Alan McClelland and Michael Hodgetts (eds), *From without the Flaminian Gate: 150 years of Roman Catholi-*

cism in England and Wales 1850–2000 (London: Darton, Longman, & Todd, 1999), pp.
108–41.

120 Susan Mumm, Stolen daughters, virgin mothers: Anglican sisterhoods in Victorian
Britain (London and New York: Leicester University Press, 1999), p. 3.

121 While still an Anglican, Newman praised convents as 'institutions which give dignity
and independence to the position of women in society' (quoted in Ian Ker, John Henry
Newman: A Biography [Oxford: Clarendon Press, 1988], pp. 189–90). Manning agreed
that convents were a good option for unmarried women, although he admitted that he
had no solution for single women who were not attracted to convent life: Robert Gray,
Cardinal Manning (New York: St. Martin's, 1985), p. 297.

122 Mumm, Stolen daughters, virgin mothers, p. 165.

123 Hill, The religious order, chapter 9; Allchin, The silent rebellion, p. 116.

124 Ullathorne, The Immaculate Conception, p. 54.

125 Theodora Jankowski, Pure resistance: queer virginity in early modern English drama
(Philadelphia: University of Pennsylvania Press, 2000), p. 84.

126 Orby Shipley, 'The Blessed Virgin', in Lee (ed.), Miscellaneous sermons, p. 215.

127 (Jane Elizabeth Leeson) The wreath of lilies: a gift for the young (London: James Burns,
1847), p. 172.

128 Lk 11: 27–8.

129 Williams, Female characters, p. 323; see also Newman, 'Our Lady in the gospel', pp.
85–6; Newman 'The glories of Mary for the sake of her son', pp. 350–1; Ullathorne, The
Immaculate Conception, p. 14.

130 The golden manual: being a guide to Catholic devotion, public and private, compiled
from approved sources (London: Burns and Oates, 1850), p. 521.

131 (Leeson) The wreath of lilies, p. 8.

132 F. C. Husenbeth, D.D., The chain of Fathers, witnesses for the doctrine of the Immaculate
Conception of the Blessed Virgin Mary, Mother of God (London: Thomas Richardson &
Son, 1860), p. 23.

133 Williams, Devotional commentary on the gospel narratives, p. 295.

134 Williams, Devotional commentary on the gospel narratives, p. 293.

135 (Leeson) The wreath of lilies, p. 168.

136 Father Sebastian, Manual of devotions, p. 45.

137 Father Sebastian, Manual of devotions, pp. 45–6.

138 Father Sebastian, Manual of devotions, p. 46.

139 (Lockhart) The Rosary of the Most Blessed Virgin Mary, p. 16; Shipley, 'The Blessed
Virgin', p. 215; William Crouch, On the invocation of saints: a paper read before the
September Synod of the Society of The Holy Cross, 1885 (Privately printed for the Society,
n.d. [?1885]), p. 19.

140 Jn 19:26–7.

141 Phillips, Manual of devotion, pp. 40–1, emphasis in original; see also Father Sebastian,
Manual of devotions, pp. 2–3; 'Dr Pusey on Marian devotion', pp. 168–9; Lockhart,
The communion of saints, pp. 53–4; Morris, Taleetha Koomee, pp. 199–200; Newman,
'Letter to Pusey', p. 444; Prayers for the conversion of the people of England; and of all
others separated from the faith and unity of the Church, set forth by the Authority of the
bishops of England, and recommended for the use of the faithful in their several dioceses,
new edn (London: Burns, Oates, & Co., n.d. [?1867]), p. 30; (Lockhart) The Rosary
of the Most Blessed Virgin Mary, pp. 14–16; Scally, A sermon on the most ancient and

venerable Order, p. 19; 'Thoughts on the Assumption', *Irish monthly* (1877), p. 502.

142 Keble, 'Mother out of sight', line 16, p. 31.

143 Shipley, 'On the cultus of the Blessed Virgin Mary', p. xxxi.

144 *A brief account of the indulgences, privileges, and favours, conferred on the Order, Confraternities, and Churches, of the Most Glorious Mother of God, the Virgin Mary of Mount Carmel: with distinct instructions for the Brothers and Sisters of the Sacred Scapular, and for all the faithful, who visit the churches of the said Order*, trans. Thomas Coleman (Dublin: Confraternity of the Holy Scapular, 1826), p. 13; Scally, *A sermon on the most ancient and venerable Order*, p. 12.

145 Noel, *Do Roman Catholics worship the Blessed Virgin Mary?*, p. 16; Chapman, *Father Faber*, pp. 148, 328.

146 J. G. Snead-Cox, *The life of Cardinal Vaughan*, 2 vols (London: Herbert & Daniel, St Louis: B. Herder, 1910), vol. 1, p. 40. Coventry Patmore reversed the equation: after his first wife's death and his conversion to Roman Catholicism, he told his children to pray to their mother if they were not yet comfortable with praying to the Virgin Mary: Kimberley van Esveld Adams, *Our Lady of Victorian feminism*, p. 97.

147 Robert O'Neil, *Cardinal Herbert Vaughan: Archbishop of Westminster, Bishop of Salford, founder of the Mill Hill Missionaries* (Tunbridge Wells: Burns & Oates, 1995), p. 16.

148 Snead-Cox, *The life of Cardinal Vaughan*, vol. 1, p. 44.

149 Snead-Cox, *The life of Cardinal Vaughan*, vol. 1, p. 42.

150 Gerard Manley Hopkins, 'The Blessed Virgin compared to the air we breathe', in Gerard Manley Hopkins, *Poems and prose*, ed. W. H. Gardner (New York: Viking Penguin, 1985), p. 56, lines 55–62.

151 Richard Challoner, *The garden of the soul, or a manual of spiritual exercises and devotions, for Christians, who, living in the world, aspire to devotion; A new edition, containing: devotions to the Blessed Sacrament, to the Sacred Heart, to St Joseph, and a collection of indulgenced prayers* (London and Derby: Thomas Richardson & Sons, 1877), p. 50, emphasis in original. The 1838 edition of *The key of Heaven* also urged the faithful to imagine Mary going to Calvary with the other women: *The key of heaven; or, a posey of prayers, selected from Catholic authors: to which are added, Gother's instructions and devotions for confession and communion*, 17th edn (London: Keating, Brown, & Co., 1834), p. 49.

152 Lk 2:35.

153 Keble, 'Mother out of sight', p. 318, line 110.

154 Newman, 'Our Lady in the gospel', p. 95.

155 L. P. Curtis Jr, *Anglo-Saxons and Celts: a study of anti-Irish prejudice in Victorian England* (Bridgeport, CT: Conference on British Studies, 1968), p. 61.

156 Catherine Sinclair, *Beatrice: or, the unknown relatives* (1852; London: Ward, Lock, & Tyler, 1890), p. 192.

157 Quoted in Richard J. Schiefen, *Nicholas Wiseman and the transformation of English Catholicism* (Shepherdstown: Patmos Press, 1984), p. 5.

158 Brenda Colloms, *Charles Kingsley: the lion of Eversley* (London: Constable, New York: Barnes and Noble, 1975), p. 49.

159 Charles Kingsley, *Yeast: a problem* (London: John W. Parker, 1851), p. 38.

160 Gill, *Women and the Church of England*, p. 97.

161 Reed, *Glorious battle*, p. 223, emphasis in original.

162 Gill, *Women and the Church of England*, p. 97.

163 Thomas Arnold, 'The Oxford malignants and Dr Hampden', *Edinburgh review*, 63 (April 1836), p. 226.

164 Kingsley made this charge in his review of Froude's *History of England* in *Macmillan's magazine* (January 1864); the review is reprinted in the Preface to the work it eventually inspired: see Newman, *Apologia pro vitâ suâ*, p. 38.

165 This prayer dates from c. 600 but did not become popular until the late tenth century: Graef, *Mary*, vol. 1, p. 230.

166 *The garden of the soul*, pp. 17, 23, 24–43, 147, 317–26; *Raccolta*, pp. 182, 189, 216; *The key of heaven; or, a posey of prayers, selected from Catholic authors: to which are added, Gother's instructions and devotions for confession and communion*, 14th edn (London: Keating, Brown, & Co., 1819), p. 34; *The key of heaven* (1834), pp. 41, 47.

167 The Rosary was a medieval devotion, allegedly given to St Dominic by the Virgin herself. The main components – the use of beads for counting the number of 'Our Fathers' and the saying of 150 'Hail Marys' and a lesser number of 'Glorias' – were present by the early twelfth century: Graef, *Mary*, vol. 1, pp. 232–3.

168 Heimann, *Catholic devotion*, p. 42. Works such as *The golden manual* and William Lockhart's *The Rosary of the Most Blessed Virgin* described the components of the Rosary and defended the devotion.

169 Jozef Vanden Bussche, *Ignatius (George) Spencer, Passionist (1799–1864), Crusader of Prayer for England and pioneer of ecumenical prayer* (Leuven, Belgium: Leuven University Press, 1991), pp. 146, 150, 152.

170 Phillips, *Manual of devotion*, p. 12.

171 (Cumming and French) *The Hammersmith Protestant discussion*, p. 265.

172 Father Sebastian, *Manual of devotions*, pp. 22, 75, 89–91, 105.

173 *Raccolta*, p. 167.

174 Challoner, *The garden of the soul*, p. 26.

175 Father Sebastian, *Manual of devotions*, p. 22.

176 *Raccolta*, p. 215.

177 *An appeal to the Associates of the Apostleship of Prayer in Great Britain and Ireland*, reprinted from *The messenger of the Sacred Heart*, July 1878 (?1878), p. 7.

178 *The key of Heaven* (1819), p. 127.

179 Newman, 'Letter to Pusey', p. 423.

180 Nicholas Wiseman, *Remarks on a letter from the Rev. W. Palmer* (London: Charles Dolman, 1841), pp. 19–23, 27–30.

181 Graef, *Mary*, vol. 2, p. 59.

182 *A novena in honour of the Most Blessed Virgin Mary of Mount Carmel, Mother of God, and our Dear Lady: together with a devout manner of reciting the Holy Rosary, as used in some of the novitiates of the Order of Mount Carmel*, translated from the Spanish (London: Burns & Lambert, 1852), p. 3.

183 F. W. Faber, letter to John Brande Morris, Easter Tuesday, 1846, reprinted in Faber, *Faber: poet and priest*, p. 147.

184 Morris, *Talectha koomee*, p. 34.

185 Margaret Pawley, *Faith and family: the life and circle of Ambrose Phillips de Lisle* (Norwich: Canterbury Press, 1993), p. 73.

186 Manning, Preface to *Meditations on the life of the Blessed Virgin*, p. xiv.

187 Wiseman, *Remarks on a letter*, p. 46; see also Newman, 'The glories of Mary for the sake of her son', pp. 349–50.

188 (A late member of Oxford University) *Four years' experience of the Catholic religion, with observations on its effects, intellectual, moral, and spiritual; and on the thraldom of Protestantism* (London: James Burns, 1849), p. 83.

189 Alphonsus Liguori, *The glories of Mary*, trans. by a father of the same (Redemptorist) congregation (New York: Edward Dunigan & Brother, 1852), p. vii.

190 (Cumming and French) *The Hammersmith Protestant discussion*, p. 333.

191 N. Wiseman, D.D., *A letter respectfully addressed to the Rev. J. H. Newman, upon some passages in his Letter to the Rev. Dr. Jelf* (London: Charles Dolman, 1841), pp. 4, 6, 9, 11–13.

192 John Lingard, *Catechetical instructions on the doctrines and worship of the Catholic Church*, rev. edn (London: Charles Dolman, 1844), pp. 134–5; Newman Papers, J. H. Newman, memorandum dated May 1846, private diary.

193 (A late member of Oxford University) *Four years' experience of the Catholic religion*, p. 81, emphasis in original.

194 *Declaration of the Catholic bishops, the vicars apostolic and their coadjutors in Great Britain*, new edn (London: Catholic Institute of Great Britain, 1838), pp. 8–11; Henry Nutcombe Oxenham, *Dr Pusey's Eirenicon considered in relation to Catholic unity: a letter to the Rev. Father Lockhart of the Institute of Charity* (London: Longmans, Green, & Co., 1866), p. 23n; Edward Waterton, *Pietas Mariana Britannica: a history of English devotion to the Most Blessed Virgin Mary, Mother of God* (London: St Joseph's Catholic Library, 1879), p. 8.

195 Challoner, *The garden of the soul* (1877), p. 10.

196 Heimann, *Catholic devotion*, pp. 42, 47.

197 See, for example, Lambeth Palace Library, London, Golightly Papers, MS 1805, letter from H. B. W. Churton to C. P. Golightly, dated St Andrews Day, 30 Nov. 1859, fols 29–30; Pusey House, Oxford, LBV 107/331, letter from E. B. Pusey to John Keble, Christ Church, Oxford, dated St Mark's Day, 1865. Some Anglicans insisted that the latter practice merely distinguished the days and did not encourage the worship of saints. See (Henry Townsend Powell) *Stretton tracts*, no. 6: Saint worship (Coventry: C. A. N. Rollason, n.d. [1840]), pp. 4–5. Samuel Wilberforce justified saints' days as serving 'to exalt the love of Christ, & the power of God's grace which caused Him to be a Saint – For this is the true glory of X's [Christ's] Saints [–] not to draw off our attention from, but to point it to Him': see Bodleian Library, Oxford, MSS Wilberforce, d. 48, fol. 122.

198 An account of the incident is found in Henry Parry Liddon, *Life of Edward Bouverie Pusey: Doctor of Divinity; Canon of Christ Church; Regius Professor of Hebrew in the University of Oxford*, 3rd edn, 4 vols (London: Longmans, 1893), vol. 3, pp. 337–8.

199 William Maskell, *A second letter on the present position of the high church party in the Church of England: the want of dogmatic teaching in the reformed English Church* (London: William Pickering, 1850), p. 39, emphasis in original.

200 Bodleian Library, Oxford, MSS Wilberforce, c. 67, letter from John H. Newman to Robert Wilberforce, 15 March 1836, fols 85–6.

201 R. J. Wilson, *A letter to the archbishop of Canterbury, on his statements made in the House of Lords, May 8th, with reference to altar cards* (Oxford: A. R. Mowbray & Co., 1874), p. 5; Shipley (ed.), *Invocation of saints and angels*, pp. xxiv–xxvi, xxix–xxx; H.N.T., *May we ask the saints to pray for us?* (London: Charles Taylor, n.d.), pp. 6–7.

202 A. P. Forbes, *An explanation of the thirty-nine articles*, 2 vols (Oxford and London: James Parker, 1868), p. 421.

203 Robert Owen, *An essay on the communion of saints, together with an examination of the cultus sanctorum, being an appendix to a work intituled 'Santorale Catholicum'* (London: C. Kegan Paul & Co., 1881), pp. 13–14.

204 Owen, *An essay on the communion of saints*, pp. 35–6.

205 H.N.T., *May we ask the saints to pray for us?*, p. 4.

206 Keble, 'The Annunciation', p. 232, line 50.

207 'Mother out of sight', p. 316, lines 48, 52–3.

208 'Mother out of sight', p. 317, lines 87–8; p. 318, line 99; 'The Annunciation', p. 232, lines 37, 43, 49. In 1845, Keble assured J. T. Coleridge, 'You see when I recommend the Ave, I mean merely the Scriptural part': quoted in Brian Martin, *John Keble: priest, professor and poet* (London: Croom Helm, 1976), p. 13.

209 Keble, 'Mother out of sight', p. 318, lines 97–100.

210 Challoner, *The garden of the soul*, pp. 24–43; *The key of heaven* (1819), p. 34.

211 Pusey House, Oxford, LBV 4, letter from John Keble to E. B. Pusey, dated P[enzance], 14 March 1865.

212 'Conversations on the catechism', *Monthly packet*, 3: 14 (February 1852), 89.

213 Shipley, *On the cultus of the Blessed Virgin*, p. xxvi.

214 Oxenham, 'Three peals of the Angelus', p. 283.

215 *Report of the inquiry*, pp. 4, 5, 27, 40, 62.

216 Mumm, *Stolen daughters, virgin mothers*, p. 31.

217 Sisterhood of St Margaret's, *Breviary offices*, p. 212. The *Sarum Missal* was the medieval missal originally used at Salisbury Cathedral and later throughout much of England, Wales, and Ireland. It was replaced by Edward VI's *First book of common prayer* (1549), but was revived in the modern period.

218 (John Henry Newman) Tract 75, *On the Roman Breviary as embodying the substance of the devotional services of the Church Catholic*, 2nd edn (London: J. G. & F. Rivington, n.d. [1837]), p. 10.

219 John Mason Neale, *Secession: a sermon preached in the Oratory of S. Margaret's, East Grinstead, November 18, 1859* (London: Joseph Masters, 1868), p. 13.

220 W. E. Gladstone, *The Vatican Decrees in their bearing on civil allegiance: a political expostulation* (London: John Murray, 1874), pp. 14–15.

221 Lord Redesdale, *Reasonings on some disputed points of doctrine*, 2nd edn (London: Rivingtons, 1874), p. 8.

222 Noel, *Do Roman Catholics worship the Blessed Virgin Mary?*, p. 14.

223 T. T. Carter, *Fellowship with the saints: a sermon preached at All Saints, Margaret Street, on the Festival of All Saints, 1868* (London: Joseph Master, 1868), pp. 7–8.

224 Carter, *Fellowship with the saints*, p. 7.

225 Pusey, *Eirenicon*, pp. 107–8.

226 George Miller, *A letter to the Rev. E. B. Pusey, D.D., in reference to his letter to the Lord Bishop of Oxford* (London: Duncan and Malcolm, 1840), p. 61.

227 Pusey House, Oxford, LBV 37, letter from Charles Pourtales Golightly to the vice-chancellor of Oxford, dated Holywell, 5 January 1846.

228 Law, *Unity, and faithful adherence*, p. 44.

229 Stephen Keenan, *Controversial Catechism: or, Protestantism refuted, and Catholicism established, by an appeal to the Holy Scriptures, the testimony of the Holy Fathers, and the dictates of reason; in which such portions of Scheffmacher's Catechism as suit modern controversy are embodied*, 3rd edn (Edinburgh: Marsh & Beattie, London and

Manchester: Charles Dolman, 1854), p. 133, emphasis in original.

230 Manning, Preface to *Meditations on the life of the Blessed Virgin*, p. xvii.

231 See, for example, Keble, 'Mother out of sight', p. 316, stanza 7; Shipley (ed.), *Invocation of saints and angels*, pp. 57–76; Nicholas Wiseman, *Lectures on the doctrines and practices of the Roman Catholic Church* (London: J. S. Hodson, 1836), p. 273; 'Devotion to the Most Holy Virgin', *Dublin review*, 21: 41 (September 1846), 41; Newman, 'On the fitness of the glories of Mary', p. 361; Frederick W. Faber, *The devout child of Mary, the Immaculate Mother of Jesus Christ* (Baltimore, MD: John Murphy & Co. and London: C. Dolman, 1855), p. 270; Pusey, *First letter to Newman*, pp. 21, 23.

232 Shipley (ed.), *Invocation of saints and angels*, p. xxxi, emphasis in original.

233 Shipley (ed.), *Invocation of saints and angels*, p. xxxi, emphasis in original.

234 Roper and Tosh, 'Historians and the politics of masculinity', p. 13.

3

The Protestant Virgin Mary

The traditional Protestant portrait of the Virgin Mary was less detailed and less effusive than the Catholic one, but was still positive. The reformers and their successors generally described Mary as an eternal virgin who, having been specially chosen by God to bear the Saviour, was a model of faith. While Protestants occasionally criticised the Virgin Mary's behaviour – for example, in the sixteenth century Hugh Latimer, the former Bishop of Worcester and future Marian martyr, blamed Mary for leaving Jesus behind in the Temple and said that this incident proved that 'they, which go about to make Mary to be without sin, are much deceived'[1] – in general Protestants did not denigrate either the person or the role of Mary, preferring merely to limit her devotional role. As Jaroslav Pelikan has noted, 'The most obvious characteristic of the picture of Mary in the Protestant Reformation was its critique and rejection of what it took to be the excesses of Medieval devotion and teaching.'[2]

This restrained yet generally positive portrait began to change in the 1830s as Protestants, especially the clergy, began to pay more attention to the Virgin Mary. Although Victorian Protestants agreed with their predecessors that Mary was 'that blessed woman'[3] who had been 'chosen from among her sex as the honoured instrument in giving him birth',[4] they generally described her as an ordinary woman who had no special role in Jesus' life beyond giving birth to him. She was neither a model disciple nor a model of human behaviour. Some Victorian Protestants went further, describing the Virgin Mary as a woman who stubbornly tried to insert herself in Jesus' ministry, to the point where he had to speak harshly to her.

The traditional Protestant portrait of the Virgin Mary was modified in the nineteenth century as a result of several factors. Most obviously, Victorian Protestants were reacting to the resurgence of the Catholic image of the Virgin Mary. In sermons, polemical pamphlets, novels, periodicals, and public addresses, they described this woman as a pagan goddess who proved that Catholicism was a corrupt form of Christianity. Theology, especially as it was implemented liturgically, was one inspiration for Protestants' dislike of the Catholic Virgin Mary and their envisioning of a more ordinary woman. Protestants' oft-stated belief that Scripture alone was authoritative meant that they were generally unwilling to imagine non-scriptural episodes. Furthermore, their emphasis on a direct personal relationship between the believer and the divine made them unwilling to imagine an expansive role for Jesus' mother, either during his life or in their own devotional lives. Protestants also were concerned that granting a human being a prominent role in salvation would lead to what they saw as the Roman Catholic error of exalting a creature over the Creator in violation of God's law.[5] Culturally, too, Marian devotion was unfamiliar to most Victorian Protestants. The only references to the Virgin Mary in the *Book of common prayer* are the few that are directly connected to Jesus, such as the Virgin Birth; dissenters would have mentioned her even less frequently in their services.

Religious disputes alone do not explain the Protestant critique of the Catholic Virgin Mary and the positing of a more ordinary woman in her place. Both the critique of the Catholic Mary and the substitution of a more ordinary woman were part of a complicated process that allowed Victorian Protestants to define woman's role and characteristics. Because Catholics represented the Virgin Mary as a woman who exhibited the very qualities that Victorian women were repeatedly told they possessed or should possess – virginity, maternal love, and spirituality – denouncing this figure as a pagan goddess allowed some Protestants, in particular the clergy, to call into question the value of those qualities, especially as they promised to give women a more prominent role in the public sphere. Even when motivated primarily by religious considerations, the effect – unintended though it may have been – of this Protestant rhetoric was to raise questions about whether possessing those qualities could give women a greater role in the public sphere. Denunciations of the Catholic Mary were frequently followed by the positing of a more ordinary and less admirable Virgin Mary, one who was the mother of several children and a faithless follower of Jesus. Asserting the historicity and desirability of this figure, even when the intention was primarily religious, allowed these Protestants to suggest that women were typically less admirable and less effectual in the public sphere than the high praise of women often voiced in Victorian culture would suggest.

The Victorian Protestants who abandoned the traditional Western model of Mary the good mother to re-envision her as an ordinary, even tedious, woman who was not particularly close to her son were representative of many denominations. Anglicans who considered their Church to be Protestant joined Methodists, Presbyterians, Baptists, Congregationalists, and even those who shunned denominational identities in describing the Virgin Mary in strikingly similar terms. Coherence was also evident in silent agreement: in an age characterised by public disputes over religious matters, no Protestants publicly opposed either the critique of the Catholic Virgin Mary or the alternative Protestant portrait. Therefore, to describe an Anglican Protestant Virgin Mary, a Methodist Virgin Mary, a Presbyterian Virgin Mary, and so on would be an exercise in redundancy. More significantly, it would unnecessarily fragment Protestant culture. While Protestants of different denominations had significant disagreements on a variety of topics, both religious and secular, they also participated in a common Protestant culture, one that feared the growth of both Roman Catholicism and Anglo-Catholicism and linked Protestantism with characteristics claimed to be integral to an English identity, including rationality, individualism, and belief in progress. It was also, the Marian discussions reveal, a culture that had reservations about the feminine ideal, the promotion of which was generally associated with Protestantism.

Mary as an ordinary woman

The Protestant portrait of the Virgin Mary was at its most positive in its depiction of her at the Annunciation, when she was described as having done God's will in bearing Jesus. James Endell Tyler, a traditional high-church and anti-Roman Catholic writer who became canon of St Paul's Cathedral in 1845, lauded Mary at the Annunciation as 'a spotless virgin, humble, pious, obedient, holy: a chosen servant of God',[6] while the Methodist minister and professor Thomas Jackson was certain that in her 'early life Mary was an example of deep piety'.[7] Drawing on legends from the early church and the Middle Ages, the nonconformist minister Henry Hamlet Dobney described the young woman whom the angel encountered as one whose 'youth had been consecrated to God. Her mind was familiar with the high and holy themes on which the psalmists and prophets of Israel had loved to dwell, and she nourished her heart with the sublime hopes that they inspired.'[8] However, the Protestant Mary exercised those virtues passively rather than actively when, with 'prompt resignation',[9] she 'meekly ... yielded up her entire self, body, soul, and spirit, to the will of the Highest'.[10] When Protestants could describe the Virgin Mary as embodying the traits they believed were inherently female – purity, obedience, maternity – they could praise her as an admirable woman. For example, at the Annunciation she closely resembled the modest, devout, young women praised in Victorian texts. Here she could be imagined as exemplifying Sarah Ann Sewell's advice that 'it is a man's place to rule, and a woman's to yield. He must be held up as the head of the house, and it is her duty to bend so unmurmuringly to his wishes.'[11] Womanly submission led to household harmony, or, as at the Annunciation, harmony between heaven and earth. It is here that we can accept Sally Cunneen's assertion: 'In part because Mary seemed so much like the Victorian ideal, especially because of her maternity, she began to receive a curiously positive reception among some distinguished Protestant writers.'[12]

Her virtues of humility, piety, and obedience notwithstanding, the Protestant Mary was not uniquely blessed by becoming the mother of Jesus. (She was not the Mother of God, a title the traditional high-church cleric Edward Wilson dismissed as an affectation,[13] but only 'the mother of our Lord's humanity'.[14]) A variety of Protestants cited Deborah's praise of Jael – 'Blessed above women shall Jael the wife of Heber be'[15] – to show that it was no extraordinary mark of praise to call a woman 'blessed'.[16] On the surface, this was simple textual criticism, evaluating one phrase in its larger context in order to argue against using even the scriptural first half of the Hail Mary. However, likening Mary to a minor biblical figure also subtly undermined even the praise she had earned at the Annunciation and thus laid the groundwork to reduce her status to that of an ordinary woman. This opportunity was taken by the writer Annette Calthrop when she argued that Jael was no heroine but a 'traitress' and a 'murderess'[17] for inviting Sisera into her tent in order to kill him. Thus she reminded her readers that Jael had done a man's work and claimed a man's honour when she took revenge on Sisera. Although Calthrop purported to contrast Mary, who had been praised by an angel, positively against Jael, who had been lauded by mere mortals, her disparaging of Jael tainted Mary also, given the tradition of equating the two women. Invoking Jael also could be a reminder of the popular stereotype of women as duplicitous, a stereotype that coexisted with and was not eradicated by the stereotype of women as morally superior to men. Finally, the comparison with Jael – who performed a symbolic rape when she murdered Sisera by driving a tent peg through his head – could subtly strengthen the criticism that Mary interfered with Jesus' work, either by trying to involve herself in his public work or by diverting attention away from him. The equating of Mary and Jael defined Jesus' mother as an unnatural woman.

Pregnancy was historically one of the markers of women's closeness to nature; it was taken to signify that women, like animals, were governed by their bodies rather than by their minds, as men constantly were claimed to be. However, the lengthy Catholic tradition of describing Mary's pregnancy as a manifestation of her unique relationship with the divine, coupled with the centrality of the Incarnation in Christian tradition and the privileging of maternity in Victorian culture, made it difficult to redefine it as a negative. Protestants rarely described the Virgin Mary in positive terms. Here their traditionally close reliance on the gospels' narrative allowed them to ignore, for the most part, Mary's pregnancy. The Protestant Mary, like the scriptural Mary, made only brief appearances while pregnant. On the rare occasions Protestants acknowledged her pregnancy, they did so usually in the manner of the traditional high-churchman Samuel Wilberforce, who in 1842 airily assured Queen Victoria and her court: 'At length the months of waiting passed away, and the gracious birth was come.'[18] (Given the Queen's dislike of childbearing, one wonders whether she had sardonically wished that the months of pregnancy were so fleeting or had scorned Wilberforce for being unrealistic.)

The anonymous author of *The Virgin Mary, a married woman* was unusual in choosing to discuss Mary's pregnancy in more detail, but he did so only to assert that she remained unchanged by her close contact with the divine. He rejected Ullathorne's thesis that the blood flowing between Mary's heart and the developing Jesus had, with every heartbeat, 'enrich[ed] her with His divinest spirit'. Instead, he argued: 'The child ... *takes from* the mother but imparts nothing to her, and not one particle of the Godhead of Jesus was imparted to Mary, nor could she by becoming His mother derive from Him any of His special attributes, whether fleshly or otherwise; nor by giving birth to the sinless did she herself attain that perfection.'[19] Describing pregnancy as a one-way process (as indeed, biologically, it was), this anonymous Protestant author subverted the traditional image of the selfless pregnant woman when he implied that the Catholic Virgin Mary was a potentially predatory mother who would steal Jesus' divinity. Having undone the connection between Mary's pregnancy and her close relationship with the divine, he may have hoped that his readers would be mindful of the negative tendencies associated with women's fertility, including their alleged susceptibility to hysteria, a medical term that itself asserts the connection between women's childbearing capacities and their irrationality. The Mary he described, who was spiritually removed from the child she carried, had all the disadvantages and none of the advantages of pregnancy. Curiously untouched by her pregnancy, she was equally detached from the divine. The rarity of this line of reasoning, however, suggests the difficulty of defining Mary's pregnancy as anything other than a positive event, in her life as well as in the Christian history of salvation. It was perhaps for this reason that Victorian Protestants usually declined to discuss Mary's pregnancy.

The growing importance of Christmas as a holiday, encouraged in part by Charles Dickens's A Christmas carol (which itself places the mother, Mrs Cratchit, at the centre of family life) and Victoria and Albert's popularisation of the Christmas tree,[20] meant that Nativity images became more common. For example, most of the references to the Virgin in Hymns ancient & modern – which, although produced by Tractarians and their sympathisers, was determinedly ecumenical – are in Christmas hymns. Images of the Virgin and Child inspired diverse reactions, tempered by an individual's position and goals. Elite Protestants, especially those with no particular public anti-Catholic agenda, were the most likely to respond neutrally to these images which, when they encountered them abroad, they could regard as aesthetic objects or local curiosities rather than devotional aids that were an affront to their own religiosity. They often noted images of the Madonna and Child in continental churches and village shrines with little, if any, negative comment.[21] They generally regarded them as charming examples of a foreign culture, albeit one that was deplorably over-emotional and ignorant of the true faith. They responded more positively to artistic images, perhaps because they could be approached as aesthetic rather than religious objects. The politician Austen Henry Layard, who was convinced that the Roman Catholic Church was filled with 'superstitions, and clogs upon the intellectual development of men',[22] nevertheless described a Giorgione painting of the Madonna and Child he saw in Madrid in 1872 as 'very charming',[23] with no mention of either goddess worship or superstition. Thirty-seven years earlier, as a young man visiting the Louvre, he had been impressed by 'a Virgin and Child by Murillo which I thought wonderful'.[24] Although the art historian and author Anna Brownell Jameson was unsympathetic to Roman Catholicism and 'the worship of the Madonna'[25] she believed it to promote, her tone softened noticeably when she discussed representations of the Madonna and Child in her Legends of the Madonna as represented in the fine arts. She decried those images, so beloved by Catholics, of the baby Jesus and Mary embracing as 'a deviation from the solemnity of the purely religious significance',[26] but she found more formal pictures of the Madonna and Child to be 'sublime conceptions'.[27] When viewing these works, she admitted, 'it is difficult, very difficult, to refrain from an Ora pro Nobis (Pray for us)'.[28]

Not everyone could accept such images of the Virgin Mary as aesthetically pleasing depictions of a loving mother or as charming foreign relics.

Those who recognised the polemical value of anti-Roman Catholicism described Mary as the anxious, unsure mother of an aloof infant. Samuel Wilberforce described an uneasy Nativity scene in which a humble and awestruck Mary made a futile attempt to understand her newborn son.

> There was the full tide of a mother's love for the Babe which slept beside her; there was the awful reverence of her pious soul for the unknown majesty of Him who of her had taken human flesh. Depths were all around her, into which her spirit searched, in which it could find no resting-place. How was He, this infant of days, the everlasting Son? How was He to make atonement for her sins and the sins of her people? When would the mystery begin to unfold itself? As yet it lay upon her thick and impenetrable; all was dark around her.[29]

This image was available also to those who, like the poet Elizabeth Barrett, were reflexively anti-Catholic but were not concerned with the polemical advantages of anti-Catholicism. Barrett's poem, 'The Virgin Mary to the child Jesus' (written well before her 1845 marriage to Robert Browning, her subsequent miscarriages, and the birth of her son in 1849), describes a Mary who understands that Jesus is divine as well as human – 'My flesh, my Lord!' – and acknowledges throughout her inferiority to this 'baby-browed/ And speechless Being'.[30] Jesus, asleep and unresponsive, does not deign to acknowledge her submission.

Wilberforce was a prominent churchman who frequently articulated his dislike of Roman Catholicism. He sought controversy as frequently as he sought preferment in the Established Church (which brought him two bishoprics and the nickname 'Soapy Sam'); today he is best remembered for debating evolution with Thomas Huxley, 'Darwin's bulldog', in 1860. In contrast, Barrett was a lay woman with only a distant relationship to organised Christianity. Her anti-Roman Catholicism was more automatic than coherent, as when, while living in Italy, she gently mocked her maid for 'light[ing] a lamp to the virgin, [and] putting up an especial prayer that the Holy Mother would not permit the Signor and Signora to stir from Florence throughout the summer'.[31] Both, however, described Mary as a distant mother who recognised her inferiority to her son. In both descriptions, the maternal love that suffused Mary was insufficient to combat her bewilderment about her son's mission. He, the vulnerable infant, held secrets that the woman who had carried him for nine months could not access. Tormented by a restless and confused spirit, she was as much awestruck worshipper as loving mother. Her spiritual and emotional separation from her baby was underscored by the physical distance between them, as he slept beside her, rather than being tenderly cradled in her arms.

It is to be doubted that Wilberforce, who adored his wife (he called her his 'most tenderly and most excessively beloved Emily'[32]), or Barrett, who ultimately found motherhood a delightful occupation, would have acknowledged the larger implications of their images of the Virgin Mary. However, it is undeniable that these twin portraits, which were publicly disseminated, posited an alternative portrait of motherhood, one in which the mother was aloof from and bewildered by the child who depended on her. In a culture heavily invested with the image of the mother as a selfless, loving woman who gently guided her children, the image of a mother who was emotionally divorced from her child had implications beyond representations of the Virgin Mary. While the figure of the Virgin Mary had less cultural authority in Protestant than in Catholic cultures, representations of her as the mother of Jesus carried more weight than those of other mothers, such as appeared in novels, conduct manuals, or parliamentary commissions. In shifting the power balance from the mother, who should have been the protector, to the son, Wilberforce and Barrett also subtly undermined the image of mothers in general as the loving and powerful protectors of their infants.

Unflattering portraits such as Wilberforce's and Barrett's were unusual, however, because it was difficult to describe any mother of a newborn, let alone the woman Christians believed to be the mother of the Saviour, in negative terms. Protestants who wished to limit the attention paid to the mother and focus on the infant usually ignored, as much as possible, the Virgin Mary at the Nativity. 'S.M.' deflected attention away from Mary when she instructed her readers in Charlotte Elizabeth's evangelical and anti-Roman Catholic *Christian lady's magazine*: 'Take notice, the wise men paid no adoration to the virgin mother, but to the child only; they fell down and worshipped HIM.'[33] When the clergyman (and friend of the Ruskins) Daniel Moore mentioned Mary in his 1854 lectures on the birth of Jesus,[34] he usually coupled her name with that of Joseph, thereby implicitly equating the relationship of mother and foster-father. Demonstrating the latent anti-Semitism characteristic of even well-educated Victorians, Moore ascribed Mary and Joseph's lack of knowledge of Micah's prophecy regarding Bethlehem to the 'very low condition ... of the whole Jewish nation, in regard to their religious intelligence, coupled with the obscurity and impoverished circumstances of Joseph and Mary'.[35] For the Protestant Mary and Joseph, poverty and obscurity were not signs of praiseworthy humility but an occasion for condemnation.

Devotional images of the Madonna and Child were another matter, however, especially for the Protestant controversialists who sought inflammatory images to support their charges that Catholicism was a pagan religion. They responded harshly to devotional images on the grounds that they made Jesus weak and superfluous, and Mary the focus of worship. Such images made Jesus, Michael Hobart Seymour charged, 'a mere appendage, to distinguish Mary – a thing introduced to point her out, and of no value but as a label to Mary'.[36] During a lengthy stay in Italy, Augustin Gaspard Edouart, a traditional high-church cleric who opposed the extremes of both Catholicism and Calvinism, was horrified to 'observe what numbers of persons fell down and worshipped before marble statues, pictures, or large *wax dolls*, which represent the Virgin Mary with the divine and omnipotent Saviour as a *feeble, helpless, babe* in her arms!'[37] Both Edouart and Seymour were reacting to Italian images. While many Roman Catholic chapels (and some Anglican chapels) had depictions of the Virgin, publicly displayed Marian statues were exceedingly rare in England, especially before 1851, in which year, in London, there was only one such statue, in St Mary's, Chelsea.[38]

Victorian culture idealised the mother–child relationship except when the mother and child in question were the Virgin Mary and Jesus. It was expected, of course, for the mother to care for her infant child. In her article 'Christmas Day', 'S.M.' acknowledged that Christ had been born 'a weak and helpless babe' who presumably required a mother's care, although in that article she ignored the Virgin Mary almost entirely and instructed her readers to do the same when she urged them: 'Take notice, the wise men paid no adoration to the virgin mother, but to the child only.'[39] Rarely if ever did Victorian discourse describe a mother caring for her infant, as she was expected to do, as a threat to masculine authority, except when the mother was the Virgin Mary. The theological significance of the Nativity, combined with the power of the idealised mother figure in Victorian culture, leads one to expect that this scene would elicit some approval for the woman who had borne and cared for the baby whom Protestants believed was her and their Saviour. However, when confronted with the figure of a woman whose maternal role had encouraged Catholics to give her great prominence, Protestants expressed serious reservations about the implications of maternal power.

Seymour's Jesuit informant, who was meant to serve as a witness to Roman Catholic corruptions, revealed the link between the Protestant Virgin Mary's limited maternal role and Protestants' anxiety about the feminine ideal. This priest, Seymour said, had assured him that

when one thinks of all the little scenes of His childhood, dwells on the little incidents of interest between the child Jesus and the mother Mary, recollects that she had him enshrined in her womb, that she used to lead him by the hand, that she had listened to all his innocent prattle, that she had observed the opening of his mind; and that during all those days of his happy childhood she, and she alone of all the world, knew that little child whom she bore in her womb and nursed at her breasts and fondled in her arms, was her God – that when a man thinks, and habitually thinks of all this, the natural result is that his affections will be more drawn out, and his feelings of devotion more elevated towards Mary.[40]

Seymour's Jesuit informant bears a striking resemblance to a stock character in both travel literature and Gothic novels, the foreigner who unwittingly indicts his own culture to an appalled Englishman or woman. Even so, he was a useful way for Seymour to remind his readers of what many of them already believed, that continental Roman Catholicism was a corrupt form of Christianity. Yet to condemn Roman Catholics as idolators he described a mother who lovingly devoted herself to her child. Seymour's denunciations of Roman Catholicism were lengthy and vitriolic even by Victorian standards; this was a man, after all, whose honeymoon in Rome produced two anti-Roman Catholic books, *A pilgrimage to Rome* and *Mornings among the Jesuits at Rome*. However, that conviction enabled Seymour to make explicit what Victorian Protestants usually only implied: that the woman who conformed to the feminine ideal could become more prominent than the man. Because they often moved from commenting on Mary to generalising about mothers, their words conveyed a broader concern that the mother would overshadow her son. Under the guise of attacking the Catholic Virgin Mary, these Protestant clergy sought to limit maternal power and prerogatives, and thus they suggested that the mother was not always a comforting, reassuring figure. They also call into question the assessment of Helsinger et al., that the 'increase of woman-worship during the Victorian period brings Mary inevitably into prominence. Since her virtues reside less in herself than in her maternal role, a culture which idealized Motherhood eulogizes Mary's innate spirituality, passivity, devotion.'[41] Instead, representatives of the culture that claimed to idealise motherhood denounced the Western tradition's prime exemplar of motherhood.

Vowed virginity and Protestant culture

One traditional indicator of the Virgin Mary's unique relationship with the divine was the belief that she had remained a virgin. This belief was shared by the reformers, including Martin Luther,[42] John Calvin,[43] and Ulrich Zwingli.[44] English reformers either stated their belief in her perpetual virginity, as did Latimer[45] and John Wesley,[46] or, like Thomas Cranmer,[47] did not address the question, suggesting that they, too, followed orthodox tradition in this area. However, Victorian Protestants departed from this tradition. Describing Mary as having borne other children,[48] they returned her to the realm of ordinary human experience. The ambiguous wording of the gospel references to Jesus' relatives allowed Protestants to argue, as did the anti-Catholic writer Catherine Sinclair, for instance: 'It is evident from the last verse of the 1st chapter of Matthew, that Mary lived afterwards with her husband Joseph as his wife.'[49] The anonymous Anglican clergyman who devoted an entire pamphlet to the topic of *The Virgin Mary, a married woman* argued: 'No restriction whatever was placed either on Joseph or Mary when the mysterious incarnation of Christ was revealed to them, but rather the contrary.'[50]

As with much of this debate, the discourse was accessible to those who did not follow theological discussions or even attend religious services: the itinerant Protestant controversialist (and former Roman Catholic) William Murphy argued in an 1868 lecture that her presence at the wedding at Cana 'proved that the Virgin Mary was favourable to marriage the same as all protestants, and was not a nun.'[51] Murphy, who was highly effective in spreading an anti-Catholic message outside of the university boundaries and the walls of churches and chapels, was deservedly described by Walter Arnstein as 'the apostle of popular anti-Catholicism in the England of the 1860s'.[52] His lectures were held in hired halls – and even, in at least one case, in a purpose-built structure that held 3,000 people[53] – and gave mayors of the cities he visited intense concern because of the propensity of his words to incite anti-Catholic riots.[54] Whether voiced by clergymen or popular speakers, references to Mary as having had other children returned her to the realm of the ordinary. Not only could she not remain a virgin–mother, but by fulfilling the woman's role of providing a man with children, she could be assigned the traditionally inferior position of the woman. Furthermore, a Mary who had borne other children was proof that life-long virginity was not divinely sanctioned, for it had not been required even of Jesus' mother.

The traditional belief in the Virgin Mary's eternal virginity was challenged at a time when female virginity became an issue in a way that it had not been previously. The insistence that women were naturally maternal devalued life-long virginity at the same time as the introduction of Roman Catholic and Anglo-Catholic convents meant that there were more opportunities for women to choose vowed virginity over marriage and a family. Protestant tradition, of course, disapproved of vowed virginity. Although Henry VIII and his daughter Elizabeth had preferred celibate priests, Article 32 asserted that 'it is lawful also for them [bishops, priests, and deacons], as for all other Christian men, to marry at their own discretion'. Dislike of vowed virginity was marked in the Victorian age, when it was described as a corruption of Christianity: the historian and anti-Tractarian writer Richard T. Hampson derided it as 'a pure relic of heathenism'.[55] However, it was also respected as a threat. Thomas Rawson Birks, an evangelical Anglican clergyman and professor of moral theology at Cambridge University, feared that 'the celibacy' of the Roman Catholic

> priesthood adds immensely to their aggressive power. It shuts them off from all the ordinary instincts of human affection; it divorces them from all mankind; and marries them to the Court of Rome. Domestic life, with its thousand gentle charities, and the love of country, with its noble aspirations, are alike forbidden them, that the current of their zeal may be confined to one channel and be directed to one sole object, the establishment of priestly dominion, and the triumph of a great ecclesiastical corruption over the consciences of Christians and the thrones of kings.[56]

Although Birks worried about men, female virginity also provoked anxiety when it was understood as giving women greater independence. This anxiety is evident in reactions to Queen Victoria, who early in her reign was a problematic figure when she was understood as being beyond her husband's control. On the eve of her marriage in 1841, a street ballad worried:

> Since the Queen has no equal, 'obey' none she need,
> So of course at the altar from such vow she's freed;
> And the women will all follow suit, so they say –
> 'Love, honour' they'll promise, but never – 'obey'.[57]

This was just one of many popular depictions of Victoria asserting authority over her new husband, often by literally wearing the pants in the family.[58] However, Victoria's early marriage, which she deliberately represented as a conventional, middle-class marriage, was meant to assuage many of her subjects' anxieties on this score.[59] Victoria insisted that she was subordinate, at least in some ways, to her husband, while an eternally virgin Mary forever reigned above her husband.[60]

The charge that Catholicism devalued or even threatened domestic life was a standard one. For the Victorian property-owning classes, as well as those who aspired to such indicators of respectability, female virginity was valued not for its own sake but for its perceived capacity to contain women, which made it key to the formation of domesticity. Unmarried women were expected to be virgins, but only as a prelude to marriage.

As Ornella Moscucci has observed, Victorians valued moral rather than physical virginity in women.[61] In fact, the spinster was a figure of ridicule in Victorian popular culture, even to the point of being the object of schemes to ship her to Australia. No similar anxiety was manifested about bachelors, however, for single women challenged the Victorian ideal of the family in a way that single men – unless they were celibate priests – did not.

The newly established convents were often greeted with hostility, for women who chose to remain single for religious reasons aroused anxiety in Victorian England in a way that other unmarried women did not. (Protestants preferred deaconesses, who were married women, over sisters.) As A. M. Allchin has noted, the Victorian attitude to Anglican sisterhoods was one of 'strong approval of their work, joined with little or no sympathy or understanding for their distinctive mode of life'.[62] One of the more famous examples of hostility being translated into actual violence was the funeral of Miss Scobel, who, against her father's wishes, joined the Sisterhood of St Margaret, the nursing order founded by John Mason Neale. Her death from scarlet fever in 1857 precipitated a riot on the eve of her funeral and then a public war of words in which Mr Scobel and Neale accused one another of abusing patriarchal authority. Roman Catholic convents were even less welcome in Victorian England. Vowed virgins represented a threat not just to individual men but to a masculine hierarchy: some Anglican bishops feared that Anglican sisters would be more popular than they themselves.[63]

An anxiety that vowed virginity could allow women a degree of independence from the family, and especially from male control, is evident in Victorian critiques of Anglican sisterhoods and Roman Catholic convents. Popular novels, for example, described nuns as failed women. In Mrs Gaskell's *North and south*, Margaret Hale is an active philanthropist, but in her longing for 'heavenly steadfastness in earthly monotony' after the deaths of her parents, she thinks: 'If I were a Roman Catholic and could deaden my heart, stun it with some great blow, I might become a nun.'[64] George Eliot's heroine Romola saw convents as a refuge for 'unhappy wives' like herself,[65] although her lack of religiosity and her desire for independence led her to reject the option. Alternatively, nuns and sisters could be described as overly feminine women when their vocation was attributed to vanity. Argemone, the ostensible heroine of Charles Kingsley's *Yeast*, longs to join an Anglican sisterhood, but her religious devotion is somewhat affected: 'She knelt and prayed at her velvet foldstool, among all the knickknacks which nowadays make a luxury of devotion.'[66] Anglican sisterhoods also appeared to be all but

Roman Catholic institutions. Echoing the charges made against Lydia Sellon in 1849, a Protestant upset by the visit Queen Victoria and two of her daughters made to Clewer in 1864 bemoaned the fact that 'professing Protestants bestow their money and influence in supporting Tractarian convents, where the errors of *confession, Mariolatry, prayers to the saints, and masses for the dead,* are taught and practised'.[67]

Manifesting the prejudice that convent life was so unnatural that women stayed only when forced to, convents were also described as prisons where Protestant as well as Catholic women were held against their will. Seymour assured his readers that his travels in Italy had taught him that a woman became 'a prisoner for life' once she took vows.[68] 'If she escapes from the monastery [convent], or attempts to fly, the laws proclaim her an outcast, and all the ministers of justice pursue her as a felon, and she is seized and punished as a criminal, and confined, if possible, still more closely than before.'[69] This attitude led to a rash of paintings depicting the nun as a beautiful woman who was turning her back on the joys of the world to be shut up in a gloomy convent.[70] It was the stereotype of the unhappy woman imprisoned in a convent that inspired Member of Parliament Charles Newdegate's decades-long campaign to open convents to inspection, on the grounds that women were held therein against their will. (When his bill was finally passed in 1870, the committee established to investigate convents and monasteries found that they held no secrets.[71]) Such erroneous depictions of convents allowed Victorians to ignore the truth that women in a convent could experience greater freedom than did their married sisters, who had little legal protection, even at the end of the century.

This discomfort with life-long virginity encouraged the Victorian Protestant emphasis on the Virgin Mary as the mother of subsequent children. Although Dobney recognised that 'the idea of *virgin purity* is instantly suggested by the very first mention of her [Mary], and is altogether inseparable from the idea of Mary', he declared that 'true inward chastity' should be the goal of Christians. 'Only, let us guard ourselves from all the influence of that merely ascetic and ecclesiastical idea, which is but a falsification and corruption of the true, and which places celibacy higher in the moral scale than ever so truly pure and honourable and noble a married life.'[72] While Protestants argued that the gospels provided evidence for Mary's subsequent children, their portrait of Mary also reflected other cultural concerns. In this case, the importance of the family in Victorian culture overrode any desire to deny female sexuality. 'Lydia' lauded matrimony, in the *Christian lady's magazine*, as 'the highest earthly gift of God to man',[73] while the author of *The Virgin Mary, a married woman* directly contradicted Neale and Frederick W. Faber when he declared that God had made marriage a more honourable state than celibacy.[74] The significance of the Virgin Mary in this defence of marriage was articulated by George Miller, the Anglo-Irish high-church divine, when he accused the recently widowed Pusey (in a work that helped inspire John Henry Newman's 'Tract 90') of a 'seemingly reluctant commendation of marriage' in calling Mary 'ever-virgin'.[75] In order to fit into the dominant Victorian social iconography, Mary had to have had a normal marriage.

Limitations on Mary's influence

Protestants generally described Mary as an ordinary mother not just in her childbearing but in her relationship to Jesus; and occasionally this could inspire praise. For example, some Protestants had kind words for the Virgin Mary's intervention at Cana, because they could interpret her actions there as being appropriately feminine. Edouart praised 'the amiable thoughtfulness exhibited by her at that time in her quick-sightedness and eagerness to have removed a difficulty which might have caused their friends not a little distress and embarrassment'.[76] Dobney agreed that 'her behaviour was altogether worthy of the true woman. The delicately sympathising endeavour to spare her humble friends the mortification of finding their supply fail before the festivities were ended led her to draw the attention of Christ to the circumstance'.[77] However, even when Protestants described the Virgin Mary as a woman properly fulfilling her domestic duties, they did not believe that her maternal authority extended into Jesus' public life. Her maternal authority ended at the wedding at Cana where, Dobney declared, Jesus 'intimated that the time was come when maternal influence over him must cease'.[78]

However, the Protestant Mary did not always gracefully relinquish her maternal authority. She 'assum[ed] too much authority over him'[79] and attempted to interfere in his mission,[80] forcing Jesus to notify her more than once of the termination of her maternal authority. He did so, they said, by repeatedly addressing her as 'Woman' rather than 'Mother', an address the evangelical clergyman William Thomas Maudson described as, 'to say the least, politely distant'[81] and Miller as 'cold'.[82] Protestants also believed, as did Maudson, that Jesus condemned his mother's behaviour with a 'harsh and unduteous' response to her at the Temple and by responding 'with apparent indifference and contempt'[83] when Mary tried to interrupt his preaching. In sum, as Francis Merewether, the Anglican clergyman and opponent of both Roman Catholicism and disestablishment, said: 'The Virgin Mother received more than once from the lips of her blessed Son, during his earthly ministry, words savouring strongly of reproof.[84] (Although the disciples were equally liable to the criticism that they misunderstood Jesus' mission, Protestant authors did not dilute their criticism of the Virgin Mary by pointing out that there was evidence that others close to Jesus did not fully understand his mission.) Nevertheless, she refused to acknowledge the severed connection and followed Jesus to the foot of the cross. There, according to Charles Thomas Longley, Archbishop of York (and subsequently of Canterbury), 'bowed down by a weight of grief such as no daughter of Eve ever bore before or since',[85] her presence multiplied her son's sufferings: 'Jesus has thus to bear not His own sufferings only, but hers as well, and seems, as it were, to be dying a double death.'[86] Michael Wheeler locates 'Christ's "hard sayings" to his mother which challenge the ideal of the Holy Family as a model for Christians to follow'[87] in the twentieth century, but in fact Victorian Protestants' interpretations of Jesus' words meant that these 'hard sayings' were well-established by the mid-nineteenth century. The Protestant Mary was no model mother, but a woman grasping to remain in her son's life when she should have gracefully relinquished him to the public world.

Deprived of an earthly role, the Protestant Mary was also denied a role in heaven. The Anglican cleric William Ford Vance, who defended the Protestant identity of the Established Church, was horrified to think that Roman Catholics 'entreat her to exercise her influence and authority over God, as a mother over her son, that he may save your souls: *"Jure matris, imperâ Redemptori": By the right of a mother, command the Redeemer!!!*'[88] Nor did Protestants consider Mary to be the mother of all Christians. Jesus assigned Mary to John's care, Sinclair said, only because she was 'a mere woman ... unable even to succour herself'.[89] The Protestant Virgin Mary, having been defined as an impediment to Jesus' work, was thus described as an ordinary woman who had no expansive sphere of influence. 'A.B.', a correspondent to the anti-Roman Catholic *Church and state gazette* who had been greatly impressed by a lecture John Cumming had given in Scarborough in 1853 condemning the Virgin Mary's position in the Roman Catholic Church, was convinced that 'it requires a large extension of faith to reconcile the superior homage to the Virgin Mary, as our Mediatrix and presiding Deity, with the woman who doubted or denied the perfectibility of her Son's mind'.[90] Protestants were confident that they were guided not just by Mary's behaviour as recorded in the gospels, but by Jesus' wishes as well. Deploring the '*Romanist* feelings'[91] expressed by the woman who praised Mary's breasts and womb, Edouart declared that Jesus, 'so far from giving encouragement to such feelings ... at once checked them'.[92] Jesus did so, taught Maudson, in order 'to

lessen the closeness, and destroy the distinction of that earthly relationship, which has been made the very ground of the especial reverence that
is rendered to the Virgin'.[93] In the mid-nineteenth century, a chorus of
Protestants agreed with Vance that Jesus had wanted 'to avoid every thing
likely to excite a feeling of undue veneration for her [Mary] in the minds
of his disciples'.[94] Protestants also claimed to be following Mary's wishes.
Cumming declared that 'if the now glorified and happy Virgin could come
down to earth, she would call on you to silence for ever the idolatrous
accents [of] Ave Maria, and teach you to breathe in language, heartfelt
and believing – Abba – Father!'[95] The Protestant Mary was, then, a model
of female self-denial; when Protestants described her as humiliated when
she tried to seize a public role, they could also have been warning women
against self-aggrandisement.

Because they did not believe that Mary's behaviour made her worthy
of devotion, Protestants rejected all forms of Marian devotion, including
the scriptural first half of the Hail Mary and prayers using that invocation,
such as the Stella Maris.[96] Protestants as various as Dobney, Edouart, and
Tyler found the King James Bible's more restrained (and, scholars now
agree, more accurate[97]) translation of the angelic greeting – 'Hail, thou
that art highly favoured' – to be more acceptable than the Catholic 'Hail
Mary, full of grace'.[98] They particularly disliked the Rosary – derided by
the Congregationalist weekly the British banner as the mindless counting
of beads 'by the million'[99] – on the grounds that it devoted more attention
to Mary than to God.[100] Seymour made obvious the underlying criticism
that the Rosary represented a challenge to God when he described unedu-
cated Italians ignoring the priest, Christ's representative, in order to say
the Rosary during Mass.[101] This view of the Rosary appeared in fiction
also. In Eliot's Romola, the Rosary is associated with Tessa, the charmingly
ignorant peasant who is assiduous in her Marian devotions (although she
sometimes falls asleep while saying the Rosary), but who knows so little of
church ritual that she does not realise her marriage to Tito is a sham.

The discomfort with the older mother, apparent when Mary was
discussed, was evident elsewhere in Victorian culture. It shaped descriptions of Queen Victoria, who was perhaps the best-known overbearing
mother of the age. As a result both of her disappointment in Bertie, the
future Edward VII, and of her reluctance to share power (which was
also manifested in her treatment of Albert during the early years of their
marriage), Queen Victoria gave her son no real responsibilities. While
Bertie's penchant for drinking, gambling, and womanising may have
justified this treatment, Victoria's subjects blamed lack of responsibility
for his extended adolescence: 'Kept in childhood beyond his time', the

future Prime Minister William Ewart Gladstone lamented, 'he is allowed to make that childhood what it should never be in a Prince, or anyone else, namely wanton.'[102] In 1867 Walter Bagehot described Bertie as 'an unemployed youth,'[103] while the radical politician Charles Bradlaugh's pamphlet *George, the Prince of Wales, with recent contrasts and coincidences*, likened Bertie to George IV, whose lengthy wait for the throne had been notoriously dissolute.[104] Bertie was unfortunately unable to imitate the example of Lord Lufton, one of the heroes of *Framley parsonage*. Lufton acknowledged that he loved and esteemed his mother, but asserted that 'nevertheless, I cannot allow her to lead me in all things. Were I to do so, I should cease to be a man.'[105] Victoria's popularity revived at her Golden and Diamond Jubilees, in 1887 and 1897, by which time her subjects perceived her as a benevolent grandmotherly figure with limited power.

Discomfort with older mothers was practically a staple of Victorian literature. Although nineteenth-century novels often deliver the message that young women were on the path to becoming mothers, they are generally marked by the absence of parents, especially mothers. Main characters – including Jane Eyre, David Copperfield, and Becky Sharp – are often orphans. Pairs of orphans are also common: in Charles Dickens's *Great expectations*, Pip and Estella are brought up by unsatisfactory surrogate mothers; in Eliot's *Adam Bede* the cousins Hetty Poyser and Dinah Morris are more fortunate in their choice of guardians. A significant number of mothers – including those of David Copperfield's two wives, and of Little Em'ly, Lucy Deane, Philip Wakem, and Mary Barton – either are dead prior to start of the story of their offspring or die during its course. Mrs May is killed in an accident brought about by her husband's careless driving early in Charlotte Yonge's *The daisy chain*, although the memory of her hovers around her husband and children like a guiding spirit. The high mortality rate of mothers is remarkable, given that almost all the heroines are progressing towards what they represented, the supposedly universal goal of women – motherhood. Certainly the lack of models for what Victorian heroines were to become reinforced the assumption that women were naturally maternal, yet a sub-plot of these novels seems to be that parents, and especially mothers, must be eliminated in the progression towards adulthood.

Older mothers are not, by any means, completely lacking in Victorian novels: Adam Bede's marginal mother, Maggie Tulliver's foolish mother, and John Thornton's disagreeable mother all outlive their husbands in Eliot's novels *Adam Bede* and *The mill on the Floss* and in Mrs Gaskell's *North and south*. However, older fathers and father-figures are in general both more prevalent and more admirable. In *The mill on the Floss*, both Lucy Deane and Philip Wakem have a father; in *The daisy chain* Dr May survives the accident that kills his wife and remains the patriarch around whom the family revolves. Adoptive fathers are sometimes depicted as superior to biological parents: such is Eppie's affection for Silas Marner, the miser who rears her after her mother dies outside of his cottage in Eliot's novel, that she does not abandon him even when she discovers her true father. Romola's mother is dead but she nevertheless loves and serves her somewhat unsatisfactory father; her childless godfather, whom she considers a second father, is in fact a better father than her biological one. Pip has two surrogate fathers: Joe Gargery provides him with emotional sustenance, while the convict Abel Magwitch provides him with the capital necessary to become a gentleman. Oliver Twist's mother dies bearing him in a workhouse, although he is later taken in by Mr Brownlow. The presence of a father or father-figure but not a mother implies that an older man could more easily be accommodated into the adult life of the young protagonist than could an older mother. In the fictional equivalent of having one's cake and eating it, too, some characters – Caroline Helston in Charlotte Brontë's *Shirley* and the heroine of Sinclair's *Beatrice*, for example – are brought up by surrogate parents but are reunited with their mothers just before the story closes. These late reunions allow the heroines to develop without a mother's guidance while still ratifying the mother–daughter relationship.

A motherless heroine perhaps offered novelists greater dramatic possibilities and was certainly not a demographic oddity. In 1841 the life expectancy was 41.18 years for women and 40.19 years for men.[106] Sheila Ryan Johanson argues that Peter Uhlenberg's conclusion that in nineteenth-century America 'only exceptional women managed to live out the "typical" life cycle, which included living long enough to marry, having children and surviving jointly with a husband until the last child married and grandchildren began arriving', can also be applied to England.[107] Nevertheless, the near-total elimination of parental figures, especially mothers, in these works that both shaped and reflected mainstream Victorian culture requires an explanation beyond the demands of realism or drama. These missing women suggest that the same culture which exalted mothers also worried that mothers who did exercise the influence they were urged to have would never allow their children – especially their sons – to become independent.

Canonical novels achieve their status by representing a culture's concerns and assumptions. Other popular works equally demonstrate a discomfort with the older mother. In fact, the absent mother was a characteristic of all genres, Carolyn Dever argues: 'To write a life, in the Victorian period, is to write the story of the loss of the mother. In fiction and biography, autobiography and poetry, the organisational logic of lived experience extends, not from the moment of birth, but from the instant of that primal loss.'[108] That an author did not need to dispatch the mother but only to ignore her is evident in Mrs Ellis's well-known advice manual *The mothers of England*. When Mrs Ellis does broach the topic of mothers and their grown children, she suggests that mothers and their adult sons continue the close relationship that was formed in childhood,[109] and even that a woman act as a surrogate mother to other young men: 'in the character of the matron of a family, all young men who are brought within the sphere of her influence, ought to feel that, to a certain extent, they have a mother'.[110] Although Mrs Ellis seems to extend a mother's role beyond the childhood of her offspring, she actually limits any power a mother might exercise by assuming throughout this book (as she does in her other works) that women are inferior to men, including their grown sons. Female equality is, she asserts, 'opposed at once to nature and religion, to philosophy and common sense'.[111] Though apparently exalting a mother's status, both in the eyes of society and in the hearts of her children, Mrs Ellis actually restricts women to the domestic sphere, where they exercise only influence, which is more easily ignored than is power.[112]

Rarely did any Victorian text make a direct connection between criticising the Virgin Mary and expressing hesitation about maternal power. To do so may have been too risky, for clichés about maternal virtue were endemic in Victorian discourse. It may also have been unnecessary: although the Virgin Mary was the subject of the critiques, the implicit criticisms of overarching maternal power could hardly have been missed. A striking exception to this general rule against overt linkage was Mrs Oliphant's novel *Madonna Mary*, serialised in *Good words* during 1866. Although this work has been cited as evidence that the Virgin Mary was a powerful role model for women in the nineteenth century,[113] such a reading ignores Mrs Oliphant's open hostility to the ostensible heroine, Mary Ochterlony, and thus to her namesake. While Mary Ochterlony is so sweet that the men of her husband's regiment call her 'Madonna Mary',[114] the author mocks her goodness as being unrealistic and even slightly tiresome. One female character belittles her as being 'a little too like Amelia in *Vanity Fair*',[115] while another scoffs at 'that ridiculous name, Madonna Mary'.[116] Even worse, Mary Ochterlony's inability to control or even influence her husband, her sister Winnie, and her youngest son leads to financial problems, estrangement among family members, and public embarrassment before harmony is finally restored at the novel's end. Far from incorporating a strong and admirable Madonna-figure into English discourse, this novel dismissed the viability of the Virgin Mary as a role model for women. *Madonna Mary* was unusual in openly expressing discomfort with the feminine ideal-cum-Madonna, but it voiced a common concern.

Protestants and the Catholic Mary

Because the Protestant Virgin Mary was conceived in part as a means by which to undermine the Catholic version, Protestants had to confront that image directly. One of their principal objections to the Catholic Virgin Mary was theological: that, by becoming an object of devotion in her own right, she claimed the attention due to the Trinity alone. Protestants frequently criticised Roman Catholics for praying to Mary in the same way as they prayed to God, thus erasing the distinction between Creator and creature.[117] The anti-Tractarian evangelical divine Edward Bickersteth (who worked to convert Jews as well as Roman Catholics) charged that 'in their ordinary worship they [Roman Catholics] intermingle devotions between God, the Virgin, and the saints'.[118] Worse still, Roman Catholics were said to ignore God in order to pray to Mary. A member of the Northampton Mission of the Protestant Reformation Society described a 'GREAT VOTARESS' of the Virgin Mary who refused to listen to any talk of God, but insisted to her Protestant interrogator 'betake yourself to the blessed *Mother of God*', whom she credited with saving souls from hell.[119] This complaint was sufficiently familiar to have appeared in fiction, as well: the Roman Catholic priest in Kingsley's novel *Yeast* prays to Mary instead of to God.[120] As William Palmer of Worcester College, Oxford – a traditional high-church cleric who was one of Froude's 'Zs' and (at the time) a friend of Newman – summed up the situation in the first of eight public letters he wrote in defence of the Church of England to Nicholas Wiseman, the Catholic Mary 'receive[d] honours which are due only to the Trinity – honours which interfere with the sole prerogatives of the Deity'.[121] Protestants described Mary as having been deified by the Roman Catholic Church,[122] being 'directly worshipped in the Roman Church',[123] and even as having been 'installed as a *fourth* person of the Godhead!'[124]

Because Protestants hardly ever publicly disagreed with the contention that Roman Catholics essentially worshipped Mary, Protestant controversialists could then argue that the powerful, prominent, Catholic Mary demonstrated 'the absolute conformity of modern popery to ancient paganism'.[125] Protestants declared that Mary was but an updated version of ancient goddesses, including Juno,[126] Venus,[127] Isis,[128] Astarte,[129] and Minerva.[130] Walter John Trower, the Anglican Bishop of Gibraltar, confided to his close friend the anti-Tractarian clergyman Charles Pourtales Golightly that his tours of the Continent had left him 'convinced that the religion of these countries (especially Spain) is virtually Semi-Pagan; & ... the worship of B[lessed] V[irgin] M[ary] is the legitimate progeny of a substitute for the worship of the Magna Dea'.[131] While Trower made his point in a private letter, the characterisation was common enough to be found in popular novels like *Romola*, in which the rededication to the Virgin Mary of Pallas Athena's Temple in Athens implied a connection between the two women.[132] The frequency and confidence of such assertions made it easy for Catherine Sinclair to conclude: 'The religion now taught by Romanists cannot be called Christianity, but is Mariolatry, a perfectly different faith'.[133]

As evidence for these charges, Protestants generally cited earlier continental rather than contemporary English devotional sources. To some extent they were forced to do so, because the relatively more restrained recusant and Victorian prayers provided few examples of the devotional fervour necessary to build their case. Additionally, continental sources allowed Protestants to depict Catholicism as a foreign religion, one that should be repudiated by good English men and women. Evidence for idolatrous Marian devotion was found in the Psalter reputedly compiled by St Bonaventure, which, as Tyler chided, 'substitut[ed] Mary's name for the God of Christians'.[134] Another favoured example was the medieval story of the two ladders. Birks warned the Bristol Protestant Alliance:

> Pictures have been printed and circulated, under the sanction of priests, in which two ladders are set up, reaching into heaven. At the top of one ladder is Christ; of the other, the Virgin. Those who strive to ascend the first, are seen falling back into the flames of hell through the inexorable severity of the Judge; but those, who choose the other ladder, are received into heaven, through the grace and intercession of the Virgin.[135]

Protestants regularly invoked this story as evidence that 'Romanism teaches that Mary is more merciful, and more willing to welcome sinners, than that Divine Saviour'.[136] The *Church and state gazette*, an Anglican weekly newspaper, went further, declaring that it offered 'proof of what the cardinal [Wiseman] and his co-religionists so often deny – namely, that the most blessed Virgin is exalted by the Romish Church into an object of worship, and invested with a power, unwarranted by Scripture, above that held by her gracious Son, our Lord and Saviour'.[137]

By far the most frequently invoked example of 'Mariolatry' was an eighteenth-century work, Alphonsus Liguori's *The glories of Mary*, a compilation of 'miracles, revelations, favours, and particular cases'[138] demonstrating the efficacy of Virgin Mary's intervention. Thomas

Hartwell Horne, an evangelical Anglican clergyman and biblical scholar, condemned Liguori's Marian devotions for exhibiting 'idolatry';[139] Charles Hastings Collette, a solicitor who wrote numerous anti-Roman Catholic works, found those devotions to be 'gross and glaring blasphemies'.[140] Palmer's conclusion that Liguori 'declares that the Virgin is a Goddess'[141] was widely shared by Protestant controversialists. One of the main objections to Liguori was his acceptance of the medieval belief, popularised by St Bernard of Clairvaux: 'No grace, no pardon, emanates from the throne of the King of kings without passing through the hands of Mary'.[142] Collette complained that, in *The glories of Mary*, 'Innumerable miracles are, likewise, said to be performed through the instrumentality of the Virgin, to attest [to] her all-powerful and omnipresent existence'.[143] Those miracles, which included securing confession for severed heads, saving a young man who sold his soul to the devil,[144] and securing the escape of birds from hawks by crying out 'Hail Mary',[145] were, the *Church and state gazette* declared, 'enough to make the hair stand on end on the head of every one who is not willingly and blindly an idolator'.[146]

Using continental sources to prove their point that the Catholic Virgin Mary was a pagan goddess allowed Victorian Protestants to argue that Roman Catholicism was a foreign religion, and thus that neither it nor Anglo-Catholicism should be countenanced by the English. Italian Marian images were most often invoked as evidence that Roman Catholics were pagan idolators. The geographical coincidence that Italy was both the seat of the Roman Catholic Church and the site of numerous pagan ruins enabled Protestants to link paganism and Roman Catholicism: they ridiculed the Pope as 'the trembling, temporising Priest of the Virgin'[147] and Italians in general as 'a superstitious people'.[148] 'If the "devotional feelings" of an Italian towards the Virgin are greater than towards his God', Palmer argued, 'I cannot but think that (whatever his faith may be *in theory*) the Virgin is practically his God';[149] while Seymour concluded that 'the religion of Italy ought to be called *the religion of Mary*, rather than *the religion of Christ*!'[150] These Victorians are the counterparts to those described by Maura O'Connor in *The romance of Italy and the English political imagination*, whose support for the political unification of Italy led them to describe the Italians as rational citizens who were worthy of self-government. Those Victorians who feared the adulteration of their Protestant religion were motivated instead to describe Italians as the childlike practitioners of a corrupt religion. As an Italian Jesuit reportedly assured Seymour, 'the Italians were a people very different from the English; that the English loved a religion of the *heart*, and the Italians a religion of the *senses*; the English a religion of the *feelings*, and the Italians a religion for the *taste*; the English *an inward and spiritual religion*, and the Italian [*sic*] *an outward and visible religion*.[151] Whether or not Seymour had an actual source for these comments, they did convey his belief, which was shared by many Victorian Protestants, that national differences manifested themselves in religious differences. Roman Catholics, who were synonymous with foreigners, were repeatedly described as practising a superficial, sensual religion, in contrast to the Protestant English, who sought a more reflective, spiritual relationship with their God.

Surprisingly, Protestants paid little attention to Ireland and France, the two countries that historically had given the English the most worry. The Irish were rarely accused of 'Mariolatry', even though many of the more baroque images of the Virgin Mary came from periodicals published in both London and Dublin (the most famous of which was the *Dublin review*). This absence was due partly to the fact that anti-Roman Catholic and anti-Irish feelings were not necessarily identified one with the other in Victorian England, for anti-Roman Catholicism was already well-established by the time waves of Irish immigrants entered England in the 1840s. Given the regularity with which the 'Irish question' intruded on Victorian Britain's politics, and the frequent intermingling of political and religious questions in the nineteenth century, this absence is also likely a result of the scarcity of Irish contributions to Victorian discourse about the role and nature of the Virgin Mary. Most of the extant sources are printed texts, which would have been the most widely circulated and thus the best means for entering the arena. None of those texts seems to have been the work of any members of the largely working-class Irish immigrant population. In addition, Roman Catholic priests usually relied on sermon notes rather than writing out their sermons,[152] and thus it would not have been easy for them to publish their sermons, as their Anglican and dissenting counterparts often did. The lack of published sermons removed a source to which Protestants could respond.

The scarcity of examples of Irish idolatry also reflected the travelling and living habits of those with the greatest access to the pulpit and the press: the English were far more likely to go to the Continent for the Grand Tour or for reasons of health or economy than to go to Ireland. (It was not until 1877 that Gladstone, whose career was so connected to the 'Irish question', made his first and, except for an extremely brief visit of several hours in 1880, only visit to Ireland; Benjamin Disraeli never crossed the Irish Sea.) Therefore, although it loomed large in the English imagination, few Victorians had any first-hand experience of Ireland. In addition, while the English had long viewed Ireland as populated by inferior people who were potentially or actually subversive, self-interest encouraged them to see the Irish as closer to being their equals, as Catholic emancipation (1829), the disestablishment of the Church of Ireland (1869), and the drive for Home Rule gave the Irish more of a role in political affairs. Furthermore, Irish peasants represented little threat to English superiority: English men and women who were worried about protecting their political, social, and cultural hegemony were threatened more by the well-born, well-educated, and prominent Anglican converts to Roman Catholicism than by Irish peasants, about only half of whom were practising Roman Catholics, and in whom Roman Catholicism was understood to be an hereditary disability rather than a conscious choice.

French devotional practices were condemned somewhat more frequently, but again less than might be expected. This has much to do with changing circumstances in which foreign policy was made. As Linda Colley has noted, by 1837 '[v]ictory at Waterloo, and the onset of peace with dominance, meant that Britons were less likely to associate the Catholic presence at home with a military threat from abroad'.[153] With the proviso that the English continued to perceive a Catholic threat to their Protestant religion, I would extend Colley's view to say that England's growing military dominance and the improvement of Anglo-French relations under Victoria – notwithstanding occasional invasion scares, as at mid-century – meant the English were less likely to fear French invasions, either military or religious. In spite of the centuries-long animosity between the English and the French, Britain and France allied themselves for the Crimean War (1853–56). After Napoleon III (r. 1850–70) came to the throne, the ruling families of Britain and France became friendly, even exchanging family visits. These developing connections, along with the anti-clericalism that had characterised a significant part of French society since the Revolution, made it in general less appealing to target the French as pagan idolaters.

As the identification of Marian devotion with other countries, especially Italy, shows, Victorian anti-Roman Catholicism was one expression of the traditional belief of the English in their national superiority, or rather of the traditional project of the English, evident since at least the eighteenth century, to convince themselves of their national superiority. In the nineteenth century this national stereotype was often expressed in racial terms. As L. P. Curtis has noted: 'Eminent Victorians, all of them intolerant to some degree, who were looking for a simple, unalterable, and universal affirmation of the superiority of English or Anglo-Saxon civilisation, clung to the notion of hierarchy or worth among the races of man.'[154] Victorian racial theories held that Anglo-Saxons were a superior group of people with a common Teutonic origin, thereby separating the

English first from the Celts and then from 'the savages of the non-Western world, in whom the Celtic character was painted with a darker brush'.[155] Victoria and Albert's clothing, including their costumes for the masked balls Albert enjoyed during the early years of their marriage, were chosen, often by Albert, to identify them as British, even Anglo-Saxon, thus asserting a shared racial past in hopes of contradicting the reality that Albert was a foreigner.[156]

English Protestants were not entirely convinced, however, that their position at the apex of the hierarchy was secure. In an age of pseudo-scientific racial theorising, Victorians worried about the contamination of Anglo-Saxon purity by other groups, including continental 'races'. They worried also that the growth of Catholicism would corrupt the Protestant religion which was integral to their sense of superiority. In 1864, the cleric Gordon Calthrop preached that the rapid growth in the number of Roman Catholic convents made it 'absurd to shut our eyes to the fact, that Romanism is lengthening her cords, and strengthening her stakes, and extending and consolidating her influence, in the very heart and centre of this Protestant opposition'.[157] As late as 1875, when anti-Roman Catholicism was waning, a Protestant journal could report: 'People are alarmed at the progress Romanism has made of late years. When they see here a convent and there a church, they lift up their hands in amazement and ask, Are the old times to return, and is Rome once more to enslave the land?'[158]

The popular depictions of English Roman Catholicism as a foreign religion had little basis in fact, especially given the continuation of the recusant spirituality that Mary Heimann has shown characterised Victorian Roman Catholicism. Although Susan O'Brien and other traditionalists have noted the influence transmitted by, for example, continental religious orders, the continued popularity of recusant devotional works throughout the nineteenth century provides strong evidence of a more moderate, and traditionally English, style of Roman Catholicism. While Protestants were far more likely to cite continental sources to buttress their portrayal of Roman Catholicism as a corrupt foreign religion, these were too fervent and florid to be typical of English Roman Catholicism. Nor were they readily available: only a few editions of Liguori's *The glories of Mary* were published in England between 1830 and 1885,[159] while the story of the two ladders was included in the former but found no place in the more popular Roman Catholic devotional manuals, such as *The garden of the soul* or the *Raccolta*. The Psalter allegedly compiled by Bonaventure, which Newman correctly concluded was mis-attributed in addition to being in 'very bad taste',[160] was even more difficult to find, as Cumming admitted: 'Last autumn I traveled over a considerable portion of France in search of modern editions of this extraordinary work, published under its proper title."[161] Ironically, Victorian Catholics were far more likely to learn about Liguori or the two ladders from Protestants, even into the 1890s. While ordinary Victorian anti-Catholics might have agreed with William James Skilton (who had been William Towry Law's curate prior to the latter's conversion to Roman Catholicism) in attributing the scarcity of these works to a conspiracy by the Roman Catholic Church,[162] in truth these types of devotion held little appeal for most English Roman Catholics. The emphasis on continental devotional practices was an attempt to deflect attention from the Oxford educations and fairly moderate devotional styles of those Roman Catholics who gave Victorians the greatest anxiety – Newman, Faber, Henry Edward Manning, and the sons of the great abolitionist William Wilberforce. Although the cleric William James Skilton argued that such men were induced to convert by 'their delusion, pride, and self-dependence, and impatience of opposition,'[163] the truth was that Roman Catholics who drew the most attention from anti-Roman Catholics had the same badges of Englishness, like class and education, as other elite men.

In the Protestant tradition generally and in the history of English Protestantism, Marian devotion was so uncommon as to be considered foreign. The contributions of Victorian Protestants to the Marian debates reinforced that sense by regularly describing Marian devotion as distant in both time and place. Furthermore, categorising Catholics as goddess worshippers feminised, and thus further marginalised, them. The result was that English Protestants – both the minority who articulated this view and the majority who consented to it, either actively by attending lectures, listening to sermons, and buying works that promoted it or passively by not challenging it – could then define themselves as modern, rational, and masculine Christians. Describing Roman Catholics as pagans also tarred advanced Anglicans with the same brush, given the frequency with which they were accused of being secret Roman Catholics. These charges could serve as a warning to advanced Anglicans to return to Protestantism or risk practising a corrupt form of Christianity.

Victorian Protestants drew on a long tradition of anti-Roman Catholicism when they described the Catholic Virgin Mary as a pagan goddess and Roman Catholics as idolaters. What is significant is not their originality or lack thereof, but their timing. Prior to the 1830s, English Protestants had paid little attention to the role of the Virgin Mary in Roman Catholicism. Certainly the growth in the English Roman Catholic population and the development of Anglo-Catholicism gave Protestants the motive and opportunity to reject Marian devotion: describing Marian devotion as a pagan legacy was one way in which to combat Catholicism, which Protestants consistently represented as a threat to biblical religion and their liberties as Englishmen. However, the timing and content of their attacks on the Catholic Virgin Mary suggest that they also saw an opportunity to voice their hesitations about whether women really were pure, selfless mothers. When they disseminated the message that the most familiar image in Western Christianity of a loving mother was actually a pagan goddess who could be legitimately rejected by the English, they undermined the suitability of the prototype for the image of woman as naturally maternal, non-sexual, and morally superior. Their discontent with representations of the ideal woman, especially as that construct of womanhood had the potential to allow women access to the public sphere, is confirmed by the alternative view of the Virgin Mary they promulgated from the 1830s onwards.

Conclusion

Ruth Vanita argues that the Protestant tradition of paying little or no attention to the Virgin Mary has, paradoxically, increased her flexibility as a symbol.

> the idea of Mary for a Protestant writer constitutes what might be called a site of free signification. A nineteenth-century English Protestant writer could not but be aware of the debates that raged around Mariology within Catholicism. But, unlike a Catholic writer, he or she was free to use the idea of Mary in transgressive ways, since Mary, not being sanctified in Protestant ideology, was not open to blasphemy in the same way.[164]

Vanita uses 'transgressive' to refer to stances supportive of same-sex communities. However, to read Victorian representations of the Virgin Mary as endorsing 'autonomous creativity, power and gentleness, women's community, sympathetic friendship with men, the joy and pain of love, and, most importantly, no father and no tying-in of childbirth with heterosexual marriage'[165] is to ignore the theological concerns of Victorian Christians. Vanita fundamentally misunderstands Christian theology[166] and the images of Mary in nineteenth-century Christian culture.[167] Furthermore, her argument is based on a small group of late-Victorian and early-Edwardian writers such as Walter Pater, Oscar Wilde, and 'Michael Field', none of whom can be considered Protestant either theologically or culturally.[168] The most compelling argument against her conclusion, however, is that Protestants' own discourse makes it clear that they felt too strongly about the Virgin to consider her 'a site of free signification'. The Virgin Mary was so identified with Catholicism that it was difficult for Protestants to recognise the Catholic Mary as anything other than a sign of Catholic corruption, as John Keble and Lydia Sellon found at mid-century. In the Victorian era, the Catholic Mary resonated with Protestants also as the embodiment of a female power that was extensive and destabilising. The Protestant response, to describe a more docile woman, further argues against Vanita's conclusion, for it confirms that the Virgin Mary, already inscribed as a symbol, could not be re-envisioned in a positive way by Protestants.

The Protestant Mary's minimal role was in keeping with the Protestant concern to focus attention on Jesus. Protestants had generally achieved that by ignoring Mary. Victorian Protestants, however, departed from Christian tradition in describing an ordinary or even problematical woman who did not merit admiration or even attention. Thus Protestants were left with, at best, a pallid version of Jesus' mother. So associated was the Virgin Mary with Roman Catholicism that any Virgin Mary could be mistaken for the Roman Catholic one, as when the narrator of Eliot's *The mill on the Floss* admitted

> I have often wondered whether those early Madonnas of Raphael, with the blond faces and somewhat stupid expression, kept their placidity undisturbed when their strong-limbed strong-willed boys got a little too old to do without clothing. I think they must have been given to feeble remonstrance, getting more and more peevish as it became more and more ineffectual.[169]

The narrator's anti-Catholicism was misplaced, for the woman described was the Protestant Virgin Mary, a mild, passive woman who was a mere vessel for the Incarnation. This inoffensive woman existed to counteract the Catholic Madonna, whose maternal identity made her the preeminent woman in Christianity and the embodiment of those virtues Victorian discourse frequently declared to be innately maternal.

Occasionally, however, the appealingly maternal Catholic Mary intruded on a Protestant's consciousness. This is unsurprising: the continuity and strength of the attacks against a small religious minority suggests that some Protestants, especially Anglican Protestants, were seeking to repress their own forbidden longings for the warmth and pageantry they considered Catholicism to offer. For example, a fundamental ambivalence about Catholicism pervades the account given by John William Burgon, a traditional high-church cleric, of

> a sailor's conduct, in the neighbourhood of Cape Misenum [southern Italy], which is not far from Baiae. On a little rocky headland there,

stands a so-called statue of the Virgo Immacolata; but it seemed to me antique – a very pretty draped figure of dazzling white marble, fished up out of the bay somewhere in the neighbourhood, probably. The devotion of the rough sailor who rowed us [to] the spot (29th May,) was really touching. He kissed the statue's feet, patted it under the chin with his finger and thumb (uttering a low sound of endearment, as if he were caressing a favourite child,) and then kissed his own fingers. I asked him if he was fond of the figure, – just by way of 'getting a rise' out of the man. He tossed up his head, as much as to say, – What a question! then waved his hand to the image, with a significant farewell smile, before beginning to descend the rock.[170]

Burgon initially seems superior to the mute, childlike Italian who mistakes a piece of pagan debris for a religious relic. Yet in admitting that he found the 'devotion of the rough sailor' to be 'really touching', Burgon shows he esteems the sailor as an affectionate and loyal man who has an appropriately complex relationship with the Virgin Mary. Echoing Mary's dual relationship with Jesus, the sailor treats the statue with familiar affection, chucking it under the chin and murmuring inarticulate endearments to it, as to an infant or small child, yet also showing it the reverence of a devotee when he kisses its feet. Burgon's insistence that devotion to a piece of marble was ridiculous could not entirely hide his longing for the sailor's relationship with both the statue and the woman it represented, a relationship that revealed his sense of place and purpose as it expanded the sailor's reality to include heaven and earth. Further thwarting the earth-bound Burgon's attempt to indicate his superiority is his failure to 'get a rise' out of the Italian. The inarticulate sailor therefore had the last word, notwithstanding Burgon's insistence that he was 'expressing no manner of approval of the occasion which called them forth. About *that* there can be but one opinion among persons who have had the happiness to be nurtured in the principles of the English communion.'[171] Burgon's attempted recovery was undone not just by the appealing figure of the sailor but by the fact that the story of the sailor was preceded by his account of seeing an Italian woman conclude her prayers by bowing before the crucifix and putting money in the box. 'It was very heathenish', he insisted, 'but it was very beautiful.'[172]

Seymour expressed the same sort of ambivalence towards Italian Marian devotion. Normally a fierce antagonist of Roman Catholicism, Seymour was nevertheless struck by the presence in Italian churches of 'some poor, shrinking, humble creature ... kneeling in some dark corner, and there gazing intently on some picture of the Virgin Mary and telling her beads'.[173] Seymour, like Burgon, immediately denied that his sentimentality implied approval of Roman Catholicism, for he almost 'wept to think of the deep darkness and ignorance' such devotion revealed.[174] Yet Seymour displayed the same longing for those women's devotion, sense of purpose, and willingness to withdraw from the world to pray. While Burgon and Seymour portrayed Roman Catholics as the pagan, superstitious, and inarticulate residents of a backward country, they could not entirely suppress their longings for the comforts they believed Roman Catholicism offered. Their fierce condemnations were as much of their own forbidden desires as of the Catholics they disparaged.

Notes

1 Hugh Latimer, 'A sermon preached in the first Sunday after Epiphany, 1552', in *The fathers of the English Church: a selection of the reformers and early Protestant divines, of the Church of England* (London: John Hatchard, 1808), vol. 2, p. 464.

2 Pelikan, *Mary through the centuries*, p. 153.

3 John E. Armstrong, *Armstrong's reply to Wiseman's pastoral letter on the Immaculate Conception* (London: Wertheim & Macintosh, 1855), p. 4.

4 W. T. Maudson, 'The dogma of the Virgin Mary's Immaculate Conception: a sermon', *Pulpit*, 67: 1,784 (8 March 1855), 236.

5 See T. R. Birks, *Modern popery: its strength and its weakness, as an aggressive power: a lecture, delivered at the request of the Bristol Protestant Alliance, at the Victoria Rooms, Clifton, on September 13, 1852* (Bristol: Whereat, 1852), p. 28; 'The religion of the Oratorians', *Church and state gazette*, 12: 617 (9 December 1853), 767; J. Endell Tyler, *The worship of the Blessed Virgin Mary in the Church of Rome contrary to Holy Scripture, and to the faith and practice of the Church of Christ through the first five centuries* (London: Richard Bentley, 1844), p. 48.

6 J. Endell Tyler, *Primitive Christian worship: or, the evidence of Holy Scripture and the Church, concerning the invocation of saints and angels, and the Blessed Virgin Mary* (London: J. G. F. & J. Rivington, 1840), p. 277. Tyler used almost the exact same phrasing in his *The worship of the Blessed Virgin Mary*, p. 81. The same passage, substituting 'pure' for 'spotless', appears in the anonymous *What is Romanism? No. X: on the worship of the Virgin Mary: evidence of Holy Scripture against it* (London: SPCK, 1846), p. 9.

7 Thomas Jackson, *A warning against popery: being an exposure of a stealthy attempt to promote the worship of the Virgin Mary, by the erection of her effigy beside the church and school of my native village* (London: Wesleyan Conference Office, 1867), p. 9.

8 H. H. Dobney, *The Virgin Mary* (London: Ward, & Co.; Maidstone: J. Brown, 1859), p. 4.

9 Annette Calthrop, 'Jael and Mary: a contrast', *Christian world magazine and family visitor*, 20: 9 (September 1884), 714.

10 Dobney, *The Virgin Mary*, p. 7; see also Jackson, *A warning against popery*, p. 9; 'Review of Edward Jewitt Robinson, *The mother of Jesus not the papal Mary*', *London quarterly review*, 45 (October 1875 and January 1876), 458.

11 Mrs S. A. Sewell, *Woman and the times we live in*, 2nd edn (Manchester: Tubbs & Brook and London: Simpkin, Marshall, & Co., 1869), pp. 28–9.

12 Cunneen, *In search of Mary*, p. 256.

13 Wilson, *Our Church calls on ritualists* (Norwich: Stevenson & Co.; London: Longman & Co., n.d. [?1871]), p. 2. The traditional high-church clergyman George Miller rejected Pusey's use of *Theotokos* on the grounds that '[w]e are taught in the Scripture that she was his mother according to the flesh, or in regard to his human nature': Miller, *A letter to the Rev. E. B. Pusey*, p. 26.

14 Armstrong, *Armstrong's reply*, p. 9; see also Edward Jewitt Robinson, *The mother of Jesus not the papal Mary* (London: Wesleyan Conference Office, 1875), pp. 4–6; Edward Wilson, *Prayer for the dead; and the 'Mater Dei': a letter respectfully addressed to His Grace the Archbishop of Canterbury* (London: Longmans, Green, & Co.; Norwich: Samuel Miller, 1870), p. 9; Dobney, *The Virgin Mary*, p. 28.

15 Judges 5:24.

16 (Cumming and French) *The Hammersmith Protestant discussion*, pp. 322–3; 'A.B.', 'Mariolatry', *Church and state gazette* (23 September 1853), 614; (Augustin Gaspard Edouart) *An address to the parishioners of Leominster upon the worship of the Virgin Mary* (London: John F. Shaw and Co., 1866), pp. 10–11; Maudson, 'The dogma of the Virgin Mary's Immaculate Conception', p. 238; Sinclair, *Popish legends*, pp. xxxiv–xxxv; William Ford Vance, *On the invocation of angels, saints, and the Virgin Mary: two sermons preached at Tavistock Chapel, Drury Lane, in the course of lectures on the points in controversy between Roman Catholics and Protestants* (London: James Nisbet, 1828), p. 38.

17 Calthrop, 'Jael and Mary', 715.

18 Samuel Wilberforce, 'The character of the Virgin Mary', *Four sermons preached before her Most Gracious Majesty, Queen Victoria, in 1841 and 1842* (London: James Burns, 1842), p. 30.

19 *The Virgin Mary, a married woman* (London: William Macintosh, n.d. [1869]), p. 13, emphasis in original.

20 J. M. Golby and A. W. Purdue, *The making of the modern Christmas* (Athens: University of Georgia Press, 1986), pp. 40, 42–3, 61.

21 See, for example, J. J. A. Boase's accounts of his continental travels in 1824, 1850, and 1851: British Library, London, Manuscript Room, Add. MSS 35045–7; J. J. A. Boase, *A ramble on the Continent in 1824*: Add. MS 35048; J. A. A. Boase, *A ramble on the Continent in 1850*: Add. MS 35049; J. A. A. Boase, *A ramble on the Continent in 1851*.

22 British Library, London, Add. MS 38972, Layard Papers, vol. 42, letter from A. H. Layard to Lady Eastlake, 1 February 1871, fol. 13.

23 British Library, London, Add. MS 38972, Layard Papers, vol. 42, letter from A. H. Layard to Lady Eastlake, 17 April 1872, fol. 24.

24 British Library, London, Add. MS 38972, Layard Papers, vol. 42, A. H. Layard, 'A journey to the Alps' (travel diary for 1835), fol. 114.

25 Anna Brownell Jameson, *Legends of the Madonna as represented in the fine arts* (London: Unit Library, 1904 [1852]), p. 2.

26 Jameson, *Legends of the Madonna*, p. 155.

27 Jameson, *Legends of the Madonna*, p. 162.

28 Jameson, *Legends of the Madonna*, p. 144.

29 Wilberforce, 'The character of the Virgin Mary', pp. 30–1.

30 Elizabeth Barrett, 'The Virgin Mary to the child Jesus', in *The complete poems of Elizabeth Barrett Browning*, ed. Charlotte Porter and Helen A. Clarke (New York: Thomas

Y. Crowell & Co., 1990), p. 72, line 2; p. 73, lines 12–13.

31 Elizabeth Barrett Browning, letter to Arabella Barrett, 15–19 April (1848), in *The letters of Elizabeth Barrett Browning to her sister Arabella*, 2 vols, ed. Scott Lewis (Waco, TX: Wedgestone Press, 2002), vol. 1, pp. 169–70.

32 Newsome, *The parting of friends*, p. 124.

33 'S.M.', 'Christmas Day', *Christian lady's magazine*, 12 (July–December 1839), 527; see also Maudson, 'The dogma of the Virgin Mary's Immaculate Conception', 238.

34 His text was Lk 2:6–7: 'And so it was, that, while they were there, the days were accomplished that she should be delivered. And she brought forth her firstborn Son, and wrapped Him in swaddling clothes, and laid Him in a manger; because there was no room for them in the inn.'

35 Daniel Moore, 'Lectures on the life of Christ: no. IV, The Nativity;' delivered in Camden Church, Camberwell, Sunday evening, 5 February 1854; reprinted in the *Pulpit*, 65 (1854), 174.

36 Seymour, *A pilgrimage to Rome*, p. 553.

37 (Edouart) *An address to the parishioners of Leominster*, p. 5, emphasis in original.

38 Chapman, *Father Faber*, p. 230.

39 'S.M.', 'Christmas Day', p. 527.

40 M. Hobart Seymour, *Mornings among the Jesuits at Rome: being notes of conversations held with certain Jesuits on the subject of religion in the city of Rome* (London: Seeleys, 1849), p. 47.

41 Helsinger et al., *The woman question*, vol. 2, p. 195.

42 Graef, *Mary*, vol. 2, p. 8.

43 Thomas A. O'Meara, *Mary in Protestant and Catholic theology* (New York: Sheed & Ward, 1996), p. 126; Graef, *Mary*, vol. 2, p. 13.

44 Graef, *Mary*, vol. 2, p. 14.

45 Hugh Latimer, *Sermons on various subjects*, 2 vols (London: T. Pitcher, 1788), vol. 1, pp. 209–10.

46 John Wesley, letter to 'a Roman Catholic', 18 July 1749, in *The letters of John Wesley*, ed. John Telford (London: Epworth, 1931), vol. 3, p. 9.

47 I am grateful to Diarmaid MacCulloch for this information.

48 In this period, some theists and atheists began to question the virgin birth. This was a fundamentally different question from that of Mary's perpetual virginity, for it questioned the divinity of Jesus. In *The life of Our Lord* (London: Associated Newspapers, 1934) Charles Dickens identified Jesus' parents as Joseph and Mary, although he bowed to Christian theology when he said that Jesus would 'grow up to be so good that God will love him as his own son' (pp. 13, 14). A theistic periodical offered another explanation: that Mary had entertained a human visitor, not an angel, nine months before Jesus' birth. See 'Lectures on the non-divinity of Jesus Christ: at the religious Discussion Hall, George Street, Euston Road, St Pancras', *Anthill's monthly chronicle and illustrated advertiser*, no. 6 (1 May 1863), 4–5; J.D.D., 'The miraculous conception', *London investigator: a monthly journal of secularism*, 1: 9 (December 1854), 129–30.

49 Sinclair, *Popish legends*, p. xxiii; see also Robinson, *The mother of Jesus*, pp. 11–12.

50 *The Virgin Mary, a married woman*, p. 7.

51 'Mr Murphy at Bacup', *Bacup times* (25 April 1868), 6; see also (Cumming and French), *The Hammersmith Protestant discussion*, p. 284.

52 Arnstein, *Protestant versus Catholic in mid-Victorian England*, p. 88.

53 Arnstein, *Protestant versus Catholic in mid-Victorian England*, p. 92.

54 For a description of Murphy's career, see Arnstein, *Protestant versus Catholic in mid-Victorian England*, chapter 7.

55 R. T. Hampson, *Religious deceptions of the Church of Rome exposed* (London: C. Mitchell, n.d.), p. 18.

56 Birks, *Modern popery*, p. 13.

57 Quoted in Margaret Homans, "'To the queen's private apartments": royal family portraiture and the construction of Victoria's sovereign obedience', *Victorian studies*, 37 (1993), 1.

58 For other examples, see Adrienne Munich, *Queen Victoria's secrets* (New York: Columbia University Press, 1996), pp. 60–2.

59 Munich, *Queen Victoria's secrets*, chapters 2–4; Homans, "'To the queen's private apartments"', 7.

60 The contested positions which both the Virgin Mary and Queen Victoria occupied in the nineteenth century, as well as the many similarities between the two figures, are nicely paralleled in the neighboring statues of these women – one above the Victoria and Albert Museum, the other looking down from the Brompton Oratory.

61 Ornella Moscucci, *The science of woman: gynaecology and gender in England 1800–1929* (Cambridge: Cambridge University Press, 1990), p. 115.

62 Allchin, *The silent rebellion*, p. 49; see also Judith Rowbotham, *Good girls make good wives: guidance for girls in Victorian fiction* (Oxford and New York: Basil Blackwell, 1989), p. 261.

63 Mumm, *Stolen daughters, virgin mothers*, p. 141. Mary Peckham Magray's *The transforming power of the nuns: women, religion, and cultural change in Ireland, 1750–1900* (New York: Oxford University Press, 1998) describes how well-born Irish nuns were able to use their family connections and economic status to defy bishops and other church authorities.

64 Mrs Gaskell, *North and south* (New York: G. P. Putnam's Sons, London: Smith, Elder, & Co., 1906 [1854]), p. 478.

65 Eliot, *Romola*, p. 322.

66 Kingsley, *Yeast*, p. 33; Kingsley's novel *Hypatia* (New York: Macmillan, 1880 [1853]) also castigates vowed virginity.

67 *The conspirators' schemes: homes, convents, confession, and education* (London: Protestant Evangelical Mission and Electoral Union, n.d. [1871]), pp. 8–9; emphasis in original.

68 Seymour, *A pilgrimage to Rome*, pp. 201–2.

69 Seymour, *A pilgrimage to Rome*, p. 202; this fate was explored in Sinclair's novel *Beatrice*.

70 Susan P. Casteras, 'Virgin vows: the early Victorian artists' portrayal of nuns and novices', *Victorian studies*, 24 (1981), 168.

71 For an account of Newdegate's campaign, see Arnstein, *Protestant versus Catholic in mid-Victorian England*.

72 Dobney, *The Virgin Mary*, p. 17; emphasis in original.

73 'Lydia', 'Female biography of Scripture: Rebekah, part I', *Christian lady's magazine*, 14 (July–December 1840), 542.

74 *The Virgin Mary, a married woman*, p. 6.

75 Miller, *A letter to the Rev. E. B. Pusey*, p. 64.

76 (Edouart) *An address to the parishioners of Leominster*, p. 7.

77 Dobney, *The Virgin Mary*, p. 9.

78 Dobney, *The Virgin Mary*, p. 9; see also Samuel (Wilberforce), Lord Bishop of Oxford. *Rome – her new dogma and our duties: a sermon, preached before the University, at St Mary's Church, Oxford, on the feast of the Annunciation of the Blessed Virgin Mary, 1855* (Oxford and London: John Henry Parker, n.d.), p. 2.

79 Vance, *On the invocation of angels, saints, and the Virgin Mary*, p. 40.

80 Maudson, 'The dogma of the Virgin Mary's Immaculate Conception', 238.

81 Maudson, 'The dogma of the Virgin Mary's Immaculate Conception', 238.

82 Miller, *A letter to the Rev. E. B. Pusey*, p. 62.

83 Maudson, 'The dogma of the Virgin Mary's Immaculate Conception', 238.

84 Francis Merewether, *Popery a new religion, compared with that of Christ and his apostles: a sermon*, 3rd edn (Loughborough and Ashby Protestant Tract Society, 1836), p. 8; see also Maudson, 'The dogma of the Virgin Mary's Immaculate Conception', 238.

85 (Longley) *Christ's dying hours*, p. 4.

86 (Longley) *Christ's dying hours*, p. 5. More often, the Protestant Mary was ignored at the crucifixion: see, for example, Hannah Sinclair's meditation on the crucifixion in her popular work, *A letter on the principles of Christian faith*, ed. Catherine Sinclair (Edinburgh: William Whyte and London: Hamilton, Adams, 1852), p. 22.

87 Michael Wheeler, *Ruskin's God* (Cambridge: Cambridge University Press, 1999), pp. 123–4.

88 Vance, *On the invocation of angels, saints, and the Virgin Mary*, p. 54; emphasis in original.

89 Sinclair, *Popish legends*, p. xxxv.

90 'A.B.', 'Mariolatry', 614.

91 (Edouart) *An address to the parishioners of Leominster*, p. 15; emphasis in original.

92 (Edouart) *An address to the parishioners of Leominster*, p. 15.

93 Maudson, 'The dogma of the Virgin Mary's Immaculate Conception', 239; see also Tyler, *Primitive Christian worship*, p. 284.

94 Vance, *On the invocation of angels, saints, and the Virgin Mary*, p. 40; see also Sinclair, *Popish legends*, p. xxxv; (Wilberforce) *Rome*, p. 2; (Edouart) *An address to the parishioners of Leominster*, p. 14; Tyler, *The worship of the Blessed Virgin Mary*, p. 83; *What is Romanism?*, p. 11.

95 (Cumming and French) *The Hammersmith Protestant discussion*, p. 252; emphasis in original.

96 See Tyler, *The worship of the Blessed Virgin Mary*, p. 8; Charles Hastings Collette, *Invocation of saints: the doctrine and practice of the Church of Rome: a lecture, delivered at the Literary Institution, Gravesend* (London: Wertheim & Macintosh, 1857), p. 13.

97 Scholars generally agree that this translation is the correct one. For a discussion on the problems of translating Lk 1:28, see Brown et al. (eds), *Mary in the New Testament*, pp. 126–32.

98 Dobney, *The Virgin Mary*, p. 6; (Edouart) *An address to the parishioners of Leominster*, pp. 10–11; Tyler, *Primitive Christian worship*, p. 276; Calthrop, 'Jael and Mary', 713.

99 'The pope and the Romans', *British banner*, 2: 53 (3 January 1849), 9.

100 Vance, *On the invocation of angels, saints, and the Virgin Mary*, p. 54; see also 'Missionary operations: Hull', *British Protestant*, 108 (December 1854), 267.

101 Seymour, *A pilgrimage to Rome*, pp. 384–5.

102 Quoted in Giles St Aubyn, *Edward VII: prince and king* (New York: Atheneum, 1979), pp. 42–3.

103 Walter Bagehot, *The English constitution* (Ithaca, NY: Cornell University Press, 1966 [1867]), p. 82.

104 Charles Bradlaugh, *George, Prince of Wales, with recent contrasts and coincidences* (London: C. Bradlaugh, n.d.).

105 Anthony Trollope, *Framley parsonage* (Ware, Hertfordshire: Wordsworth, 1994 [1861]), p. 150.

106 J. A. and Olive Banks, *Feminism and family planning in Victorian England* (NY: Schocken Books, 1964), p. 28.

107 Johansson, 'Demographic contributions', p. 260.

108 Carolyn Dever, *Death and the mother from Dickens to Freud: Victorian fiction and the anxiety of origins* (Cambridge: Cambridge University Press, 1998), p. 1.

109 Mrs (Sarah) Ellis, *The mothers of England: their influence and responsibility* (New York: D. Appleton and Philadelphia, PA: George S. Appleton, 1844), p. 167.

110 Ellis, *The mothers of England*, p. 185.

111 Ellis, *The mothers of England*, p. 164.

112 Ellis, *The mothers of England*, pp. 58, 167.

113 Cunneen, *In search of Mary*, chapter 7; Helsinger et al., *The woman question*, vol. 2, pp. 194–6.

114 Mrs Oliphant, 'Madonna Mary', *Good words*, 7 (1866), 300, 376, 433, 517, 586.

115 Oliphant, 'Madonna Mary', 8.

116 Oliphant, 'Madonna Mary', 586.

117 See Collette, *Invocation of saints*, p. 13; E.T., 'Mariolatry', *Wesleyan–Methodist magazine* (3rd series), 20 (September 1841), 741.

118 Edward Bickersteth, *Come out of Rome; the voice from Heaven to the people of God: a sermon preached before the Protestant Association, on Wednesday evening, April 22, 1840, at St Clement Danes Church* (London: Protestant Asociation, 1840), p. 11; see also Seymour, *Mornings among the Jesuits*, p. 52; Vance, *On the invocation of angels, saints, and the Virgin Mary*, pp. 52–3.

119 'Interesting cases of conversion from Romanism', *British Protestant*, 104 (August 1854), 198; emphasis in original. This was an unusual extension of the traditional Roman Catholic belief that Mary interceded for souls in purgatory. See also Seymour, *A pilgrimage to Rome*, p. 507; C. P. Golightly, *Look at home, or, short and easy method with the Roman Catholics* (Oxford: J. H. Parker and London: J. G. and F. Rivington, 1837), p. 8; 'Missionary operations: Broadway, Worcestershire', *British Protestant*, 108 (December 1854), 263.

120 Kingsley, *Yeast*, p. 283.

121 William Palmer, *A letter to N. Wiseman, D.D. (calling himself bishop of Melipotamus) containing remarks on his letter to Mr Newman* (Oxford: John Henry Parker, 1841), p. 14.

122 'Review of Robinson's *The mother of Jesus*', 438; see also Dobney, *The Virgin Mary*, p. 29.

123 E.T., 'Mariolatry', 740; see also 'France', *Baptist magazine*, 45: 201 (September 1854), 557; Walter Farquhar Hook, *The novelties of Romanism: or, popery refuted by tradition: a sermon, preached in St Andrew's Church, Manchester* (London: F. C. & J. Rivington and

London: J. Burns, 1840), p. 18; John C. Miller, 'The Immaculate Conception: a sermon', *Pulpit*, 67: 1,793 (10 May 1855), 427; Birks, *Modern popery*, p. 27; (Powell) *Stretton tracts*, no. 6, p. 9.

124 'Illustrations of the invocation and worship of the Blessed Virgin Mary, in the churches of Belgium', *Congregational magazine*, 26: 7 (September 1843), 626, emphasis in original.

125 Hampson, *Religious deceptions of the Church of Rome*, p. iv. See also Thomas Edward Evans, *The glories of Jesus or the glories of Mary?* (London: James Nisbet & Co., 1865), p. 70; Sinclair, *Popish legends*, p. 32; Sinclair, *Beatrice*, pp. 211–12; John Poynder, *Popery in alliance with heathenism: Letters proving that where the Bible is wholly unknown, as in the heathen world, or only partially known, as in the Romish Church, idolatry and superstition are inevitable*, 2nd edn (London: J. Hatchard & Son, 1835), pp. 22, 30–3, 39, 55–7; Seymour, *A pilgrimage to Rome*, pp. 98–9.

126 Hampson, *Religious deceptions of the Church of Rome*, p. 47; Seymour, *A pilgrimage to Rome*, p. 597; Sinclair, *Popish legends*, p. xxxii.

127 Birks, *Modern popery*, p. 19; Bodleian Library, Oxford, MSS Wilberforce, e. 9, Samuel Wilberforce's diary of a holiday in Europe, fol. 38.

128 Birks, *Modern popery*, p. 19; Hampson, *Religious deceptions of the Church of Rome*, p. 4; emphasis in original.

129 Birks, *Modern popery*, p. 19.

130 Seymour, *A pilgrimage to Rome*, p. 99; see also Tyler, *Primitive Christian worship*, pp. 243–4.

131 Lambeth Palace Library, London, Golightly Papers, MS 1810, Walter John Trower, letter to C. P. Golightly, 26 October 1865, fols 164v–5.

132 Eliot, *Romola*, p. 67.

133 Sinclair, *Popish legends*, p. xxi. 'Mariolatry' was so common a charge against the Roman Catholic Church that it frequently appeared in titles: see, for example, John Evans, *The origin and progress of Mariolatry; being intended as a companion to the Rev. T. H. Horne's 'Mariolatry'* (London: William Edward Painter, 1852); (Thomas Hartwell Horne) *Mariolatry: or, facts and evidences demonstrating the worship of the Blessed Virgin Mary by the Church of Rome, derived from the testimonies of her reputed saints and doctors, from her breviary, and other authorized Romish formularies of devotion, confirmed by the attestations of travellers*, 2nd edn (London: William Edward Painter, 1841); 'A.B.', 'Mariolatry', 614; E.T., 'Mariolatry'.

134 Tyler, *Primitive Christian worship*, p. 367.

135 Birks, *Modern popery*, p. 28; this story is also mentioned in Cumming's letter to the editor of *The Times*, reprinted in *Church and state gazette*, 12: 606 (23 September 1853), 593.

136 Sinclair, *Popish legends*, pp. xxxv–xxxvi; see also (Edouart) *An address to the parishioners of Leominster*, p. 22; Seymour, *Mornings among the Jesuits*, p. 56.

137 'Cardinal Wiseman on the worship of the Virgin', *Church and state gazette*, 12: 606 (23 September 1853), 596.

138 Liguori, *The glories of Mary*, p. ii.

139 (Horne) *Mariolatry*, p. 75; see also (Cumming and French) *The Hammersmith Protestant discussion*, p. 291.

140 Collette, *Invocation of saints*, p. 15.

141 Palmer, *Letter to Wiseman*, p. 23; see also Birks, *Modern popery*, pp. 33–4.

142 Palmer, *Fifth letter to Wiseman*, p. 81, quoting Liguori, *The glories of Mary* (Dublin 1837); see also 'Missionary operations: Westminster', *British Protestant*, 105 (September 1854), 212.

143 Collette, *Invocation of saints*, p. 19; see also (Edouart) *An address to the parishioners of Leominster*, p. 22.

144 Noel, *Do Roman Catholics worship the Blessed Virgin Mary?*, pp. 12–13.

145 'Mr Murphy at Bacup', 6.

146 'Cardinal Wiseman on the worship of the Virgin', 596.

147 'The retrospect of 1849', *British banner*, 3: 105 (2 January 1850), 3.

148 Seymour, *A pilgrimage to Rome*, p. 564.

149 Palmer, *Letter to Wiseman*, p. 45; emphasis in original.

150 Seymour, *Mornings among the Jesuits*, p. 45; emphasis in original.

151 Seymour, *Mornings among the Jesuits*, pp. 36–7; emphasis in original.

152 I am indebted to the late Gerard Tracey of the Birmingham Oratory for this information.

153 Colley, *Britons*, p. 332.

154 Curtis, *Anglo-Saxons and Celts*, p. 119.

155 George W. Stocking Jr, *Victorian anthropology* (New York: Free Press and London: Collier, Macmillan, 1987), p. 63.

156 Munich, *Queen Victoria's secrets*, chapter 2.

157 Gordon Calthrop, *The secret of Rome's strength: a sermon preached at the parish church, Islington, on Sunday morning, November 20th, 1864, on behalf of the Islington Protestant Institute* (London: William Hunt, n.d. [?1864]), p. 6; for a similar concern with the growing numbers of Roman Catholic convents, see 'Romish ritualism', 1000.

158 'Roman Catholic London', *Christian world magazine and family visitor*, 11: 2 (February 1875), 154.

159 The British Library and the Cambridge University Library have combined holdings of three copies of *The glories of Mary* (published in 1852, 1854, 1868), as well as one copy of excerpts from *The glories of Mary*, published as *The month of Mary* (London: Burns, Oates & Co., 1872).

160 John Henry Newman, *The letters and diaries of John Henry Newman*, vol. 16, ed. Charles Stephen Dessain (London: Thomas Nelson & Sons, 1965), p. 343.

161 *The psalter of the Blessed Virgin, written by St Bonaventure*, ed. John Cumming (London: British Reformation Society, 1852), p. iii. A search of the catalogues of the copyright libraries confirms the scarcity of nineteenth-century copies of *The psalter*. The British Library has an 1872 edition; both the British Library and the Bodleian Library, Oxford, have copies edited by Cumming; no copies are in the Cambridge University Library.

162 W. J. Skilton, *Neither inconsistency, nor unfaithfulness to the word of God, justly charge-able upon the authorised teaching of the Church of England: a letter to the parishioners of Harbone, from the Rev. W. J. Skilton, M.A., late curate of that parish, with reference to some statements contained in a recently-published letter of the Hon. and Rev. W. T. Law, M.A.* (London: F. and J. Rivington and Birmingham: H. C. Langbridge, 1852), pp. 6–7. The depiction of continental Catholicism as the true Catholicism was common among Victorian Protestants. Writing to his English parishioners while living in Italy, Edouart assured them: 'Here it is to be seen in its true and native colours, not modified and disguised, as in England': *An address to the parishioners of Leominster*, p. 4.

163 Skilton, *Neither inconsistency, nor unfaithfulness*, p. 6.

164 Ruth Vanita, *Sappho and the Virgin Mary: same-sex love and the English literary imagination* (New York: Columbia University Press, 1996), pp. 19–20.

165 Vanita, *Sappho and the Virgin Mary*, p. 7.

166 For example, she repeatedly confuses the Immaculate Conception and the Virgin Birth: see *Sappho and the Virgin Mary*, pp. 7, 46, 51, 81, 98; Vanita also describes Mary as having 'had a child out of wedlock' (p. 147). In the gospel accounts, Mary conceived Jesus while betrothed, but she had married Joseph by the time Jesus was born.

167 For example, with regard to Marian debates in Victorian England, her assertion that the 'general tone was hysterically misogynist' (p. 16) ignores the complexities of the issues, while her claim that the Virgin Mary represents 'autonomous female joy and creativity' (p. 50) ignores the universal Christian belief that Mary conceived under the power of the Holy Spirit. Mary can be seen as autonomous only if God is written out of the narrative, and such a reading was unimaginable to Christians.

168 Michael Field was the pseudonym for the lesbian couple Katherine Bradley and her niece Edith Cooper; they converted to Roman Catholicism in 1907. Oscar Wilde may well have converted on his deathbed.

169 George Eliot, *The mill on the Floss* (London: Penguin, 1979 [1860]), p. 62.

170 John W. Burgon, *Letters from Rome to friends in England* (London: John Murray, 1862), pp. 62–3.

171 Burgon, *Letters from Rome*, pp. 62–3; emphasis in original.

172 Burgon, *Letters from Rome*, p. 62.

173 Seymour, *A pilgrimage to Rome*, p. 381.

174 Seymour, *A pilgrimage to Rome*, p. 381.

4

Sex, sin, and salvation: the debate over the Immaculate Conception

I n 1854 the discussions about the Catholic and Protestant images of the Virgin Mary became more contentious and more complicated than at any time in English history as a result of Pope Pius IX's promulgation of the Immaculate Conception, which declared that the Virgin Mary had been conceived without the stain of original sin. That pronouncement drew more participants than did any other aspect of the Victorian Marian debates, partly because it was publicised in the general-interest press; one was not required to visit churches or chapels, read prayerbooks, or listen to sermons to know about it. In addition, it provided a specific opportunity for Victorian Christians to consider a single question, albeit one with broad implications. In periodicals, pamphlets, speeches, sermons, hymns, and private letters, famous and obscure Victorians seized this opportunity to enter the Marian debates. Dissenting contributions increased notably, especially in articles in periodicals.

Conflict over the Immaculate Conception was one part of the debate about theology among Victorian Christians; it was also an aspect of the conversation about the nature of woman. Roman Catholics, who were required to believe in the Immaculate Conception once it had been made dogmatic, defined a woman who was unchanging in her sinlessness, while Protestants asserted that sinfulness was integral to each human being. Advanced Anglicans were very hesitant about the dogma; they generally preferred to describe a woman who was born, but not conceived, without sin. Besides marking a distinction (although not always a sharp one) between the Roman Catholic and advanced Anglican images of the Virgin Mary, the debate is significant because, in defining original sin and identifying how it was transmitted, Victorian Christians articulated their beliefs about the relationship between sexual intercourse and original sin. Roman Catholics generally separated the two, whereas Protestants did not. This was not an arcane theological discussion, but was one that had implications for how people viewed their bodies, and thus had an impact beyond church and chapel.

Sin and the Victorians

The Immaculate Conception was a divisive issue in part because it concerned sin, a topic that pervaded the consciousness of Victorian Christians. While all Christians believed that humanity was fallen, the Victorians were distinguished from their eighteenth-century predecessors by their profound concern with sin, their own as well as that of others. These feelings were encouraged by public and private exhortations. Even Canon Frederic W. Farrar of Westminster Abbey, who questioned the existence of hell, cautioned his congregation in 1877 that 'because of the frailty of our nature, because of the strength of passion and temptation, – not loving, but loathing it – not seeking, but resisting it – not acquiescing in, but fighting and struggling against it, – we all sometimes fall' into sin,[1] a habit Catherine Sinclair's sister Hannah attributed to 'the deep depravity and corruption of human nature'.[2] Victorian churchgoers would have heard clergymen detail a lengthy list of sins. In one sermon alone, Dean Richard William Church of St Paul's Cathedral preached against drunkenness, lying, pride, lust, uncleanliness, hatred, malice, carelessness, idleness, and loving the things of this world,[3] while on another occasion John Henry Newman warned against pride, hurting others, exhibiting 'ill-temper, and sullenness', possessing 'an *unforgiving spirit*', envy, denominational friction, and 'love of singularity', or novelty.[4] More daringly, Edward Bouverie Pusey warned Oxford undergraduates not to 'first fever your own frames, and then, in a way which Christ forbids and hates, remove that feverishness'.[5] Churchgoers would also have learned of the awful consequences of sin. Newman warned sinners that they were 'in training for future disobedience, and anticipating the misery of hell',[6] while the Anglican minister William Hay Macdowall Aitken ominously informed his congregation that if intoxication, Sabbath-breaking, and swearing 'were proved against you, nothing else would be required – that would be quite enough to seal your doom!'[7] For all their theological, liturgical, and cultural differences, Protestants and Catholics shared a deep consciousness of human sinfulness and its consequences. Their awareness of human sinfulness had diverse sources, including the evangelicals' stress on an individual conversion experience and the subsequent leading of a holy life, the Oxford Movement's attention to human corruption, and the adoption by Victorian Roman Catholicism of what Mary Heimann terms 'an excitable approach to sin and grace'.[8] The popularity of hell-fire sermons throughout the Victorian age, the upsurge in philanthropy among middle-class Victorians, and even the self-punishment endured by men like Pusey and William Ewart Gladstone testify to this preoccupation with sin.

The preoccupation with sin and its consequences was evident in the conflict over the efficacy of baptism that had engaged Anglicans since the early nineteenth century. This long-running dispute reached a head in the Gorham controversy, which began in 1847 as a debate over the theology of original sin and baptism, and ended in 1851 as a question of ecclesiastical authority. The controversy began when Henry Phillpotts, the pugnacious Bishop of Exeter who had convened the hearing on the practices at Lydia Sellon's convent and orphanage in 1849, asked George Cornelius Gorham to submit to a series of questions to determine his doctrinal orthodoxy on the topic of infant baptism before instituting him to the living at Brampford Speke. Rejecting the high church belief in the efficacy of infant baptism, Gorham argued that baptism was not effective unless it was accompanied by a change of heart:

> Our church holds, and I hold, that no spiritual grace is conveyed
> in Baptism, except to *worthy recipients*; and as infants are by nature
> *un*worthy recipients, 'being born in sin, and the children of wrath', they
> cannot receive any benefit from Baptism, except there shall have been
> a prevenient act of grace to make them worthy. Baptism is the sign or
> seal, either of the grace already given, or of repentance and faith, which
> are stipulated, and must be hereafter exercised.[9]

Dissenters agreed with Gorham, and with evangelical Anglicans generally, that baptism was a sign – rather than the means – of grace, although they did not deny that baptised children could receive divine grace. As the nonconformist minister Henry Hamlet Dobney argued, 'Not that the mere ordinance [baptism] effected anything; but it was the outward and visible sign which gave a certain fixity, as it were, and visibleness to the inward and spiritual grace, or reality.'[10] The 'Thirty-nine articles' appear to confirm this view: Article 27 describes baptism as 'a sign of regeneration and new birth', rather than as the means of that regeneration. The controversy was settled in favour of the evangelicals in 1851, when the Privy Council's lay Judicial Committee's decision that Gorham should be instituted to his living essentially undercut ecclesiastical authority within the Church of England by taking away decisions about church teaching from the Bishop. This decision, of course, was the impetus for the conversions of Henry Edward Manning, Robert Isaac Wilberforce, and William Maskell, among others. (However, had the Gorham decision favoured Philpotts, up to 6,000 Evangelical clergymen would have left the Church of England.[11])

The Gorham controversy was heated partly because of the personalities involved: neither Gorham nor Philpotts was the type to avoid a confrontation. The significance of the issues involved – including ecclesiastical authority, the role of ritual, and the importance of an individual conversion experience – also contributed to the fervour with which the battle was waged. But at the root of the controversy lay a disagreement over how and when the stain of original sin could be removed from a human soul. Thus the Gorham controversy pushed the questions of original sin and redemption to the forefront of Anglican consciousness at mid-century, just before the Roman Catholic Church defined the Immaculate Conception.

Ineffabilis Deus

On 8 December 1854, Pope Pius IX promulgated *Ineffabilis Deus*, which declared that the Virgin Mary had been preserved from original sin in anticipation 'of the merits of Jesus Christ, the Saviour of mankind'.[12] This declaration reversed the Marian beliefs of the early Christian church: the Church Fathers, if they spoke of Mary at all, either stated explicitly or else implied that she had been conceived and born with original sin; some even said she had committed actual sin.[13] John Duns Scotus in the early fourteenth century had been the first to formulate, in the face of long-established opposition, a convincing argument for the Immaculate Conception of Mary. The Feast of Mary's Conception began to be widely celebrated in the mid-fourteenth century and was officially confirmed in the following century by Sixtus IV (r. 1471–84). In 1693 Innocent XII extended the celebration of the Feast to the whole Church; Clement XI made the Feast a holy day of obligation in 1708. However, debates over the Immaculate Conception continued among theologians throughout the eighteenth century, and it was not until the beginning of the nineteenth century that the papacy began to move towards defining the belief.[14]

Encouraged by the immediate predecessors of Pope Pius IX, Roman Catholic bishops and religious orders at the beginning of the nineteenth century increasingly petitioned for the definition of the Immaculate Conception. The popular acceptance of the belief was evidenced by the response to the visions Catherine Labouré, a Sister of Charity, reported having had of Mary surrounded by the words, 'Oh Mary, conceived without sin, pray for us who have recourse to thee', in her convent on the Rue de Bac, Paris, in 1830.[15] The 'miraculous medal' that was struck from this image was widely copied around the world. The medal's popularity lends some credence to Newman's statement about the Immaculate

Conception: '[Roman] Catholics have not come to believe it because it is defined, but it was defined because they believed it'.[16] The image Catherine Labouré reported having seen would have been familiar even to those English Roman Catholics who did not possess a medal: it appeared at the head of Father Ignatius Spencer's *Association paper*, the publication of the prayer association he founded in 1852,[17] as well on the frontispeace of works such as Frederick W. Faber's *The devout child of Mary* and Bishop William Bernard Ullathorne's *The Immaculate Conception of the Mother of God*.

In 1849 Pius IX began to define the doctrine, a process that culminated in his reading the decree on 8 December 1854, the day that had been celebrated as the Feast of Mary's Conception and was now to be celebrated as that of her Immaculate Conception. The official reports of the popular response were overwhelmingly positive. Nicholas Wiseman, who was present in St Peter's Basilica when the declaration was read, assured English Roman Catholics that 'scarcely a dry eye was to be seen among those who witnessed this touching scene', while outside St Peter's 'every mark of sincere joy was exhibited by the devout Roman people'.[18] In a sermon delivered at the Second Provincial Council of Westminster the following year, Manning assured the Cardinal and his fellow Roman Catholics that not only the English but the entire Roman Catholic world had answered Wiseman's call to rejoice:

> Never since the great Council of Ephesus, which invested the Blessed Virgin with the august title of Mother of God, has so vivid and universal a joy broken forth from the heart of the Catholic Church. The publication of this Dogma has given form and articulation to the thoughts and desires of the faithful throughout the world.[19]

Ten years later, Newman confirmed Manning's assessment in his recollection that the doctrine 'was received every where on its promulgation with the greatest enthusiasm'.[20]

These optimistic reports of the doctrine's reception ignored the reluctance of some English Roman Catholics to accept a belief that, as recently as 1840, Peter Baines, the Western Vicar-Apostolic in England, had dismissed as being 'peculiarly obnoxious to protestants, which belongs not to the code of defined dogmas, and which Catholics, therefore, may without censure reject'.[21] Certainly Wiseman anticipated objections that the doctrine was a new one, for he assured his flock that

> the Church pretends to no new revelations ... the immunity of the ever blessed Virgin, Mother of God, the eternal Word incarnate, and the spotless Lamb, had been a doctrine revealed from the beginning, and

if hitherto only received in implicit faith, henceforth, by virtue of his decree to be believed by all with explicit faith, that is, as a distinct and separate dogma, no longer involved in the general belief of what the Church teaches.[22]

Wiseman must not have been entirely convincing, for several months later Faber – who also believed the doctrine was an apostlic one[23] – informed Ullathorne [*The Immaculate Conception of the Mother of God*], 'We found many good lay folks, frequenters of the sacraments, who were *scandalised* at the definition, and on different grounds: and your book meets every one of the objections we have met, and that not in a dry way, but so as to breed devotion.'[24] Four days later, he told Newman that Wiseman was 'perturbed at the difficulties about the definition.'[25] Faber was convinced that 'the difficulty lies *rarely* in the Immaculate Conception, but in the matter of defining.'[26] Possibly Faber's parishioners, like some bishops, believed that the timing of the definition was inopportune, rather than that the dogma itself was objectionable.[27] Regardless of any resistance, the doctrine was quickly incorporated into English devotional manuals: the 1857 English edition of the *Raccolta* promised 100 days' indulgence for saying one of two 'Ejaculations in Honour of the Immaculate Conception,'[28] and the belief appeared in the English 'Penny Catechism' by 1859.[29]

Heimann sees the incorporation of the Immaculate Conception as helping to emphasise 'the distinct and exclusive character of membership in the [Roman] Catholic Church.'[30] Certainly this new dogma reminded other English Christians that Roman Catholics had beliefs and sources of authority different from theirs, and a hierarchy based in Rome. Not surprisingly, Roman Catholics made those differences positive matters. Because the Immaculate Conception was the first binding doctrine without scriptural proof, the Roman Catholic hierarchy claimed that, as Wiseman said, the Church had relied on 'the unfailing assistance of the Holy Spirit' in asserting the doctrine.[31] The lack of scriptural evidence was taken as a sign that, as Faber said, the 'Church alone is infallible, and it is the Church alone whom the Holy Ghost leads into all truth'.[32] A decade after the promulgation of *Ineffabilis Deus*, Manning would argue, in *The workings of the Holy Spirit in the Church of England*, that 'the Catholic and Roman Church' was 'the sole authoritative interpreter of Scripture and of antiquity'[33] and suggest that there was more unbelief than truth in the Church into which he had been born.[34] In 1855 he argued the corollary to this position when he positively rejoiced in the lack of scriptural evidence as demonstrating that the Holy Spirit operated in the Church he had recently joined: *Ineffabilis Deus* does not say that it [the Immaculate Conception] is true, it offers no logical or historical proofs of its truth; it declares that it is revealed: that it was contained in the Revelation of the Day of Pentecost. And we receive it, not upon argument or criticism, but upon the witness of the Church, which is the sole witness of the mind of God, for 'The things that are of God no man knoweth but the Spirit of God.'[35]

The invocation of the Holy Spirit is more commonly associated with evangelicalism, but the language of *Ineffabilis Deus* and its English defenders is a reminder that Roman Catholics also believed that the Holy Spirit worked in their Church. Citing the authority of the Holy Spirit also allowed Roman Catholics to define their Church as the privileged receptacle of divine revelation and thus as superior to other Christian churches.

Although the Roman Catholic hierarchy declared itself unconcerned with the lack of scriptural support for the doctrine, such support was sought, most often through an alternate translation of Gen. 3:15. Substituting *ipsa* (her) for *ipse* (its), Roman Catholics translated God's curse on the serpent as 'She [Mary] will bruise thy head, and thou shalt bruise her heel', rather than 'it [the seed; i.e., Jesus] will bruise thy head, and thou shalt bruise its heel'. Pius IX twice referred to this passage in justifying the proclamation of Mary as immaculate.[36] Ullathorne interpreted several Old Testament passages, including Prov. 8:22–4 – 'The Lord possessed me in the beginning of His ways. Before He made anything from the beginning. The depths were not as yet, and I was already conceived' – in reference to the Virgin Mary.[37] The convert John Jerome referenced the metaphorical proofs cited by Alban Butler, an eighteenth-century author and chaplain to the Duke of Norfolk, of Mary's sinlessness in the Song of Solomon 4:12: 'She was the *enclosed garden* which the serpent could never enter; and *the sealed fountain* which he never defiled.'[38] Such citations were, however, relatively unimportant in either the establishment or the defence of the doctrine: the first scriptural reference does not come until about a quarter of the way through *Ineffabilis Deus*, and there are only two other scriptural references in the entire document. The lack of scriptural backing, and the general lack of Roman Catholic concern in that area, reflected one of the fundamental differences between Catholics, who sought authority in tradition as well as in Scripture, and Protestants, who professed to be guided by *sola Scriptura*.

Because they valued tradition as well as Scripture, Roman Catholics sought to enlist the Church Fathers as defenders of the Immaculate Conception, even though, as the *Dublin review* was forced to acknowledge, 'the doctrine of the Virgin's Immaculate Conception was never formally and explicitly proposed to Christian antiquity'.[39] Disregarding the lack of precedent, the ultramontane journal nevertheless hypothesised that Mary's purity was an apostolic belief that could have been forgotten by the fifth century[40] and insisted that at any rate the belief 'is virtually and implicitly contained in those very epithets which antiquity delighted to emulate upon the Mother of God'.[41] Ignoring the Church Fathers who had declared that Mary had been marked by original sin, Manning asserted that the early church recognised Mary as 'the spotless one' who 'was declared to be free from sin, and from all contact with sin'.[42] Newman, Faber, and Ullathorne found that Augustine was the most amenable to citation, thanks to his famous statement in *De natura et gratia*, 'that when he spoke of sin he did not intend to include our Blessed Lady in any thing he said'.[43]

Roman Catholics also invoked *recapitulation*, a patristic trope that extended Paul's description of Jesus as the Second Adam[44] to identify Mary as the second Eve. As Newman explained to Arthur Osborne Alleyne, a Roman Catholic who had converted to Anglicanism, 'when St Irenaeus says, "mankind is surrendered to death by a *Virgin*, and is saved by a *Virgin*", he surely implies that as Eve was without sin, so was Mary. Why indeed is it difficult to suppose that Mary had at least the privilege of Eve? – and Eve had an immaculate conception and birth'.[45] Roman Catholics repeatedly argued that the frequency with which the Church Fathers applied recapitulation to Mary demonstrated their belief in her sinlessness. More than a decade before the dogma had been declared, Wiseman assured his adversary the traditional high-church clergyman William Palmer of Worcester College, Oxford: 'This comparison between Mary and Eve, in the same manner as Christ and Adam are compared, is so common among the older writers, that, from St Irenaeus downwards, it would be easy to fill pages with quotations'.[46] The year after the dogma had been issued, Manning said that for the first 1,000 years members of the church had repeatedly declared the Virgin Mary 'to be free from sin, and from all contact with sin ... As the second Eve she was all that the first Eve was, and of a higher dignity, inasmuch as in all things she is greater'.[47]

In addition to seeking support for the belief in Scripture, tradition, and divine inspiration, Roman Catholics deduced the Immaculate Conception from Mary's motherhood. Believing that her motherhood was the greatest honour conferred on any individual, Newman reasoned that Mary needed to be conceived without sin to ensure that she was above the other saints in the heavenly hierarchy.[48] A more common argument, which Newman contended also had patristic support,[49] was that Jesus' sinless body could not have gestated in a sinful womb. 'Can the faith of Jesus permit us to regard His own Blessed Mother in such a light [i.e., having original sin], even for a moment?' Ullathorne asked rhetorically. 'Did the Holy Ghost commingle His spirit with such a flesh? Did Jesus take flesh from a being like this?'[50] The Catholic celebration of the close physical relationship between Jesus and Mary, evident in Ullathorne's meditation on the blood that flowed back and forth between Mary and the embryonic Jesus, almost demanded the declaration of the Immaculate Conception. Faber (whose hymn, 'O Mother! I could weep for mirth', was written in honour of the Feast of the Immaculate Conception[51]) shuddered 'to think that the matter of the Precious Blood had ever been itself corrupted with the taint of sin, that it had once been part of the devil's kingdom, that what was to supply the free price of our redemption was once enslaved to God's darkest, foulest enemy'.[52] Therefore, Faber argued, Christians must believe that 'the Mother of God ... always belonged to God, and to none but Him: that she was never under a curse, or in the power of the devil, or his slave, which she would have been if she had been conceived in original sin'.[53]

Faber's argument was open to challenge on the grounds that Christians believed Mary's parents to have had original sin. In order to avoid having to project an entire lineage of sinless forebears back into eternity, Roman Catholics also asserted that, even were it possible for a sinful mother to bear a sinless son, Jesus so loved his mother that he conferred on her the honour of immaculate conception. Drawing on the medieval formula *Potuit, decuit, ergo fecit* (God could do it, it was fitting to do it, and therefore he did it), Ullathorne contended that filial love and divine prerogative ensured Mary's immaculate conception.

> [W]hen we consider, once more, the infinite holiness of Jesus, and His filial consanguinity with Mary; what other conclusion is open to us, than that He who could make His Mother immaculate, did not abandon her to His enemy, but in the view of His own merits did make her most pure, and full of grace, and immaculate? ... [C]an we say that He contemplated her as *defiled*, as *unclean*, as a *child of wrath*, as *the servant of sin*, as *brought under the power of the devil*?[54]

Mary's motherhood, then, was Roman Catholics' primary justification for positing her immaculate conception. They concluded that the purity of the mother, which they believed was a gift from the son, was necessary in order to protect her son from the taint of sin. His purity Christians believed to be essential not just because he was divine but because the sacrifice on the cross had to be made by a pure being. Roman Catholics' belief in the Immaculate Conception, however hesitantly the dogma initially was accepted in England, had been prepared for over several centuries by the growing popular belief, especially on the Continent, in Mary's sinlessness. It was also consistent with the regular invocation in Victorian popular culture of the ideal of woman as both morally superior and defined by her maternal instincts, although Roman Catholics exaggerated those characteristics as they confined them to a single woman. However, because Roman Catholic tradition had defined Mary as sinless well before 1854, it is more accurate to reverse the equation to note that popular Victorian culture had, in describing women as being more spiritual and moral than men, defined a more limited version of the Roman Catholic Mary.

Having addressed, at least to their own satisfaction, the lack of direct scriptural evidence by relying on scriptural metaphors, tradition, and the logic of Mary's motherhood, Roman Catholics had to deal with the question of the nature and means of the transmission of original sin. Roman Catholics were prepared to accept the doctrine of the Immaculate Conception because, as Newman explained to Alleyne, they understood original sin as a passive disability, 'the deprivation of the grace of God, which was a gift external and superadded to Adam's nature'. Therefore, 'the entrance of grace into the soul, as a presence, ipso facto destroys Original Sin'.[55] This view of original sin, which was first propounded by Thomas Aquinas, held that Adam and Eve had been endowed with supernatural grace, and that the fall had returned them to a natural state. Original sin was, then, not a fatal wound but the absence of grace.

Roman Catholics were also prepared to accept the dogma because they did not believe original sin to be transmitted via sexual intercourse. Although apocrypha from the early church and later legends presented Mary's parents as exceptionally good and pure, and Mary's conception as being achieved through a kiss, officially Roman Catholicism attributed her sinlessness not to her parents' virtues or actions but to God's miraculous intervention. In 1567 Pope Pius V condemned the link between original sin and concupiscence, leaving Roman Catholics with no formula for explaining the transmission of original sin, as Newman noted.

[B]y us (though nothing on the *mode* of the transmission of Original Sin has been determined by the Church) concupiscence is viewed as a mere token or badge of Original Sin, which goes *with* the descent from parent to child ... We believe then, that, in a matter of fact, the Blessed Virgin's conception was of this kind; – her mother conceived as other mothers, in concupiscence, but that concupiscence was not a token, in that particular case, of the transmission of spiritual disabilities to herself, the child conceived.[56]

In fact, belief in the Immaculate Conception was impossible without separating original sin from sexual intercourse, so it is no coincidence that the link with sexual intercourse was severed in Roman Catholic doctrine about two centuries after belief in Mary's immaculate conception began to gain adherents. There is no evidence, however, that separating original sin from sexual intercourse gave Roman Catholics a more positive attitude towards human sexuality, and the purpose of sexual intercourse was restricted to procreation until the Second Vatican Council (1962–65).

A logical objection to the Immaculate Conception could be made on the basis of chronology: Mary was conceived well before Jesus' death on the cross, a sacrifice Christians believed removed the eternal (although not the temporal) consequences of original sin. Roman Catholics addressed this problem by utilising an elastic conception of time. Acknowledging that Mary's sinless conception predated Jesus' death, they insisted that it was nevertheless obtained, as Faber said, 'by the precious blood of Jesus Christ'.[57] She had, in other words, been saved in the same manner as all humans, but out of time.[58] 'She is indisputably among those whom our Lord suffered for and saved; she not only fell in Adam, but she rose in Christ, before she began to be',[59] Newman informed Alleyne. An alternative explanation that relied on an equally elastic view of time was to posit, as Jerome did, that Mary had been created under the same conditions as had been Adam and Eve. 'Hence there was no *new* creation, or an existence under new conditions of original purity, but rather an *ordinary* creation under the primoeval condition of purity.'[60] No matter how the timing of Mary's preservation from original sin was explained, these creative chronologies must have had a jarring impact on Victorian culture, in which linear time was omnipresent in daily life in the form of, for example, railway timetables and factory whistles. Advances in geology and evolutionary theories would have further impressed on Victorians the linear nature of time. Yet a flexible chronology was necessary in order to argue that a sinless Mary was fully human: as Jerome argued, Mary, 'being generated according to the ordinary laws of nature, inherited, like others, all the conditions of that nature, without forfeiting, like others, the original presence and indwelling of the Creator with his creature, which exemption implies inherent grace and spotless purity.'[61]

Although Roman Catholics were often accused by Protestants of focusing on Mary at the expense of God, ultimately they understood the Immaculate Conception as a Christological belief and not as distinct from their other Christian beliefs. For nineteenth-century Roman Catholics, as for their predecessors, the Immaculate Conception was, as Faber said, 'plainly a doctrine which, from its own nature, intimately concerns the glory of God, the honour of Jesus Christ, and the eminence of His ever-virgin Mother'.[62] Its primary aim was not, Jerome cautioned, to exalt Mary, but to honour Christ: 'God ... preserved her from the taint of original corruption for the honour of his Son, whose humanity was to be formed out of the Virgin's flesh'.[63] Therefore, Roman Catholics said, the doctrine led not to Mary, but to God, because those who prayed to Mary would learn to love God. The *Dublin review* urged its readers to

> remember that every Catholic regards Mary as absolutely free from the slightest approach to moral imperfection of any imaginable kind; and that her contemplation, therefore, is among the most powerful correctives of every inordinate and irregular passion. But, in proportion as every inordinate and irregular passion is corrected, in that very proportion the love of God is fostered and promoted; and the love of God, therefore, instead of being impeded, is promoted with singular efficacy by prayer to the Most Holy Virgin.[64]

Whereas all Catholics thought of Mary throughout her earthly life as a model for their own behaviour, Roman Catholics also saw in her the hope that one day they, too would be free of sin. 'In truth', Newman assured Alleyne, '[Roman] Catholics consider her as the signal and chiefest instance of the power and fullness of redeeming grace; for her Son merited for her that initial grace which was the prevention of Original Sin.'[65] That Victorian Roman Catholics found in Mary's immaculate conception not just a reminder of their sinfulness but also the promise of their own salvation further explains her usefulness in their devotional lives. If her power was not accessible to ordinary Christians, in her sinlessness she embodied what they hoped to attain.

Although in some ways the Catholic Mary seemed to affirm the popular idealised depictions of woman, especially the more domestic version that predominated before the 1860s, the declaration of the Immaculate Conception widened the gap between these two figures, for even the most effusive depictions of the feminine ideal never declared her to be free of sin, either original or actual. Furthermore, the representations of this internally contradictory, evolving ideal were never as static as an eternally sinless woman was. The Immaculate Conception represented Mary as fixed in her sinlessness, whereas fictional representations of the feminine ideal almost always presented her as someone who had to grow into the role of the ideal woman. The stringent and contradictory demands of the feminine ideal meant that no living woman could hope to meet that standard of behaviour. The declaration of the Immaculate Conception also removed Mary further from the experience of ordinary women: the emphasis on sin and redemption in Christian doctrine meant that no other human being could aspire to sinlessness. Yet Roman Catholics continued to turn to this powerful woman who was solitary in her sinlessness; for them she was a comfort rather than a challenge.

Advanced Anglicans and the Immaculate Conception

Advanced Anglicans generally, although not invariably, rejected the Immaculate Conception. This position had a strategic value for them, for it allowed them an opportunity to deny that they were secret Roman Catholics. Referring to the doctrine, Richard Frederick Littledale, the ritualist priest and controversialist, insisted: 'Ritualists do not teach even *one* of the doctrines and practices which are special and peculiar to the Church of Rome, distinguishing it from other ancient Churches ... therefore Ritualism is *not* Romanism in the most essential particulars.'[66] However, their reservations were more substantive than strategic. Most of their objections derived from the fact that the doctrine had, as Keble said to Robert Isaac Wilberforce in 1851, 'not a shadow of appearance in antiquity or in Scripture either.'[67] Although in 1845 Keble had made his friends anxious about the extent of his Marian devotion, he reiterated his uneasiness regarding the Immaculate Conception to Gladstone in 1858: 'I have a most intense dread and dislike of the new doctrines and practices (new since the last Oecumenical council at any rate, and some of them since 4 or 5 years ago) in relation to the B[lessed] V[irgin] M[ary].'[68] Gladstone himself called the doctrine 'an act of violence' that had dealt 'a deadly blow ... at the old historic, scientific, and moderate school' within the Roman Catholic Church,[69] while John Mason Neale reminded the sisters at East Grinstead that St Bernard of Clairvaux 'wrote against what he calls the blasphemy of the Immaculate Conception.'[70]

Pusey's response to *Ineffabilis Deus* exemplified the liminal position of advanced Anglicans: although he thought it 'intrinsically probable' that Mary had been cleansed after her conception but while still in the womb,[71] he believed the doctrine to be 'an obstacle' to reunion between the Church of England and the Roman Catholic Church[72] and argued that it was based not on tradition but on 'an appeal to feeling'.[73] Pusey detailed a history of non-belief in the proposition, beginning with Augustine, in his *First letter to Newman*. Of Augustine and his contemporaries, Pusey wrote that 'the multiplicity of minds who hold the same language, as to the universality of original sin ... seems to me the more to evince the absence of any tradition that there was any other exception besides our Lord, or that any one born according to the law of our birth was excepted'.[74] Confessing to Newman in a private letter that 'the Imm. Conc. is a perplexity',[75] Pusey insisted in a subsequent letter that he had not denied the belief itself: 'But I do not think that I have said any thing against any thing which is held to be de fide, unless indeed it is the Immaculate Conception, and I do not think that I have, in terms, denied this.'[76] Pusey essentially shared the Roman Catholic belief: he wanted the Roman Catholic Church to state explicitly that the belief referred to the conception of Mary's soul only,[77] as Ullathorne said that it did.[78] Yet Pusey, who justly feared being labelled a traitor to his Church and who envisioned Mary as a less powerful woman than most did Roman Catholics, did not accept Ullathorne's reassurance. By likening Mary to John the Baptist and St Jeremiah, both of whom Catholics believed had been cleansed in the womb, he described her as unusually but not uniquely blessed.

In general, advanced Anglicans followed Pusey in approaching but never fully accepting the Immaculate Conception. The Tractarian Isaac Williams partially invoked the patristic trope of recapitulation: he contrasted Eve's want of faith with Mary's being guided by faith, but left out the Roman Catholic corollary that both had been born without sin.[79] In an 1856 sermon, the Tractarian Thomas Thelluson Carter skirted the boundaries of admitting a belief in the Immaculate Conception when he described Mary as being

> so far as was ever given to a child of Eve (One only excepted) blessed among women, honoured of Angels, and highly favoured of God. She was the pattern of all those who, in their several degrees, nurtured in Christian homes, and shielded from the impurities of the world, have never fallen away from their first grace, ever drawing nearer to the perfect vision of God.[80]

Carter refused to delineate Mary's status precisely, other than to say that she was so 'highly favoured of God' that she was inferior only to Jesus. However, he seemed to describe her as a very good rather than a sinless person when he said that she was the model for those who were never exposed to the world's wickedness and who therefore 'have never fallen away from their first grace'.

A very few advanced Anglicans did welcome the doctrine. 'De Q', a Tractarian who hoped for reunion with the Roman Catholic Church, rejected the ambiguity of 'first grace', which could refer to either childhood innocence or the grace that Christians believed had characterised Paradise. He argued that the Immaculate Conception should be accepted on the basis of the historical celebration of the feast of Mary's conception by the Church of England, of the Roman Catholic and Eastern Orthodox acceptance of the belief, and the belief in the immaculate nativity of John the Baptist and Jeremiah.[81] Robert Owen, a Tractarian who also hoped for reunion, wrote of the Tractarians' favorite poet: 'Wordsworth could imply the Immaculate Conception, when he sang of Mary as – Woman! above all women glorified!/ Our tainted nature's solitary boast, &c.'[82] Ignoring Keble's rejection of the doctrine, Owen also interpreted Keble's 'Ave Maria; blessèd Maid!/ Lily of Eden's fragrant shade'[83] as expressing the belief that Mary had been conceived without sin.[84]

The debate among advanced Anglicans over the Immaculate Conception is a reminder of how the lack of a supreme authority, such as the pope in the Roman Catholic Church, could lead to unresolved theological questions. This debate was less significant than other debates that have gripped the Church of England, such as that over the nature of the Eucharist in the nineteenth century or over clerical homosexuality today, but it illuminates the same fact about the structure of the Anglican Church. Founded on compromise, the Anglican Church was open to conflict about fundamental matters of belief. The advanced Anglican responses to the Immaculate Conception showed the existence of a middle ground, between acceptance and outright rejection of the Immaculate Conception. This new dogma had appeal for advanced Anglicans, but not enough to allow them to overcome their qualms about its lack of foundation in either Scripture or early church tradition. Ambivalent about the doctrine, advanced Anglicans were left in a liminal position in terms of their denominational identification.

Protestants and the Immaculate Conception

The Catholics who defended the Immaculate Conception or even the immaculate birth of the Virgin Mary were an embattled minority, for public opinion in Victorian England was overwhelmingly hostile to the belief. When *Ineffabilis Deus* was promulgated, the *Wesleyan–Methodist magazine* reported that 'the Protestant world rang with indignation at this new instance of presumption'.[85] This assessment was not entirely hyperbolic, for the Immaculate Conception inspired a larger number of dissenting participants than did any other aspect of the Marian debates. This increased participation was due to some extent to the fact that the promulgation of the dogma gave dissenters a specific event to which they could react, but it can be attributed also to the fact that the dogma involved three elements that shaped the self-identity of all Protestants: it touched on the question of whether women were morally superior to men; it addressed the issue of how Christian beliefs were determined; and, because the doctrine was promulgated by the pope, it was a reminder that the Roman Catholic hierarchy was based outside of England.

Protestant opponents of the doctrine, which the Presbyterian controversialist John Cumming denounced as an 'act of idolatry',[86] often began
their critiques by referring to the Bible. The Irish Anglican clergyman
George Croly, who opposed Catholicism as well as dissent, complained
that the doctrine was 'destitute of all ground in Scripture',[87] while the
evangelical clergyman William Thomas Maudson said positively: "The
Bible contradicts it, both by silence and by words.'[88] It had even been
defined, according to the *Church and state gazette*, 'in defiance of holy
Scripture'.[89] Delivering the annual sermon for the Protestant Association
in 1885, the evangelical Anglican John C. Miller declared: 'There is not one
single passage in the whole of the New Testament – I need not say there
is no single passage of the Old – of which it can with the slightest show of
reason and of common sense be alleged, that it is a sufficient foundation
to bear this dogma.'[90] The *Wesleyan–Methodist magazine* charged that
'the Church of Rome cannot claim any authority for the new dogma from
the word of God'.[91] The lack of scriptural evidence, the Anglican minister
John Echlin Armstrong concluded, 'settles the point with the *faithful*'.[92]

The scriptural verse cited most often against the dogma was Mary's
declaration at the beginning of the Magnificat: 'My spirit rejoices in God my
Saviour.'[93] Protestants claimed that this admission made the Virgin Mary a
witness against the dogma. 'W.J.S.', a Methodist, argued that 'Mary herself
point-blank contradicts ... Pius IX., the Cardinals, and a large number
of Popish Bishops' who had asserted the Immaculate Conception,[94]
while Armstrong argued that 'if Jesus was the Virgin's *Saviour*, it was
that He might save her from *her sins*. *Therefore*, she had sins. *Therefore*,
the Immaculate Conception is a figment.'[95] Thomas John Lingwood, a
clergyman who defended the Protestant identity of the Church of England
and opposed the Oxford Movement, agreed: 'When, then, we find Mary
rejoicing in spirit at the prospect of a Saviour, we must needs conclude she
had sins for which she grieved, and from which she hoped to be saved by
Him.'[96] It was this view of the Virgin Mary that Samuel Wilberforce had
incorporated into his Christmastime sermon preached before the Queen,
when he imagined Mary gazing at her infant and wondering: 'How was He
to make atonement for her sins and the sins of her people?'[97]

Protestants found further evidence of Mary's sinful nature in her
going to the Temple to be purified after the birth of Jesus. Miller asked
rhetorically whether it was

> probable that the Virgin mother would have been directed by the Spirit
> of God – impelled by the impulses of her own pious heart, wrought
> upon by that Spirit dwelling within her as a saint of God – to go like

any other woman, and present her offering in the temple for purification after childbirth, if she had been in every sense and in every degree without sin?[98]

Maudson used the same argument in a sermon preached six weeks after the doctrine was promulgated:

> But if Mary was free from sin, why did she thus present the sacrifices by which it was acknowledged and typically atoned for? and if, particularly, exempt from *original* sin, why did she present them on an occasion, which was evidently purposely selected by God, as an intimation that we are *born* in sin and *conceived* in iniquity?[99]

Jesus as well as Mary became a witness against the Immaculate Conception when the Anglican clergyman William Ford Vance said that by addressing his mother as 'Woman' Jesus provided 'proof that she was nothing more than a human being, born of the stock of fallen Adam, and deriving from him a mortal and sinful nature'.[100]

Just as Roman Catholics pointed to *Ineffabilis Deus* as evidence that their Church was 'the sole witness of the mind of God',[101] Protestants interpreted the doctrine as proof, as Armstrong informed Roman Catholics, that 'your church does not exalt the hearing and the keeping of God's Word'.[102] The *Quarterly review* agreed that the doctrine was 'but a small addition to the heterogeneous mass of fiction with which Rome has overlaid the simplicity of the Gospel'.[103] Rejecting the Roman Catholic explanation that *Ineffabilis Deus* merely defined beliefs that had belonged to the early church, Maudson castigated the Roman Catholic Church for having 'virtually adopted that scheme of *development* put forth by an eminent pervert [Newman] to her communion; and no longer venturing to affirm that she holds and teaches the identical truths delivered by the great founders of Christianity'.[104] This corruption of Christianity demonstrated by *Ineffabilis Deus*, Cumming said,

> must convince the disciples of the recent seceders from the Protestant Church, that if there be defects where they are – and no visible church is perfect – there are brands and marks of apostasy so deep and now so indelible in the Romish Church, that nothing but ignorance or fanaticism can [convince one to] leave a Protestant Church and enter her communion.[105]

Protestants' professed reliance on *sola Scriptura* meant that it was impossible for them to accept the doctrine; and by contesting it on scriptural grounds, they were able to reinforce the traditional charge that Roman Catholics paid scant attention to the Bible, a charge that allowed Protestants to assert that they were rational readers of the Bible capable of distinguishing fiction from the word of God. Protestants were genuinely motivated by theological concerns, but they were as adept as were Roman Catholics in exploiting this dogma for propagandistic purposes.

In spite of their professed reliance on *sola Scriptura*, Protestants, like Roman Catholics, also turned to patristic writings to support their position. The traditional high-church clerics Wilberforce and James Endell Tyler agreed with John C. Miller that Augustine had rejected the Immaculate Conception.[106] (In truth, Augustine was ambivalent, declaring both that all humans bore the burden of original sin and exempting the Virgin Mary from his declaration without positively asserting that she had been conceived without original sin.) Protestant opponents of the doctrine also delighted in reminding Roman Catholics that later tradition offered no consensus on the state of Mary's soul at conception. Referring to the medieval dispute between the followers of Thomas Aquinas and those of Duns Scotus over whether the Virgin had been born or conceived immaculate, Catherine Sinclair noted pointedly the 'Dominicans differ from the Franciscans on an important point respecting the Virgin Mary',[107] a dispute which the Anglican cleric William James Skilton rather gleefully said was characterised by 'bitterness and animosity'.[108] Yet neither acknowledged that the division between the Franciscans and the Dominicans was about whether she had been conceived or merely born without sin. While the dispute was not unimportant theologically, it did not concern the ultimate question of Mary's sinlessness. And, of course, by the mid-nineteenth century, many advanced Anglicans had adopted the original Dominican position that she had been born, if not conceived, without original sin.

Protestants' rejection of the Immaculate Conception was consistent with their defining the Virgin Mary as an ordinary woman. To be human, they believed, was to be sinful. As Thomas Hartwell Horne argued, Mary 'was one of Adam's fallen race, and ... must have been a partaker of the sins and infirmities, in which all, so descended, deeply share'.[109] The alternative, Protestants saw, was to conclude that Jesus' sacrificial death and resurrection had been unnecessary: if Mary had been conceived without sin, Maudson worried, 'then the inheritance of a fallen nature is not *necessarily* attached to man at all, and the need of a Deliverer for the race is incapable of being shown'.[110] Belief in the Immaculate Conception also required, Lingwood argued, that one believe

> that Mary, and not Christ, was the first sinless human being; that freedom from the corruption and taint of sin was accomplished before the birth of Jesus; and that sinless humanity existed without the incarnation of the Son of God, and independently of the union of the Divine

and human nature in His person, which is directly opposed to the statements of God's Holy Word.[111]

The fear that an immaculately conceived Mary would usurp Christ's position was similar to the Protestant objection that the Catholic Virgin Mary interfered in Jesus' work on earth. Wilberforce thundered that 'this dangerous delusion is a part, and the crowning part, of a whole system which does thus place on the Mediator's throne the Virgin mother instead of the incarnate Son'.[112]

Victorian Protestants could never accept the Immaculate Conception, because there was no direct scriptural support for it and because they feared that it allowed Mary to usurp Jesus' role and stature. They also had to reject the doctrine because they understood original sin as a corruption of human nature, a defilement of the soul.[113] This view, which dates back to the early church and was adopted by Protestant reformers, was codified in Article 9, which described original sin as an 'infection of nature'.[114] The seventeenth-century divine Thomas Jackson used the language of corruption and sickness in his treatise on original sin, which was reprinted in the nineteenth century: *Original Sin is more then [sic] a meer Privation; more then a meer want of Original justice; [it is] a multiplicity of wounds or diseases in our nature*.[115] Victorians themselves used similar language: Aitken likened original sin to 'a fatal moral disease, [which] has entered our nature',[116] while Hannah Sinclair described it as *a deep pollution*; a total alienation from the heart of God, which is most culpable, and wholly inexcusable, in his sight'.[117] The result, the Anglican Protestant minister Charles Bradley declared, was that '[w]e are a company of guilty and polluted creatures, whom God has condemned for their crimes to everlasting wretchedness'.[118]

The universality of original sin, Victorian Protestants believed, was ensured because original sin was transmitted through sexual intercourse. As evidence they could cite Ps. 51:5: 'Behold, I was shapen in iniquity, and in sin did my mother conceive me.' In linking original sin and sexual intercourse they were in agreement with Augustine and other Church Fathers.[119] Christ's sinless human nature was dependent in part on his miraculous conception, Miller explained: 'It was, I say, because He had no human sire, but because the power of the Holy One overshadowed the Virgin, that therefore the flesh of Jesus Christ, and the soul of Jesus Christ, and the mind of Jesus Christ, were preserved absolutely free from all taint of sin'.[120] Thus Protestants agreed with advanced Anglicans that the mechanics of human conception guaranteed the universality of original sin.

These arguments reveal different, and unexpected, understandings of sexual intercourse and original sin in Victorian England. That celibate priests, including Newman, Ullathorne, and Faber, did not ascribe the transmission of original sin to sexual intercourse, while married men with children, including Pusey, Tyler, and Wilberforce, did suggests again that personal experience did not necessarily dictate one's theology. Protestants' and advanced Anglicans' reliance on the Augustinian explanation that original sin was transmitted through sexual intercourse reinforced the generally negative light in which sexual intercourse was held in Victorian public culture. Victorians, especially educated and church-going Victorians, would certainly have known of the link between sexual intercourse and original sin because those ideas were not limited to theological texts but reached a wider audience by being incorporated into sermons and periodical articles. These arguments thus challenge Michael Mason's thesis that in nineteenth-century England 'explicit anti-sensual attitudes tended above all to emanate from secularist and progressive quarters', rather than from Christian denominations.[121] Instead, it is clear that 'anti-sensual attitudes' were also promulgated by clergymen.

Even when evolutionary theory called into question the historical Adam and Eve, Victorian Christians continued to understand original sin as a hereditary disability. This view was consistent with the belief in the inheritance of acquired characteristics, which many educated people in the nineteenth century believed was the means by which species evolved. In a sermon delivered several years before *Ineffebilis Deus* was issued, the popular Anglican cleric Frederick W. Robertson (who disassociated himself from all church parties) asserted that

> he who would deny original sin must contradict all experience in the transmission of qualities. The very hound transmits his peculiarities learned by education, and the horse of Spain his paces taught by art to his offspring, as a part of their nature ... It is plain that the first man must have exerted on his race an influence quite peculiar: that his acts must have biassed [sic] their acts. And this bias or tendency is what we call original sin.[122]

Certainly Protestants consistently rejected any Catholic belief that elevated the Virgin Mary's stature above that of other humans. Even if they had not feared committing idolatry, their understanding of original sin as integral to human flesh as well as to the soul made it impossible for them to accept that any person was sinless.

Rejecting the Immaculate Conception was also useful polemically, as it provided an opportunity to portray Roman Catholics as lacking free will. Although Manning spoke of the Church's role in defining Mary's immaculate conception, in fact *Ineffabilis Deus* testified to the increase of papal power that occurred during the nineteenth century: the declaration was made by the pope alone, and Barbara Corrado Pope argues that it was a gesture of defiance against the forces of rationalism and modernity.[123] Protestants shared that view of the dogma: the Congregationalist weekly newspaper the *British banner* asserted that it was 'in perfect keeping with Papal logic, that to *say* a thing is thus and thus, is to *make* a thing thus and thus, although it was not so before'.[124] Demonstrating a penchant for conspiracy theorising, Croly argued that the real purpose of convening the bishops in Rome for the reading of *Ineffabilis Deus* was actually 'for a mustering of the whole force of Popery in Europe for some new onslaught on Protestant institutions'. If that were the case, he continued, the Vatican 'could not adopt a more popular pretext among the Popish millions, than the seeming offer of honours to the great Popish deity, the Virgin'.[125]

Rejecting the Immaculate Conception was one facet of the argument that only Protestants were truly English and truly Christian. Armstrong, who opposed both Anglo-Catholicism and Roman Catholicism, accused the Roman Catholic Church of trying to 'thrust [the dogma] ... down the throats of Bible-reading English Christians'.[126] Protestants used the dogma as evidence that the Roman Catholic Church neither followed Scripture nor valued liberty of conscience, both of which were central to Protestant England's idea of itself. The approach was typical of Victorian anti-Roman Catholic writings, which often contrasted servile Roman Catholics to 'free-born Englishmen'. Ignoring the fact that Scottish law differed from English law, Catherine Sinclair was reassured by the thought that the 'laws of England ... give liberty to every individual in Britain',[127] and then contrasted free Britons to abject Roman Catholics who were 'without will, thought, liberty, or intelligence, except through the despotic sway of their priest'.[128] Cumming's professed hope that 'our Roman Catholic fellow-countrymen' would be 'emancipat[ed] into the principles and liberty of that religion ... which we believe and can prove to be the inspiration and force and peace of the best men in our world, and the foundation of the noblest and surest hopes for another'[129] was meant more as a reminder of assumed Roman Catholic ignorance than as a cry for conversions, as is evident from his lack of interest throughout his career in converting Roman Catholics, as well as from the smug tone of this blast against Roman Catholicism.

The contrast between the images of free, rational Protestants and ignorant, superstitious Roman Catholics has a long history in England, dating back to the Reformations of the sixteenth century and reaching its peak in the opposition to Charles I and James II, whose religious sympathies (and in James' case, conversion) and ruling styles confirmed for Protestants the link many believed existed between Roman Catholicism and absolutism. The depiction of Roman Catholics as under the despotic rule of the pope or his local enforcers, priests and nuns, made them, no matter how English by birth or heredity, foreigners in England. The assertion of any authority akin to the expanding papal authority was unknown in England in the nineteenth century, when the power of the monarch was gradually eroded.

Protestants' rejection of the Virgin Mary as a sinless woman also meant that they were more in accord with mainstream Victorian culture. Peter Gay's acknowledgment of 'the divorce of private experience and public discussion in the bourgeois century'[130] should serve as a warning that the profusion of literature insisting that women were morally superior does not mean that all, or even many, Victorians believed this to be the case.[131] In fact, the abundance of these writings suggests that the Victorians were not convinced that this was so. Even those classic promulgations of the feminine ideal, such as Sarah Ellis's popular advice manuals and John Ruskin's 'Of Queens' Gardens', were riven with doubt that women were truly virtuous. This anxiety was encouraged by the Protestant insistence that the Virgin Mary, traditionally the exemplar of female virtues even among the reformers, was a sinful woman.

The ideal of the virtuous woman, constructed to combat the traditional fear that woman was more corrupt than man, was potentially problematical in that she could pose a threat to male superiority. The fear was expressed in one of the main arguments against the Immaculate Conception, that a sinless Mary would challenge Jesus' unique identity and would ultimately usurp his throne. This was a particular concern for clergymen: if woman was innately morally superior, she could undermine clerical authority from the pulpit. Certainly Victorian Protestants would not have accepted the Immaculate Conception, but the terms on which they denied it – emphasising not just the sinfulness of all humanity, but the sinfulness of a particular woman, who, historically, had been the exemplar of human love for the divine – suggests that they had concerns in addition to theological ones. Even when the Reformation shifted attention away from the Virgin Mary, the goal was to ignore her more than it was to condemn her. Victorian Protestants were, however, more overtly hostile. Religion was certainly one source of that hostility: a non-scriptural doctrine offended them, and critiquing it could also help combat the allure they feared Roman Catholicism held for some English men and women.

The language in which their critique was couched, however, was noteworthy in a culture that repeatedly described women as morally superior. Insisting on Mary's sinfulness could also undermine the image of women as morally superior to men, especially given the lack of images of other good women in the sermons, speeches, and other texts against the Immaculate Conception. Protestants did not object to the Immaculate Conception merely in order to envision women as equally sinful as men, but when they described Mary as sinful, like all humans, they connected this question to the discourse that described women as morally superior to men. While they were genuinely outraged by a non-scriptural belief, the result of their rejection of the Immaculate Conception was to deploy an image of a sinful woman, one that could be used as a counterpoint to the more widely available image of woman as morally superior.

Notes

1 Frederic W. Farrar, *Eternal hope: five sermons preached in Westminster Abbey, November and December, 1877* (New York: E. P. Dutton & Co., 1878), p. 131.

2 Sinclair, *A letter on the principles of Christian faith*, pp. 9–10.

3 Church, *Village sermons preached at Whatley*, p. 37.

4 John Henry Newman, *Sermons 1824–1843*, vol. 2: *Sermons on biblical history, sin and justification, the Christian way of life, and biblical theology*, ed. Vincent Ferrer Blehl, S.J. (Oxford: Clarendon Press, 1993), pp. 280–2.

5 Pusey, *The Presence of Christ in the Holy Eucharist*, p. 70.

6 Newman, *Sermons 1824–1843*, vol. 2, p. 314.

7 W. Hay M. H. Aitken, *Mission sermons*, 3rd edn (London: John F. Shaw & Co., n.d. [?1880]), p. 112.

8 Heimann, *Catholic devotion*, p. 146.

9 Quoted in J. C. S. Nias, *Gorham and the Bishop of Exeter* (London: SPCK, 1951), p. 18; emphasis in original.

10 H. H. Dobney. *Free Churches: a tract for my own congregation* (London: Strahan & Co., 1871), p. 40.

11 Kenneth Hylson-Smith, *Evangelicals in the Church of England 1734–1984* (Edinburgh: T. & T. Clark, 1988), p. 125.

12 Pius IX, *Ineffabilis Deus: official documents connected with the definition of the dogma of the Immaculate Conception of the Blessed Virgin Mary* (Baltimore, MD: John Murray & Co. and London: Charles Dolman, 1855), p. 95.

13 Origen, St Athanasius, St Basil, St. Gregory Nazianzen, Irenaeus, St Gregory of Nyssa, St John Chrysostom, St Ephraem, St Cyril of Alexandria, Tertullian, and St Cyprian were among those who denied that Mary was without sin: George Joussard, 'The Fathers of the Church and the Immaculate Conception', in Edward Dennis O'Connor (ed.), *The dogma of the Immaculate Conception: history and significance* (Notre Dame, IN: University of Notre Dame Press, 1958), pp. 51–85; Graef, *Mary*, vol. 1, pp. 40–3.

14 For an analysis of the historical role of the papacy in the definition of the Immaculate Conception, see René Laurentin, 'The role of the papal magisterium in the development of the dogma of the Immaculate Conception', trans. and abridged Charles E. Sheedy and Edward S. Shea, in O'Connor (ed.), *The dogma of the Immaculate Conception*, pp. 271–324.

15 The more famous apparition connected to the belief in the Immaculate Conception was that reported by Bernadette Soubirous, that a woman who identified herself only as the Immaculate Conception had appeared to her on several occasions in a grotto near Lourdes in 1858. For accounts of the apparitions at Rue de Bac and Lourdes, see David Blackbourn, *Marpingen: apparitions of the Virgin Mary in nineteenth-century Germany* (New York: Alfred Knopf, 1994), chapter 1; Pope, 'Immaculate and powerful'; Zimdars-Swartz, *Encountering Mary*, chapter 1.

16 Newman, *Apologia pro vitâ suâ*, p. 330.

17 Bussche, *Ignatius (George) Spencer*, p. 196.

18 Nicholas Wiseman, *Pastoral letter of His Eminence Cardinal Wiseman, Archbishop of Westminster, announcing the definition of the Immaculate Conception of the Blessed Virgin Mary* (London: T. Jones, 1855), p. 7.

19 Henry Edward Manning, 'Dogmatic authority: supernatural and infallible', *Sermons on ecclesiastical subjects* (Dublin: James Duffy, 1863), vol. 1, p. 122.

20 Newman, *Apologia pro vitâ suâ*, p. 330.

21 British Library, London, shelfmark m15.4499, unpublished MS by P. A. Baines, 'A history of the pastoral addressed to the faithful of the Western District, on occasion of the Fast of Lent 1840', p. 20; a fuller discussion of the controversy is found in Bossy, *The English Catholic community*, pp. 388–90.

22 Wiseman, *Pastoral letter*, pp. 4–5.

23 Faber, 'The doctrine and definition of the Immaculate Conception', p. 271.

24 Faber, *Faber: poet and priest*, p. 270; emphasis in original.

25 Faber, *Faber: poet and priest*, p. 270.

26 Faber, *Faber: poet and priest*, p. 271; emphasis in original.

27 'Of the 603 Bishops consulted [by Pope Pius IX in 1849], 546 favored definition; 56 or 57 opposed it for various reasons; only four or five opposed *definability*; 24 were undecided on the question of opportuneness; about ten desired an indirect definition, without condemnation of the contrary opinion as heretical. A final group would make no judgment': Laurentin, 'The role of the papal magisterium', p. 309; emphasis in original.

28 *Raccolta*, pp. 166–7.

29 Heimann, *Catholic devotion*, pp. 112–13.

30 Heimann, *Catholic devotion*, p. 114.

31 Wiseman, *Pastoral letter*, p. 4.

32 Faber, 'The doctrine and definition of the Immaculate Conception', p. 272.

33 Henry Edward Manning, *The workings of the Holy Spirit in the Church of England: a letter to the Rev. E. B. Pusey, D.D.* (London: Longman, Green, Longman, Roberts, & Green, 1864), p. 5.

34 Manning, *The workings of the Holy Spirit*, p. 6.

35 Manning, 'Dogmatic authority', p. 121.

36 Pius IX, *Ineffabilis Deus*, pp. 78, 79, 84–5.

37 Ullathorne, *The Immaculate Conception*, p. 61–4.

38 Jerome, *Cuddesden versus Vatican*, p. 12, emphasis in original.

39 'Passaglia on the prerogatives of Mary', *Dublin review*, 41 (September 1856), 131.

40 'Dr Pusey on Marian doctrine: peace through truth', *Dublin review* (new series), 7: 14 (October 1866), 469, 473.

41 'Passaglia on the prerogatives of Mary', 131.

42 Manning, 'Dogmatic authority', pp. 124.
43 Faber, 'The doctrine and definition of the Immaculate Conception', p. 276; John Henry Newman, *The letters and diaries of John Henry Newman*, vol. 19, ed. Charles Stephen Dessain (London: Thomas Nelson & Sons, 1969), p. 347; Ullathorne, *The Immaculate Conception*, p. 109.
44 Rom. 5:20.
45 Newman, *The letters and diaries of John Henry Newman*, vol. 19, p. 347, emphasis in original. Newman expressed the same idea several years later, in his *Letter to Pusey*, p. 396.
46 Wiseman, *Remarks on a letter*, p. 24.
47 Manning, 'Dogmatic authority', p. 124.
48 Newman, 'On the fitness of the glories of Mary', p. 370.
49 Newman contended that the Church Fathers had believed not only that Mary was conceived immaculate but that it was necessary for her to be immaculate in order for the Annunciation to occur: Newman, 'Our Lady in the gospel', p. 89.
50 Ullathorne, *The Immaculate Conception*, p. 80.
51 Faber, *Faber: poet and priest*, p. 269.
52 Frederick William Faber, *The precious blood: or, the price of our salvation* (London: Thomas Richardson & Son, 1860), p. 29.
53 Faber, 'The doctrine and definition of the Immaculate Conception', p. 269.
54 Ullathorne, *The Immaculate Conception*, pp. 82–3; emphasis in original.
55 Newman, *The letters and diaries of John Henry Newman*, vol. 19, p. 363; see also Newman, *Letter to Pusey*, p. 398.
56 Newman, *The letters and diaries of John Henry Newman*, vol. 19, pp. 365–6; emphasis in original; see also Newman, *Letter to Pusey*, p. 397.
57 Faber, 'The doctrine and definition of the Immaculate Conception', p. 269.
58 'Dr Pusey on Marian doctrine', 484; Ullathorne, *The Immaculate Conception*, pp. 84, 197.
59 Newman, *The letters and diaries of John Henry Newman*, vol. 19, p. 368.
60 Jerome, *Cuddesden versus Vatican*, pp. 20–1; emphasis in original.
61 Jerome, *Cuddesden versus Vatican*, p. 20.
62 Faber, 'The doctrine and definition of the Immaculate Conception', p. 274; see also Newman, *The letters and diaries of John Henry Newman*, vol. 19, p. 362.
63 Jerome, *Cuddesden versus Vatican*, p. 11; also p. 17.
64 'Dr Pusey on Marian devotion', 162.
65 Newman, *The letters and diaries of John Henry Newman*, vol. 19, p. 368; also Newman, 'The glories of Mary for the sake of her son', p. 352.
66 Littledale, *Ritualists not Romanists*, p. 2; emphasis in original.
67 Bodleian Library, Oxford, MSS Wilberforce, c. 67, letter from John Keble to Robert Isaac Wilberforce (transcription), undated (?1851), fol. 209.
68 British Library, London, Gladstone Papers, vol. 299, letter from John Keble to W. E. Gladstone (copy; in Keble's hand?), 8 October 1858, fol. 189.
69 W. E. Gladstone, 'The Vatican Decrees in their bearing on civil allegiance: a political expostulation', *Rome and the newest fashions in religion: three tracts* (London: John Murray, 1875), p. xxvi.
70 Neale, *Secession*, p. 10.
71 Pusey, *First letter to Newman*, pp. 52, 392.

72 Pusey, *First letter to Newman*, pp. 76–7; W. T. Maudson also interpreted the Immaculate Conception as a sign that reunion with the Roman Catholic Church was becoming less likely: Maudson, 'The dogma of the Virgin Mary's Immaculate Conception', 235–6.

73 Pusey, *First letter to Newman*, p. 291.

74 Pusey, *First letter to Newman*, p. 108.

75 Pusey House, Oxford, LBV 121/14, letter from E. B. Pusey to J. H. Newman, 2 November 1865.

76 Pusey House, Oxford, LBV 121/33, letter from E. B. Pusey to J. H. Newman, 19 November 1866.

77 Pusey House, Oxford, LBV 121/33, letter from E. B. Pusey to John Henry Newman, undated (18 or 19 January 1866); Pusey, *First letter to Newman*, pp. 63, 76–7.

78 Ullathorne, *The Immaculate Conception*, pp. 99, 126–7.

79 Williams, *Female characters*, p. 324.

80 T. T. Carter, *Mercy for the fallen: two sermons in aid of the House of Mercy, Clewer* (London: Joseph Masters, 1856), pp. 15–16.

81 De Q., 'The conception of the Blessed Virgin Mary', *Union review: a magazine of Catholic literature and art*, 6 (1868), 513–14, 518, 526.

82 Owen, *An essay on the communion of saints*, p. 56.

83 Keble, 'The Annunciation', p. 232, lines 37–8.

84 Owen, *An essay on the communion of saints*, p. 56.

85 'The Immaculate Conception', *Wesleyan–Methodist magazine*, 1: 6 (June 1855), 523.

86 Cumming, *The Immaculate Conception*, p. 5.

87 (George Croly) 'The new article of "faith"', *Wesleyan–Methodist magazine* (5th series), 1: 1 (January 1855), 80; see also 'The Feast of the Conception', *Quarterly review*, 98 (1856), 152; 'The Feast of the Conception', *Quarterly review*, 97: 193 (June 1855), 149; *Papal infallibility* (London: Rivingtons, 1872), p. 4; 'The religion of the Oratorians', *Church and state gazette*, 12: 167 (9 December 1853), 765; Robinson, *The mother of Jesus*, pp. 11–13; *The Virgin Mary: a married woman*, p. 14; 'The Immaculate Conception', *Watchman and Wesleyan advertiser* (new series), 5 (27 December 1854), 421.

88 Maudson, 'The dogma of the Virgin Mary's Immaculate Conception', 237.

89 'The great fallacy', *Church and state gazette*, 13: 665 (10 November 1854), 710; emphasis in original.

90 Miller, 'The Immaculate Conception', 426; see also 'The Immaculate Conception', *Wesleyan times*, 7: 335 (12 February 1855), 108.

91 'The Immaculate Conception', *Wesleyan–Methodist magazine*, 527.

92 Armstrong, *Armstrong's reply*, p. 4; emphasis in original.

93 Lk. 1:47.

94 W.J.S., 'Fragments on the "Immaculate Conception"', *Wesleyan–Methodist magazine* (5th series), 1: 2 (February 1855), 150.

95 Armstrong, *Armstong's reply*, p. 4; emphasis in original. This was a common argument: see 'The Immaculate Conception', *Wesleyan times*, 109; 'Southwark mission: missionary report', *British Protestant; or, journal of the Special Mission to Roman Catholics in Great Britain*, 116 (August 1855), 218.

96 Thomas J. Lingwood, *Was the Virgin Mary Immaculate, and born without sin? A sermon, preached in the Chapel of St Andrew and St Mary, Maidenhead, on Sunday, October the 15th, 1871* (London: William Hunt & Co., 1872), p. 4.

97 Wilberforce, 'The character of the Virgin Mary', p. 31.

98 Miller, 'The Immaculate Conception', 428.
99 Maudson, 'The dogma of the Virgin Mary's Immaculate Conception', 238; emphasis in original.
100 Vance, *On the invocation of angels, saints, and the Virgin Mary*, p. 40.
101 Manning, 'Dogmatic authority', 121.
102 Armstrong, *Armstrong's reply*, pp. 9–10; emphasis in original.
103 'The Feast of the Conception', *Quarterly review*, 98, 148.
104 Maudson, 'The dogma of the Virgin Mary's Immaculate Conception', 235; emphasis in original.
105 Cumming, *The Immaculate Conception*, p. 6.
106 Miller, 'The Immaculate Conception', 428; Tyler, *The worship of the Blessed Virgin Mary*, p. 287; (Wilberforce) *Rome*, p. 6. In this they were joined by the Italian apostate priest Gavazzi, as reported in 'The Immaculate Conception', *Wesleyan times*, 109.
107 Sinclair, *Popish legends*, p. xii.
108 Skilton, *Neither inconsistency, nor unfaithfulness*, p. 22.
109 (Horne) *Mariolatry*, p. 37. See also (Croly) 'The new article of "faith"', 80; 'The Immaculate Conception', *Wesleyan–Methodist magazine*, 531; (Francis Sitwell) *The recent Decree on the Immaculate Conception of the Blessed Virgin Mary: a sign of the present time. A sermon preached at Albury, on the twenty-fifth of December, 1854* (London: Thomas Bosworth, 1855), p. 14.
110 Maudson, 'The dogma of the Virgin Mary's Immaculate Conception', 237; emphasis in original.
111 Lingwood, *Was the Virgin Mary Immaculate?*, p. 15.
112 (Wilberforce) *Rome*, p. 22.
113 For more on the differences between Protestant and Roman Catholic beliefs on original sin, see Linwood Urban, *A short history of Christian thought*, rev. and expanded edn (New York and Oxford: Oxford University Press, 1995), pp. 144–5; and Edward Yarnold, S.J., *The theology of original sin* (Notre Dame, IN: Fides Publishers, 1971), p. 79.
114 Protestants did not cite Article 15, 'Of Christ alone without sin', which was directed against the Anabaptists and probably not intended to counteract belief in the Immaculate Conception: E. J. Bicknell, *A theological introduction to the thirty-nine articles of the Church of England*, 2nd edn (London: Longmans, Green, & Co., 1925), p. 220.
115 Thomas Jackson, *The works of the reverend, learned, and pious divine, Thomas Jackson, D.D.* (London: John Martin, Richard Chiswell, and Joseph Clark, 1673), vol. 3, p. 6; emphasis in original.
116 Aitken, *Mission sermons*, p. 113.
117 Sinclair, *A letter on the principles of Christian faith*, p. 10; emphasis in original.
118 Bradley, *Practical and parochial sermons* (New York: Appleton, 1849), p. 179.
119 Although Augustine has often been blamed for imposing a negative view of human sexuality on the West, in fact he thought that human sexuality had been part of Paradise. Augustine saw post-lapsarian human sexuality as one sign of humanity's fallen nature because it was uncontrollable, not because it was evil in and of itself. He does, however, strongly condemn concupiscence, and there are suggestions in both his *Confessions* and *The city of God* that original sin is transmitted through sexual intercourse, an argument he made in part to combat the Pelagians' contention that original sin was acquired, not inherited: Peter Brown, *The body and society: men, women, and sexual renunciation in early Christianity* (New York: Columbia University Press, 1988),

chapter 19; Yarnold, *The theology of original sin*, pp. 28, 57, 78–9. This belief was shared by other Church Fathers: Ambrose, for example, believed that Christ would not have been without sin had he been conceived in the normal way: Yarnold, *The theology of original sin*, p. 28.

120 Miller, 'The Immaculate Conception', 427; see also Maudson, 'The dogma of the Virgin Mary's Immaculate Conception', 236.

121 Michael Mason, *The making of Victorian sexual attitudes* (Oxford and New York: Oxford University Press, 1994), p. 3.

122 Frederick W. Robertson, *Sermons on Christian doctrine* (London and Toronto: J. M. Dent & Sons and New York: E. P. Dutton, 1921), pp. 26–7.

123 Pope, 'Immaculate and powerful', pp. 181–2.

124 'The pope's encyclical letter', *British banner*, 2: 69 (25 April 1849), 266; emphasis in original.

125 (Croly) 'The new article of "faith"', 80.

126 Armstrong, *Armstrong's reply*, p. 9.

127 Sinclair, *Beatrice*, p. 70.

128 Sinclair, *Beatrice*, p. 83; also pp. 86, 87.

129 Cumming, *The Immaculate Conception*, pp. 6–7.

130 Gay, *The bourgeois experience*, vol. 1, p. 140.

131 Other historians who have strongly questioned the incorporation of this ideal into private life include Carl Degler, 'What ought to be and what was: women's sexuality in the nineteenth century', *American historical review*, 79 (1974), 1467–90; and Peterson, *Family, love and work*.

5

The Virgin Mary and the formation
of Victorian masculinities

Victorian religion was, at the official level, largely a masculine enterprise. In neither church nor chapel (with a few exceptions) could women preach or hold positions of authority; their role in religious assemblies as in the home was to support male authority. The clergy would appear to have been well-positioned to take advantage of the religious endorsement of masculine authority, given the sanction of their profession as well as their sex. However, in the nineteenth century clerical authority began to diminish as church attendance declined, women began to take more prominent roles within organised religion, and Christian beliefs were challenged by secular forces, especially advances in scientific knowledge. One of the paradoxes of this religious age was that although Christianity apparently ratified masculine authority, the clergy were feeling besieged. Some attempted to retrench their authority by working with or for the poor and working classes who were often unchurched: they advocated church-building programmes, especially in urban areas where there was a severe shortage of pews, as Edward Bouverie Pusey did in Leeds; they wrote in support of them, as Charles Kingsley did under the pseudonym 'Parson Lot'; they supported their strikes, as Henry Edward Manning did; they served poor parishes, as did Charles Fuge Lowder of St Peter's, London docks. Others responded intellectually: they opposed new ideas that they believed threatened truths historically regarded to be central to Christianity, as Samuel Wilberforce did in his famous 1860 debate with Thomas Huxley; or they sought to eliminate the challenge posed by scientific ideas by arguing that those ideas represented no real threat to Christian truths.

This chapter considers another, previously unexamined, response of the clergy to their declining authority: some clerics defined the Catholic Virgin Mary in such a way that they could then define a masculine self-identity that would withstand the challenges of contemporary society.

(The Protestant Mary was not a strong enough figure for either Catholic men to react against or Protestant men to champion.) Whether the clergy defined their masculine identity against the Catholic Virgin Mary or in conjunction with her, this was a two-way process: they defined her in order to define themselves. I am not suggesting a simple equation in which they seized on representations of the Virgin Mary as a way to bolster their authority as men or as clerics. However, the different ways in which they chose to define the Virgin Mary, while influenced by theology, their own religious traditions, and the culture in which they lived, also enabled them to assert their authority as men. Useful to understanding this process are the 'two key propositions' articulated by Michael Roper and John Tosh: that 'masculinity (like femininity) is a *relational* construct, incomprehensible apart from the totality of gender relations; and that it is shaped in relation to men's social power'.[1]

In examining four individuals who constructed different types of clerical self-identity when they described the Virgin Mary, this chapter offers a microcosmic view of the arguments laid out more broadly in chapters 2–4. These four different types of masculinity are not necessarily the only ones that could be shaped in response to this iconographic woman, but they are deserving of detailed study because they were articulated by men whose public profiles ensured that their self-fashionings would be widely disseminated. Furthermore, each of these men left behind extensive documentation about his attitudes towards gender relations in general, making it possible to situate his image of the Virgin Mary in a larger context. The common Protestant position was the repression of the feminine within. This was the position of men like Charles Kingsley who were initially drawn to the maternal nurture the Virgin Mary represented but who subsequently felt compelled to reject both her and what they saw as their own weakness. A more nuanced position, exemplified by Edward Bouverie Pusey, was to define women as praiseworthy but ultimately subordinate to men. Commending the Virgin Mary for her uniquely feminine qualities while limiting her public role allowed these men to honour the feminine while retaining their authority within the Church and the family. A less common but no less effective approach was that taken by Frederick W. Faber, who celebrated the Virgin Mary as a superior but unique woman so that the feminine could be accessed but her power could not be shared by other women. Finally, there was the masculine self-identity exemplified by John Henry Newman, one that, less anxious about gender roles and distinctions, accepted the feminine and the masculine as compatible rather than competitive.

Examining these four types helps to fill a gap in masculinity studies:

notwithstanding the cultural significance of Christianity in Victorian England, studies of Victorian masculinity rarely include clergymen among their subjects. When they do, they generally consider them as men, not as clerics. Brian Heeney's *A different kind of gentleman*[2] and Anthony Russell's *The clerical profession*[3] both examine, as their titles suggest, clergymen as professionals without considering how their formation of a masculine identity differed from that of other gentlemen. John Tosh has offered an insightful analysis of the types of masculinity developed by the Benson men, yet he treats Edward Benson's clerical occupation as just another profession, rather than one that posed special problems for developing a masculine self-identity.[4] James Eli Adams classes clergymen with those whose labours were intellectual, with the consequence that he considers one part of the challenge but not all of it. Notable exceptions to this approach are recent essays by Philip Healy, Lori M. Miller, and Frederick S. Roden that analyse the roles of theology and spirituality in the shaping of a masculine identity.[5] These exceptions should become the norm as scholars recognise that the clerical profession posed specific problems in the formation of a masculine identity. The Marian debates reveal that the clerical profession provided unique opportunities for its members to define a masculine identity that, while distinct from the more common models with a greater reliance on worldly success or physical strength, was potentially more able to withstand feminist challenges.

Masculinity and Christianity

In the nineteenth century clerical authority declined as Christian beliefs, and the biblical backing on which they depended, were increasingly challenged by a variety of new ways of thinking, including evolutionary theories and the development of Higher Criticism. Clerical authority was challenged also by the laity within the Established Church, as was shown by Parliament's decision to abolish many of the Irish bishoprics in 1833 (the impetus for Keble's 'National apostacy' sermon that marks the beginning of the Oxford Movement) and by the lay Privy Council's Gorham decision. Furthermore, declining church attendance meant that fewer people heard, or apparently even thought they needed to hear, the sermons that constituted a primary means by which clergymen exerted their authority. The 1851 religious census revealed that only about half the people in England and Wales attended church services.[6] The downwards trend continued over the course of the nineteenth century, especially in urban areas. By the beginning of the twentieth century only about 20 per cent of London's population regularly attended church.

Another, albeit more nebulous, potential challenge to the authority of the clergy was the popular notion that women were more spiritual than men. Crediting women with a higher spirituality was not intended to challenge clerical authority, because female influence was supposed to be simple and confined to the domestic sphere, leaving public pronouncements and the study of theology to men. However, in practice it could do so: if women were innately spiritual, they might reasonably conclude that they had no need to subordinate themselves to male religious guidance. A few women did seem to reach that conclusion: in 1860 Catherine Booth began preaching alongside, and sometimes in place of, her husband (a decision that eventually allowed other Salvation Army women to preach), and Florence Nightingale recorded her heterodox religious views in *Suggestions for thought* (the proofs of which led Manning to discourage her from converting to Roman Catholicism[7]). Scholars have described some Victorian women writers, including Christina Rossetti, Harriet and Jemima Newman, and Charlotte Yonge, as theologians, arguing that their contributions to religious discussions merit that title.[8] This valorising of women's fiction and poetry would likely not have been understood by their Victorian readers or perhaps even by the women themselves. However, the limited number of public challenges to male religious authority did not necessarily lessen the clergy's perception that the spiritual woman was a competitor. Certainly Protestant clergymen's highlighting Jesus' rebuke of Mary when she interfered in his public work suggests an anxiety that a stated belief in women's moral superiority could allow women to challenge men's monopoly on religion in the public sphere. While Catholicism's emphasis on priestly authority could forestall a feminist challenge, Protestants found it difficult to access that option, given their less exalted view of the clerical role and the fact that some Protestant denominations either allowed women to preach or had done in the recent past.

The erosion of clerical authority was especially evident in the Church of England's loss of cultural and political as well as religious authority throughout the nineteenth century. Anglicans lost their monopoly on parliamentary seats from 1828 onwards, when dissenters were admitted, followed by Roman Catholics (1829), Jews (1858), and atheists (1886). They lost their monopoly on the ancient universities in 1854, with the abolition of religious tests at Cambridge and Oxford. The problem of lay authority over the Church, exercised through Parliament and the Privy Council, was compounded when non-Anglican laity entered those bodies. As Paz notes, in the nineteenth century 'the Church [of England] had an embattled mentality, largely because it really was threatened from all sides'.[9]

The secular world offered little support to clergy undergoing this erosion of authority. Clerics were unable to conform to the dominant Victorian models of masculinity, which demanded worldly success and stature that were at odds with many of the professed values of Christianity. The erosion of clerical authority was also related to the decline of men's domestic authority, as the ideology of separate spheres designated the home as the woman's sphere. This occurred in spite of the fact that the unstable ideology of separate spheres was not, nor could ever be, fully implemented. Nevertheless, it was a powerful cultural force, especially for the middle and upper classes who were most associated with it. John Tosh has shown that separate spheres were maintained even in middle-class families where the father worked in or close to the home: 'the separation of spheres was centrally a matter of mental compartmentalisation which did not necessarily depend on a physical gulf between home and work. Whether the husband worked at home or used it merely as a refuge, he had little to do with domestic labour or domestic management.'[10] This does not mean that domesticity was divorced from masculinity. On the contrary, as Tosh has persuasively argued, domesticity was a key factor in asserting a masculine self-identity, beginning with the process of establishing a household.[11] Nevertheless, the psychological gulf created in part by men's overall lack of involvement in the daily household management would have been more likely to affirm, rather than to contest, the ideology of separate spheres on the individual level. The effects of industrialisation, including the increasing separation of home and work and the gradual withdrawal of children from the labour force, would also have led, especially in the working classes, to the father's growing distance from his children. This the educated classes had already experienced: boys of the elite could be sent to boarding school as early as the age of 3. Certainly many of the men who wrote about the Virgin Mary, including Pusey and Kingsley, experienced this distance from their fathers. It does not seem to have determined their views of the Virgin Mary, however, as Pusey had, in general, a positive view of her, while Kingsley ultimately saw her as a threat to masculine self-rule.

Laymen from the middle and working classes could respond to these changes by emphasising characteristics designated masculine, especially competitiveness, physicality, and an aggressive sexuality. Victorian clergymen, however, found it increasingly difficult to conform to the dominant models of masculinity, thanks in large part to the evangelical revival, which began in the second half of the eighteenth century, and the Oxford Movement. Both movements emphasised personal holiness and discouraged clergymen from pursuits that were typically masculine (at least for the educated and property-owning classes) such as riding, shooting and hunting, dancing, and gambling. Mark Robarts, the cleric in Anthony Trollope's *Framley parsonage*, illustrates the dilemma men in his profession faced: as he is drawn into the aristocratic world of debts, high-priced horses, and dubious morals, he is uncomfortably aware that all of this is especially forbidden to him. His patroness, Lady Lufton, condemns him with her remark: 'Mr Robarts' character as a clergyman should have kept him from such troubles, if no other feeling did so.'[12] Pusey, though never so gay a figure as Mark Robarts, avoided such chastisement when he gave up pleasures such as hunting and novel-reading following his encounters with Pietists in Germany.[13]

Since clerics were generally barred from demonstrating physical prowess – or at least this was not a source of stature for them – some sought to define their intellectual work as masculine against the common perception that it was feminine and passive. As Adams has noted, they could do so by emphasising their self-discipline and identifying themselves as gentlemen: 'The gentleman was thereby rendered compatible with a masculinity understood as a strenuous psychic regimen, which could be affirmed outside the eco nomic arena, but nonetheless would be embodied as a charismatic self-mastery akin to that of the daring yet disciplined entrepreneur.'[14] A more obvious role model for clergymen was Jesus. Unfortunately for them, however, traditional representations of Jesus bore little resemblance to the ideal Victorian man: 'the meek and lowly Jesus',[15] as an anonymous female writer described him at mid-century, was born into poverty, lived in relative obscurity, and died one of the most disgraceful deaths the Roman Empire could impose. He was a far cry from the ideal Victorian man who was supposed to strive and win, first on the playing fields, and then in the brutally competitive marketplace, in the military, or in Parliament.

Jesus' apparent celibacy placed him further at odds with the masculine ideal. The importance of the family meant that life-long celibacy was not a Victorian value, especially for men. This was clear in the accusations that priestly celibacy – which was mandatory for Roman Catholics and increasingly popular among advanced Anglicans – was unnatural. Kingsley condemned Roman Catholic priests as 'prurient celibates' and scorned celibate men as 'not God's ideal of a man, but an effeminate shaveling's ideal',[16] while the historian Richard T. Hampson was convinced that the '*Celibacy* of priests is of Pagan origin and signification'.[17] The vast majority of Victorian Christians who rejected life-long celibacy had to acknowledge, however, that Jesus was apparently a celibate. There is no suggestion in Scripture that he had a wife or children, which in any case would have enormously complicated Christian theology by positing a race of semi-divine descendants. In order to allow a celibate Jesus to fulfill the masculine role of creating a family, Protestants insisted that his dismissive response to his mother and brothers' interruption of his preaching demonstrated that he had abandoned his biological family for the spiritual one he had formed. Jesus, William Thomas Maudson declared, 'took occasion from the circumstance, to disparage, and almost to disclaim, this earthly relationship, and to represent it as decidedly inferior to that resulting from a spiritual connexion'.[18]

In spite of the gulf between the biblical Jesus and the ideal Victorian man, the Victorian church witnessed the curious attempt to merge the two, or at least to make them compatible. Muscular Christianity, described by Adams as a 'peculiar amalgam of athletic and devotional rhetoric',[19] was more significant in its cultural outreach to working-class men than in its reconfiguring of Jesus' image, but it was nevertheless important as a symptom of the anxiety some Victorian men felt about their self-identity. One of the classic expressions of this attempt to describe Jesus as the premier example of masculinity was Thomas Hughes's 'arresting little book',[20] *The Manliness of Christ*. Better known as the author of the Tom Brown books, Hughes found Christ to be 'the true model of the courage and manliness'[21] because he was patient, disciplined, focused, and reliable. Although Hughes believed that '[t]rue manliness is as likely to be found in a weak as in a strong body',[22] he hoped that Jesus' cleansing of the Temple 'should satisfy those who think courage best proved by physical daring'.[23]

Muscular Christianity had at best limited success in redefining the image of Jesus. Peter Gay has argued that the Jesus described by Hughes did not exemplify muscular Christianity because his masculinity was ultimately premissed on his suffering.[24] I would broaden the focus to argue that the suffering of Hughes's Jesus was only the final example of his submission to God's will, for Hughes describes Jesus as being 'in perfect accord with the will of God'[25] throughout his life. While submission to the will of another was hardly a hallmark of Victorian masculinity, the noted Brighton preacher Frederick W. Robertson attempted to redefine it as a masculine quality by describing Jesus' suffering as exemplifying masculine self-sufficiency:

[T]he strength that is in a man can be only learnt when he is thrown upon his own resources and left alone. What a man can do in conjunction with others does not test the man ... It is one thing to rush on to danger with the shouts and the sympathy of numbers: it is another thing when the lonely chieftain of the sinking ship sees the last boatful disengage itself, and folds his arms to go down into the majesty of darkness, crushed, but not subdued.

Such and greater far was the strength and majesty of the Saviour's solitariness.[26]

Robertson's image was unconvincing because the comparison was inexact. While Robertson deemed the captain who drowned rather than to take up a place in a rescue boat noble and courageous, at the most – and this part is not clear – the captain may have allowed someone else to be saved. In contrast, Christians believed that Jesus' death saved all of humanity. Because Robertson does not explicitly say that the captain gave up his life to save another's, an alternative but equally plausible reading of his analogy is to conclude that the captain's death was an act of self-destruction in the guise of noble sacrifice. While Robertson's example illustrates the difficulty of finding contemporary comparisons to Jesus' suffering as described in all four gospels, the problem lay in the attempt generally, rather than in the specific example. In fact, all of the efforts to define Jesus as an impressively self-reliant man failed, because the gospels describe a man whose actions and sense of self are at odds with the values of muscular Christianity.

The impossibility of remaking the image of Jesus to conform to the demands of muscular Christianity was only the most obvious reason for the failure of that movement. Another was that defining both Christ and his worshippers as masculine excluded women, who made up the majority of worshippers. When the Anglican cleric George Croly determined that Christianity was 'a manly religion, addressed to manly understandings, and to be taught in manly language,'[27] and called for 'a large body of active, vigorous, and learned men, superintending the Establishment, and especially marshalling its learning and ability, for the contest with Sectarianism,'[28] or when Hughes assured his audience that the 'conscience of every man recognises courage as the foundation of manliness, and manliness as the perfection of human character,'[29] they blatantly ignored more than half of their congregations. Even when Hughes acknowledged the reality of female Christians he did not modify his basic understanding of Christianity as a masculine religion: 'And then comes one of the most searching of all trials of courage and manliness, when a man or woman is called to stand by what approves itself to their consciences as true, and to protest for it through evil report and good report, against all discouragement and opposition from those they love or respect.'[30] He left his audience with the ludicrous image of a woman undergoing 'trials of courage and manliness'. Furthermore, the vigorous, at times even martial, language of those clergy who preached muscular Christianity left little room for traditional

Christian virtues such as patience, humility, and charity.

Finally, by positing a more limited and rigid definition of masculinity that virtually excluded women, muscular Christianity created the opportunity for a separate feminine presence to emerge; and that may have been an underlying factor in the failure of the movement. In part to avoid this complication, Victorian Christians often abandoned the manly Jesus in favour of a Saviour who was described in feminine terms,[31] a project that had a counterpart in Victorian paintings – including William Holman Hunt's *The Light of the World*, *The shadow of death*, and *The finding of the Saviour in the Temple*; Ford Madox Brown's *Christ washing Peter's feet*; and John Everett Millais's *Jesus in the house of his parents* – that depicted Jesus as feminine, or even effeminate.[32] Mrs Ellis defined Jesus, in *The daughters of England*, as the exemplar of feminine virtues to the extent that, as Claudia Nelson has argued: 'By the climax of the book, indeed, she is implicitly comparing women to Christ, the only man ever to exhibit the feminine self-sacrifice, pure devotion, and "capacity for exquisite and intense enjoyment."'[33] The nonconformist cleric Henry Hamlet Dobney found Jesus to be 'the compassionate Redeemer'[34] and assured Victorians that artists generally 'assume a predominance of the feminine in him',[35] while the traditional high-church cleric Augustin Gaspard Edouart relied on 'the Lord Jesus's boundless mercy, tender love, and abundant compassion',[36] and praised Jesus as 'an omniscient, merciful, all-powerful, tenderly loving Mediator, who is exactly suited to our need and requirements'.[37]

Feminine and masculine qualities alternated here, as if Edouart wanted to insist that they were as completely intermingled as were Jesus' human and divine natures. The Victorian stereotype of the loving mother as the counterpoint to the stern father who went out into the brutal world of the marketplace provided the antidote to the brutal competition associated with the public sphere. Jesus, as he was traditionally represented, did not require a feminine counterpoint to his work of salvation, which ignored the boundary between public and private, as he himself was represented in the gospels and in the Christian tradition as obscuring the distinctions between masculine and feminine. Describing Jesus as both masculine and feminine eliminated Mary (and the feminine generally) as a competitor to the masculine as embodied by the Saviour, the role model especially for the clergy. It did not, however, solve the problem for Victorian clerics, who did not generally see themselves as embodying feminine as well as masculine traits. A more promising solution to the quandary of their declining authority was to define the Virgin Mary as a particular type of the feminine, against or in conjunction with which they could define themselves as independent men.

Repression of the feminine within: Charles Kingsley

The most famous practitioner of muscular Christianity was Charles Kingsley. Although Kingsley loathed the term that Hughes embraced,[38] Protestant Christianity and an exuberant approach to life were both essential to his ideal man. Kingsley's ideal of manhood, as defined in his sermons, novels, essays, and personal correspondence, was a married Protestant who was privileged but sympathetic towards workers, physically fit, and confident without being arrogant. He was honest, chivalrous, and eager to leave domestic comforts for unknown parts of the world. Perhaps it was this love of adventure that prompted Kingsley to have his heroes bearded: presumably men wandering the world have little time to shave. The beard, though, also gave Kingsley's characters another opportunity to assert their manliness. Claude Mellot, who embodies a type of muscular Christianity in *Yeast*, defends his beard as 'natural'[39] and thus as an indicator of Protestant manliness:

> I wear it for a testimony and a sign that a man has no right to be ashamed of the mark of manhood. Oh, that one or two of your Protestant clergymen, who ought to be the perfect ideal man, would have the courage to get into the pulpit in a long beard, and testify that the very essential idea of Protestantism is the dignity and divinity of man as God made him! Our forefathers were not ashamed of their beards; but now ... in proportion to a man's piety he wears less hair, from the young curate who shaves off his whiskers, to the Popish priest who shaves his crown.[40]

Kingsley, like Mellot, believed that the antithesis of the good (and, generally, good-looking) English Protestant man was a Catholic – usually Roman Catholic, but sometimes Anglo-Catholic. Catholic men, in Kingsley's worldview, were, quite simply, effeminate, with all that that word implied to the Victorians: they were dishonest, physically unimpressive, and celibate. Perhaps his best-known, and ill-fated, expression of anti-Catholicism was his 1863 attack on Newman, 'What, then does Doctor Newman mean?' Kingsley's off-handed jibe – 'Truth for its own sake has never been a virtue of the Roman clergy. Father Newman informs us that it need not and on the whole ought not to be'[41] – inspired a flurry of correspondence between Newman, the publisher, and Kingsley; Newman's final salvo, in 1864, was *Apologia pro vitâ suâ*, the chronicle of his spiritual development until his conversion.

A key weapon in Kingsley's campaign to define Catholic men as effeminate was the depiction of the Virgin Mary as a powerful woman whom Catholics invoked more often than Jesus. In *Westward Ho!*, one of the primary Catholic figures is Eustace Leigh, a weak and deceitful man who eventually becomes a Jesuit priest (the epitome, in the Victorian age, of Roman Catholic deviousness). His priestly vocation is delayed, however, by his unsuccessful courtship of Rose, the novel's first heroine. His attempts at love-making, which resemble stalking more than romancing, are preceded by mumbled consultations with the Virgin, suggesting, if not that Mary encouraged men to treat women badly, at least that men who did not respect female virtue were likely to be drawn to the Virgin Mary. Failing to win Rose's love, Eustace Leigh then attempts to win her for his Church, one represented by the Virgin Mary. He begs Rose to enter 'the bosom of that Church where a Virgin Mother stands stretching forth soft arms to embrace her wandering daughter, and cries to you all day long, "Come unto me, ye that are weary and heavy laden, and I will give you rest!"'.[42] Placing Jesus' words from Mt 11:28 in Mary's mouth was a less-than-subtle way of making the familiar point that Catholics replaced Jesus with his mother. Rose, who remains a faithful English Protestant even though by this point she is married to a Spanish Roman Catholic, rejects his clumsy attempts at proselytising as she had previously rejected his offers of love.

Yeast, a novel Kingsley wrote to defend 'the faith of our forefathers'[43] against the twin threats of Catholicism and scepticism,[44] also described the Virgin as a powerful mother who diverted attention away from God. It stated more clearly the corollary, one often specified by Protestants, that such a woman appealed to men who wished to renounce maturity and reason. Luke,[45] a Tractarian priest who in the course of the novel converts to Roman Catholicism, personifies the effeminate man Kingsley associated with Marian devotion. Luke is a pathetic creature who admits, between long dramatic pauses, that the Virgin Mary satisfies his desire for a mother who will guide and protect him:

> I am weak ... I am longing to be once more an infant on a mother's breast ... I am a weary child, who knows nothing ... Will you reproach me because when I see a soft cradle lying open for me ... with a Virgin Mother's face smiling down all woman['s] love above it ... I long to crawl into it, and sleep awhile? I want loving, indulgent sympathy ... I want detailed, explicit guidance.[46]

Throughout the novel, Luke reiterates his desire to seek the Virgin Mary, even when it means abandoning his bankrupt father. Lancelot Smith, one of the novel's examplars of manly Christianity, rejects his cousin's retreat into infancy: 'I am not a child, but a man; I want not a mother to pet, but a man to rule me.'[47] That Lancelot's views were Kingsley's is confirmed by a letter, written to a country rector at about the same time, in which he complained of the Roman Catholic Church's 'substituting a Virgin Mary, who is to *nurse* them like infants, for a Father in whom they are men and brothers'.[48] Instead, Kingsley urged Christians to turn 'to the strong *man*, Christ Jesus – stern because loving – who does not shrink from punishing, and yet does it as a man would do it, "*mighty* to save"'.[49] Masculine chastisement, in other words, was both necessary for salvation and evidence of Jesus' love. Kingsley condemned Catholics for wrongly seeking a human mother rather than a divine redeemer, and a woman instead of a man. Kingsley's implication that only a man was strong enough to turn to the man who would, if necessary, punish him made both worshipper and God masculine. The association between Catholics (*Yeast* being an anti-Tractarian as well as anti-Roman Catholic novel) and the Virgin Mary allowed Kingsley to argue that real men – which is to say real Englishmen – were Protestant.

Kingsley's depiction of the Catholic Virgin Mary as a semi-pagan goddess who replaced Jesus as the focus of worship was one aspect of his well-known anti-Catholicism. That prejudice, which was an integral part of his personal and professional identity, permeates his writing in all genres. Kingsley's anti-Catholicism had several sources. When he first met his future wife, Fanny Grenfell, she was considering joining Pusey's Anglican sisterhood, a fate he rescued her from by allowing her to save him from unbelief.[50] He also despised the Roman Catholic Church's high valuation of celibacy and its obstruction of Italian unifica-tion. What is psychologically significant, especially in the context of his Marian representations, is that Kingsley's anti-Catholicism was also an attempt to repudiate his own early attraction to Catholicism. He once, he confessed, had 'longed for Rome, and boldly faced the consequences of joining Rome'.[51] So strong was this attraction that his biographer, Brenda Colloms, wrote: 'It is by no means inconceivable that if Charles Kingsley had not met Fanny Grenville, and had remained a bachelor, he would not have become an Anglo-Catholic – he was always attracted by the style and ceremony of the Catholic service'.[52]

Thus in order to fashion an identity as an independent and rational man, Kingsley had to deny aspects of his own personality, of which his attraction to Catholicism was one manifestation. Catholicism, especially Roman Catholicism, was popularly stereotyped as an irrational, emotional, and highly decorative religion that particularly appealed to women and unmanly men. Kingsley, for all his rhetorical championing of manly Protestantism, fell far short of that ideal. He was engaged in intellectual work – writing, preaching, and lecturing – and was often in poor health; he had eight breakdowns between 1848 and 1859, and a final one in 1864.[53] A trip to the West Indies in 1869–70 and a lecture tour in North America in 1874 were his only excursions abroad; he was not even bearded. More damning for his masculine self-identity, his contemporaries often saw him as emotional and even womanly. As Adams has noted, 'Kingsley's obsessive, furious attacks on "Jesuit" effeminacy and treachery, not only in his famous controversy with Newman but throughout novels, periodical articles, sermons, and letters, have suggested to many commentators a nearly hysterical disavowal of unsettling features of his own character.'[54]

It was no wonder, then, that he felt compelled to reject vociferously the most feminine part of this allegedly effeminate religion. Kingsley was not just denouncing the Catholic Mary; he was repudiating what he considered to be his own weakness and error in desiring Rome. And he did so in order to define himself as the type of man he celebrated: a rational, independent, Protestant man. This self-definition depended on depicting women as weaker than men and, in their weakness, potentially dangerous to those men they wished to remake in their image. Although Kingsley described the Virgin Mary as an overpowering mother, more often he saw women as threatening in their weakness. This is the drama that is enacted in *Yeast*: Argemone, the woman Lancelot loves, is a threat to masculinity, as evidenced by her Tractarianism and her campaign against Mellot's beard. Her death at the end of the novel, even though occasioned by editorial constraints rather than authorial vision, frees the men to go on a quest for knowledge. Even her plainer but more useful sister Honoria is sacrificed at the end, confirming that the artificial limits the feminine imposed on the masculine must be repudiated, by death if necessary. The Virgin Mary, of course, could not be dismissed so easily. However, her presence served Kingsley's purposes better than did Argemone's absence: his caricature of the Virgin Mary as an overbearing mother who infantilised men allowed Kingsley to set up rational Protestant men in opposition to her.

Kingsley's ambivalence towards the Catholic Virgin Mary also reflected his relationship with his own mother, a strong-willed woman. For the first several years of his life, Kingsley was a sickly boy who often slept in his mother's bedroom, while she doted on him to the extent that she wrote down his boyish sermons and proudly showed them to the bishop. At the end of her life, she came to live with the Kingsleys at Eversley. Kingsley, then, knew what it was like to have an overbearing mother, and there are indications that he sought to distance himself from her. For example, when he went to the West Indies near the end of his life, he ignored his mother's request to visit her family's homestead. Kingsley's desire for a strong masculine figure may also have been the result of his awareness of his parents' unhappy marriage, the failure of which, Chitty speculates, may have resulted from 'the contrast between her husband's ineffectual personality and her own bustling and organising one'.[55]

Kingsley's desire to celebrate masculine strength and to distance himself from feminine weakness, however, was not easily achieved. Consciously or unconsciously, he sabotaged his own attempts to align himself with the independent male. While overtly rejecting the nurturing mother who encouraged perpetual infancy, in *Yeast* Kingsley actually provided a sympathetic portrait of the mother who would shelter the 'weary child'. While the reader was meant to disdain Luke's unmanly desires, there is evidence that Kingsley, too, was struggling to reject them. This ambivalence emerges more clearly in the portrait of Mrs Leigh, mother of Amyas Leigh, the hero of *Westward Ho!* Although the Virgin Mary is associated with Jesuits and the Spanish enemy in Kingsley's novel, he draws a sympathetic portrait of a Madonna-like mother in the figure of Mrs Leigh. Her Protestant credentials are impeccable, being the daughter of 'one of Queen Catherine's bedchamber women, and the bosom friend and disciple of Anne Askew',[56] a Protestant martyr under Henry VIII. The narrator praised her as being 'one of those noble old English church-women, without superstition, and without severity, who are among the fairest features of that heroic time'.[57] She loves her sons and regrets their leaving for the New World, although she does not attempt to hinder their going. Even when a blinded Amyas returns from his adventures, she does not try to keep him within her sphere of influence; in fact, she helps to civilise Ayancora so that she will be a suitable wife for Amyas.

Mrs Leigh, then, was the stereotypical good Protestant mother who allowed her son to grow into an independent man. However, Kingsley's self-discipline slipped early in the novel, when he drew an intimate portrait of the relationship between mother and son. The scene when Amyas Leigh rises in the middle of the night to join his mother, who is kneeling in prayer in her bedroom, is both a love scene and a scene of worship, resonant of medieval chivalric scenes in which the acolyte's adoration of the Madonna echoed that of the knight's prostration before the maiden:

> At last she rose, and standing above him, parted the yellow locks from off his brow, and looked long and lovingly into his face. There was nothing to be spoken, for there was nothing to be concealed between these two souls as clear as glass. Each knew all which the other meant; each knew that its own thoughts were known. At last the mutual gaze

was over; she stooped and kissed him on the brow, and was in the act to turn away, as a tear dropped on his forehead. Her bare little feet were peeping out from under her dress. He bent down and kissed them again and again; and then looking up, as if to excuse himself, – 'You have such pretty feet, mother!' ... 'What is that to you, silly boy? Will you play the lover with an old mother? Go and take your walk, and think of younger ladies, if you can think of any worthy of you.'[58]

This could easily be mistaken for a love scene: it takes place at night, in a woman's bedroom, between 'two souls' who understand each other without speaking. Mrs Leigh's somewhat awkward injunction to her son not to mistake her for a lover only underscores the repressed eroticism, or at least romance, of the encounter. It is also a devotional scene, with Amyas Leigh gazing up worshipfully into the eyes of the mother before kissing her tiny feet, just as Catholic worshippers sometimes kissed the feet of a statue (to the horror of those Victorian Protestants who witnessed such scenes during their continental travels). Kingsley attempted to justify this worship, first by having the Protestant hero worship his mother rather than the Madonna, and then by having the mother reject such worship. However, what clearly emerges is Kingsley's desire to worship the mother, which in this case was channelled towards a more acceptable Protestant mother who gently teased her beloved son as she stepped down from the pedestal which both Amyas Leigh and Kingsley thought she deserved. The lasting impression left by the scene is not, however, Mrs Leigh's injunction to her son to find a suitable woman, but the intense communion between idealised mother and worshipping son. Their ability to communicate with looks rather than words is an indictment of Amyas's relationship with Ayancora, when at the end of the novel the now-blinded lover is unable to share with his future wife the intense, wordless communication he enjoyed with his mother.

Kingsley's ambivalence towards the Catholic Virgin Mary was similar to that expressed by John William Burgon and Michael Hobart Seymour on their visits to Italy. All three men briefly indulged their desires for a loving mother before recovering enough to reject this apparent threat to masculine self-sufficiency and maturity. Their desires, admitted and then rejected, showed the utility of the Virgin Mary to men who wished to draw a sharp line between masculine and feminine: rejecting her, they also renounced their own desires for a strong maternal presence in order to position themselves as independent Protestant men.

The feminine exalted and restrained: Edward Bouverie Pusey

Pusey was less conflicted about his masculine identity than was Kingsley, and thus he approached the Virgin Mary more calmly. As a theologian, his view of the Virgin Mary was more overtly grounded in Scripture and tradition than was Kingsley's. He described her as a virtuous woman who was blessed in being the mother of Jesus and even as a model Christian. Nevertheless, he also defined the Virgin Mary as an example of subordinate womanhood. He was able to solidify masculine authority not by questioning Mary's virtues or her maternal role but by limiting her sphere of influence to private life, which he achieved largely by contrasting the divine realm with the human one. In his two major works that addressed Marian devotion in the Roman Catholic Church, the *Eirenicon* and the *First letter to Newman*, as well as in sermons and private letters, Pusey articulated his esteem for the Virgin Mary while sharply limiting any action that might seem to interfere with Jesus' prerogatives. In so doing, he defined a masculine self-identity that was more assured and less strident than was Kingsley's, and so was better able to dismiss women as competitors.

Overall, Pusey exemplified the restrained Marian devotion typical of Anglo-Catholics. Confident that through her motherhood God had 'brought [her] to a nearness to Himself above all created beings',[59] Pusey was comfortable discussing the physical realities of Mary's relationship with Jesus, beginning with her pregnancy. He did not think that Mary's role was one of passive acceptance, but that she had an active part in the redemption of humanity, that she was 'a *moral* instrument of our common redemption'.[60] He held that her activity and her special status continued in heaven: both publicly and privately Pusey reiterated his belief that Mary, 'with all the inhabitants of heaven, and she more eminently than all, does pray for us',[61] although he wished to ensure that prayers to Mary and all the saints would not 'interfere with the all-sufficiency of the Intercession of our Divine Redeemer'.[62] Putting a high value on virginity, Pusey accepted the ancient legends that she had remained intact during the birth of Jesus.[63]

Catholics described Mary as an active participant in salvation in order to emphasise her virtues and her independence, all of which were dependent on her fidelity to God. However, Pusey's Marian devotion was threaded with a reluctance to accord her too much power. This was clear in his ambivalence about the extent of Mary's participation in the Incarnation. In the mid-1860s Pusey stated that 'not even the Incarnation should take place without the cooperation of His creature's free will'.[64]

Several years later, however, he retreated from this position when he argued that Mary could not have declined the angel's invitation because God had prepared her to say yes: 'He, in all eternity ... foreordained her who was to be Theotokos, Genitrix Dei, the Mother of God'.[65] Pusey further reduced the significance of Mary's participation when he stated that God's plan would not have been thwarted even had Mary refused to bear Jesus: 'the Incarnation might have been delayed for a while; it could not have failed'.[66] Thus, while not intending to question Mary's virtues, Pusey limited the scope of her actions in order to assert that God's will was not dependent on a human's response.

In general, Pusey was uncomfortable with Mary wherever she seemed to take precedence over the Trinity. For example, while he characterised Mary as the *Theotokos*, he did not consider that this title gave her any power or influence over Jesus.[67] Nor did he approve of the trope that Mary was the mother of all believers: he feared that 'this introduces a new personal relation of the Blessed Virgin to us, not indirectly through the Lord, but directly as given to her by Him'.[68] To some extent, statements like this were inspired by Church politics as well as aesthetic inclination. Pusey's more restrained description of Mary's role enabled him to position himself as a defender of Catholicism while denying that he was a secret Roman Catholic. To that end, Pusey also attacked the more flamboyant Roman Catholic devotional writers. His usual targets were continental priests like Alphonsus Liguori and Francisco de Suarez, although he was also irritated by Faber, who, Pusey complained, was 'always bringing in the devotion to the Blessed Virgin'.[69] These writers had in common a florid style and an apparent tendency to make Mary the focus of devotion (although they would have denied that the latter was either their intention or the result of their devotional writings).

Pusey was concerned with defending what he believed to be orthodox. Thus he absolutely rejected Faber's Marian devotion because he thought it assumed that Jesus was 'not willing to hear us, unless we seek a Mediatrix with Him, who is to dispose Him to hear us'.[70] Related to Pusey's concern with orthodoxy was his professed desire for reunion between the Anglican and the Roman Catholic Church. Somewhat disingenuously, he assured Newman that his goal in writing the misnamed *Eirenicon* was to find out what the Roman Catholic Church insisted was *de fide* in Marian devotion, in order to hasten Anglican–Roman Catholic reunion. If this were true, he did not begin with an open mind: he was convinced that 'this system [of Marian devotion] is the great barrier and ground of alienation of pious minds in England'.[71] Finally, we must not overlook aesthetic considerations: the relatively ascetic Pusey had a deep distaste for the unrestrained style typical of Liguori, Suarez, and Faber. Pusey's attacks on the Virgin Mary's role in the Roman Catholic Church were more about defending Anglo-Catholicism and seeking possible grounds for reunion between the Church of England and the Roman Catholic Church. More revealing of both his theology and his masculine self-identity were his positive views of the Virgin Mary. Pusey's view of Mary was akin to the more passive version of the feminine ideal that flourished in the early Victorian years: she was a devout woman whose major achievement was motherhood, yet whose maternal power was somewhat limited.

Pusey valued intellectual discipline and self-denial more than athletic displays of power; he fought in the fields of theological controversies and university politics. (In one such contest, he vanquished Kingsley: in 1863 he blocked Kingsley from getting an honourary degree at Oxford University on the grounds that his novel *Hypatia* was immoral.) Pusey's high valuation of chastity (without opposing a married clergy) seems at odds with Kingsley's almost obsessive celebration of human sexuality. However, Pusey, too, was obsessed with sexuality in that his extreme preference for celibacy, in others as well as in himself, made celibacy a negative virtue, a denial of sexuality rather than an expression of self-sufficiency or commitment to God. Although Pusey's aristocratic family imbued him with the ideal of service, his construction of masculinity owed more to the university, which privileged intellectual achievement and self-discipline and which was the environment in which he spent most of his life. Pusey's model man excelled in learning, especially theological learning, was devoutly Christian (but Catholic rather than Protestant), was chaste, loyal, honest, and disdainful of material things. Pusey's desire to limit Mary's devotional role was also consistent with his persistent attempts to maintain masculine authority in the Church: his emphasis on priestly authority, especially through the celebration of the sacraments, was another way to achieve this goal.

Even though Pusey generally lauded Mary's maternal role, he believed that excessive praise of her could lead to Christians wrongly assuming she had a large sphere of influence, one that would impinge on Jesus' work. Discomfort with the idea that Mary had any real power was consistent with Pusey's general reluctance to allow women autonomy, a reluctance that he had learned at home. Pusey's father, the 'autocratic'[72] Philip Bouverie Pusey, was 52 when he married a woman twenty-four years younger than himself. Pusey's biographer Henry Parry Liddon attributes to the age-gap and Philip's extended bachelorhood the 'certain formal stiffness, – perhaps even an austerity' that characterised the household of Pusey's youth.[73] Pusey's mother, Lady Lucy, was self-controlled to the point that she 'gave people the impression of being a very practical and unsentimental person.'[74] Somewhat surprisingly for such a reserved mother and son, the two adored each other. 'Pusey consistently attributed the greatest blessings which he had received from Almighty God to his mother's influence,'[75] although even the hagiographic Liddon suggests that Pusey may well have idealised his late mother.[76] On her side, Lady Lucy 'used to say that no child could be more obedient or industrious: she used to speak of him as her "angelic" son, a phrase which in a person of her reserved and prosaic temper was by no means a flower of rhetoric.'[77]

Pusey's upbringing had taught him a conventional model of marital harmony: the husband directed and the wife acquiesced. Liddon describes Lady Lucy as the ideal Victorian wife: 'She was a devoted wife, consulting her husband's prejudices, at whatever inconvenience to herself; she shared to the full his benevolent instincts; she reinforced, or more probably she adopted, his precise and methodical ways, and heartily carried out his wishes.'[78] Pusey implemented the pattern in his own marriage. He deeply loved his wife, Maria Barker, whom he had met when he was almost 18. Opposition from both sets of parents ensured a courtship of nine years,[79] during which time Pusey educated Maria about the theology and history of Christianity.[80] This hierarchical relationship continued in their marriage. His authority over his household was evident in his insistence that the children be punished severely for minor infractions; he also required the family to fast even when his wife was dying of tuberculosis and their children were ill.[81] While Liddon somewhat patronisingly remarks that 'the growth of her character during the eleven years of her married life was a remarkable testimony to the strength and nature of her husband's influence', as she surrendered her interest in society events and light reading for religious devotion and assisting her husband's scholarship,[82] Forrester has convincingly argued that the Puseys' marriage was a process of Pusey's breaking Maria's will so that she would conform to his outlook, to the extent that she argued with the doctor who tried to prevent her sick children from fasting.[83]

Pusey's support of Anglican sisterhoods beginning in the 1840s seems at odds with his treatment of his wife. Both Michael Hill and Susan Mumm have noted his stated belief that women should have primary control over sisterhoods.[84] Yet here he evinced a similar pattern of control: Pusey had been involved in the foundation of the Sisters of Mercy, and he continued to exercise pastoral and administrative supervision over them. Although Lydia Sellon has been deemed 'autocratic',[85] she called him 'Father' as a sign both of his pastoral authority and of their personal relationship. Mumm argues that 'Pusey had a consistently detrimental effect on any community with which he got involved', in part because of 'his love of interfering'.[86] Pusey's role in establishing sisterhoods makes it clear that his support for women's autonomy was conditional in that it was extended only to those who followed the sort of celibate, communal life he envisioned for them and who were engaged in domestic or quasi-domestic work, such as caring for orphans or the sick. He never allowed complete independence to the sisterhoods with which he was associated. Pusey's support of Anglican sisterhoods, then, was consistent with his belief in male authority, a belief that was apparent in his view of Mary.

Although Pusey's persona was less aggressively masculine than was his sometime rival's, he was more successful than Kingsley in defending a sphere of masculine authority. Because Pusey's serious and austere personality manifested no hint of any feminine tendencies, his reaction to the presence of the Virgin Mary was unmarred by hysterical disavowal of what he feared in himself. Imagining the Virgin as a model of devout femininity enabled Pusey to depict her activities as limited to those that supported masculine and divine authority. Describing Mary allowed Pusey to describe a world in which the male was the public person and the virtuous woman was subordinate. It also allowed Pusey, as priest, to associate himself with the public, authoritative man.

Celebration of the feminine: Frederick W. Faber

Both Kingsley and Pusey defined a masculine identity that, because it rejected the figure of a powerful woman, was independent and in control. Outright rejection of the woman as competitor was not, however, the only option for men who sought to define an independent manliness. As Faber showed, celebrating the Virgin as the embodiment of maternal love could also enable a man to define himself as independent.

Faber had a highly sentimental and romanticised image of the Virgin. He described her as Jesus' loving mother, who was so intimately connected with her son throughout his earthly life that she became the central figure – after the Trinity – in the story of salvation. As we saw in chapter 2, Faber delighted in imagining the emotional and physical connections between Mary and her infant. Unlike most Catholics, Faber extended Mary's involvement in Jesus' life well past the wedding at Cana. Ignoring the lack of scriptural evidence, he was certain that the final face Jesus had seen from the cross was Mary's[87] and that Jesus had appeared to his mother immediately after his resurrection.[88] Faber saw Mary as the perfect mother, and thus he seemed never able to exhaust his praise for her. 'God's dear Mother'[89] was 'the mother beyond all other mothers'[90] who was blessed with an 'excess of heavenly light which shone unsettingly upon her sinless soul'.[91] Nevertheless, Faber was typically Roman Catholic in that he understood Mary as a visible sign of God's love and goodness, rather than as an object of worship herself. As he asked rhetorically in his hymn, 'The Most Holy Trinity': 'If Mary is so beautiful,/ What must her Maker be?'[92] Moreover, Faber approached Mary as the way to God rather than believing her to be an end in herself: 'There is no time lost in seeking Him, if we go at once to Mary; for He is always there, always at home ... She is the short road to Him.'[93]

Faber was drawn towards Marian devotion while still an Anglican. In 1843 he described Mary as a reliable intercessor for the faithful,[94] and, as noted in chapter 1, at least twice in 1844 he asked Newman for permission to pray to the Virgin.[95] Marian devotion characterised the Brothers of the Will of God, the short-lived order he founded immediately after his conversion. One of the members recalled that

> certainly in those early days we seemed to live almost in the companionship of the Saints and of the Madonna ... We adopted many Italian customs and practices in devotion, especially to the Madonna. The devotion of Maria Desolata was observed every week from Friday evening to Sunday morning. On the Vigil of the Assumption the Chapel was adorned with an abundance of candles and fir trees.[96]

As a Roman Catholic, Faber was freed to become an ardent champion of Marian devotion. Telling the faithful that they could 'never have enough devotion to her, that, so far as degree is concerned, there is no possibility of excess',[97] he was convinced that the solution to England's private and public woes was 'an immense increase of devotion to our Blessed Lady'.[98]

From the beginning of his life as a Roman Catholic, Faber's Marian devotion caused concern. Roman Catholic priests who visited the Brothers of the Will of God looked askance at his addressing the Virgin as 'Mamma'.[99] After he had been ordained a Roman Catholic priest in 1847 and had founded the Oratory of St Philip Neri in London, his fellow priests became uneasy about his decorating the Lady altar with flowers and putting candles in front of pictures of the Virgin.[100] Some English priests complained to Rome that All for Jesus 'contained heresy'.[101] Impervious to the criticism, Faber told his friend the Marchese Leopoldo Bartolomei: 'Some of the old Catholics say I shall fall away and become an Apostate because I push devotion to our Blessed Lady too far.'[102]

The most controversial aspect of Faber's intense Marian devotion was his heterodox assertion that Mary's participation in Jesus' work of salvation did not end at Calvary. He believed that the physical bond between mother and son endured eternally, so that Mary's body and blood were present in the eucharistic sacrifice:

> [T]here is some portion of the Precious Blood which once was Mary's own blood, and which remains still in our Blessed Lord, incredibly exalted by its union with His Divine Person, yet still the same. This portion of Himself, it is piously believed, has not been allowed to undergo the usual changes of human substance. At this moment in heaven He retains something which once was His Mother's, and which is possibly visible, as such, to the saints and angels. He vouchsafed at mass to show to St Ignatius the very part of the Host which had once belonged to the substance of Mary.[103]

Advanced Anglicans as well as most Roman Catholics rejected this exalted role for Mary. Pusey was appalled by the notion that Mary's body and blood were in any way present in the Eucharist,[104] while Newman noted that Faber's view of the Eucharist was not approved by the Roman Catholic Church. Protesting that Mary's 'name is not heard in the administration of the sacraments',[105] Newman argued that the Church actively suppressed such heresies: 'I recollect hearing in Gregory XVI's time ... of measures taken against the shocking notion that the Blessed Mary is present in the Holy Eucharist'.[106] Nevertheless, Faber's 'pious belief', which was more typical of continental than of English Roman Catholicism,[107] illustrates his view that the mother was forever connected to her son.

The most obvious source of Faber's fervent Marian devotion was the exceptionally close relationship he had with his mother. Faber was born into a devout Anglican family in 1814, a year after two siblings had died on the same day. Not surprisingly, he was indulged by his mother, who saw him as a consolation gift for the loss of his elder siblings.[108] A deep bond formed between the two, and Faber was devastated when his mother died in 1829, when he was away at school. The Virgin Mary was certainly an emotional replacement for his mother.

Faber's Marian devotion was also a manifestation of his excessively emotional nature. He was a prolific writer and his works (the majority of which were not about Mary) were suffused with emotion. More significantly for those Victorian Protestants who sought to depict Roman Catholicism as a foreign religion, Faber's writings were popular in England, and many of them went through multiple editions.[109] Faber's style as well as his popularity made him, Chapman argues, typically Victorian:

> Faber is most nearly akin to Dickens. The reaction of Dickens [to industrialisation and utilitarianism] was the emotional reaction of the

natural man, Faber's was the emotional reaction of the spiritual man. Is it fantastic to say that what Christmas was to Dickens, Marian devotions were to Faber? It was the attempt in both cases to redress the balance, to bring back into life what had been driven out by Bentham – in the one case human brotherhood ... in the other the religion of love. The one was of his age no less than the other. Faber shows himself to be a Victorian in a hundred different ways. He is betrayed by his style, by his optimism, by his sugary taste, by his sentimentality. We don't like his referring to Our Lady as Mamma ... But, then, we also don't like Little Nell.[110]

Faber's Marian prayers were no more fervent than his other prayers. His biographer Ronald Chapman finds 'pure gold' in his devotional writings but is nevertheless forced to concede that they are 'florid',[111] 'exuberant',[112] and even 'repetitive and sentimental to an extraordinary extent'.[113] Effusions like Faber's anticipation of salvation as the resting 'forever in the Bosom of God in an endless rapture of insatiable contentment'[114] lead one to agree with Chapman.

Faber's contemporaries deemed him effeminate because of his highly emotional nature. He lacked the restraint and moderation considered essential in a culture that equated manliness with self-control. As Chapman acknowledges, 'Above all he lacked moderation. His love of exaggeration was too strong.'[115] Faber's ideal of manliness was unabashedly emotional, but it was also homosocial, and his biographers have noted the 'homosexual element in Faber's early friendships'.[116] He spent most of his life living in community with other males: first at school, then at Oxford University. As an advanced Anglican he founded an order for men, which was replaced by the Brothers of the Will of God for a short period after his conversion. Most of his life as a Roman Catholic was spent as head of the Oratory of St Philip Neri in London, which he had founded. Self-control and athleticism were not, for Faber, markers of manliness, as they were for so many Victorians of his class. However, being in control was: Faber never hesitated to let those around him know that he was in charge of the London Oratory. This led to many conflicts with Newman, whom he had once idolised, and between the London and Brompton Oratories.

It is tempting to see Faber, as a Christian and as a man, as the antithesis of Kingsley and Pusey, both of whom insisted on preserving male authority by subordinating the female. However, Faber actually shared their conservative views of gender relations. Although Faber's Victorian opponents charged that his praise of Mary undermined male authority, the opposite was true. Claiming Mary as his mother reinforced Faber's priestly identification with Jesus: if they shared a mother as well as a heavenly

Father, they were truly brothers. While the Roman Catholic identification of Mary as the mother of all meant that this familial relationship was open to all, the authority it conveyed was not. In the case of Faber and other Roman Catholic priests, whose role was that of God's representative on earth, this identification strengthened their association with Jesus, and thus their claim to speak for him on earth.

Nor did the Virgin Mary provide a model for female leadership in Faber's theology. Mary's unique role as divine mother meant that her authority was not transferrable to other women. Her example did not lift her earthly sisters from their traditional place as the inferior daughters of Eve, for they could not access the divine motherhood that was the Virgin Mary's source of authority. Faber's invocation of the Virgin Mary, then, allowed him to accomplish in one way what Pusey and Kingsley had in another. While Faber linked himself with Jesus by asserting that they shared a mother, Pusey and Kingsley identified themselves with Jesus by protecting his prerogatives and his realm of action against the usurping woman. While Faber eliminated female virtue as a challenge to male authority by embracing the Virgin Mary and highlighting her unique qualities, Pusey and Kingsley accomplished the same goal by minimising or denying those same qualities. Although Kingsley's hysterical reaction to the Virgin Mary suggested her potential for destabilising Victorian gender norms, Pusey's and Faber's praise of Mary revealed the means by which that danger could be minimised or eliminated. The Catholic Virgin Mary was therefore not so dangerous as some Victorian Protestants believed her to be. Rather than necessarily being a subversive figure who jeopardised the gender distinctions which Victorian culture strived to maintain, she could prove useful in a variety of ways to confirm male superiority.

Complementary masculinity and femininity: John Henry Newman

Kingsley, Pusey, and Faber ultimately ratified the Victorian attempt to distinguish the masculine from the feminine even if, as in Faber's case, it was done by first idealising the feminine. While this goal was typically Victorian, another option was evident in the Marian devotion of John Newman. His rich yet balanced view of Mary defined her, and by extension women in general, as complementary to men. Unlike Faber, he avoided bathos and sentimentality; unlike Pusey, he evinced no latent fear that a powerful woman might need to be restrained; unlike Kingsley, he was not torn between desire and dismay. Newman praised the Virgin

Mary as a woman chosen by God to be the Mother of God and a model for Christians, but because he saw her role as intimately connected to the divine, he had no fear that she would usurp divine prerogatives.

Although Newman's Marian devotion deepened after he converted, even as an Anglican he had had an appreciation of Mary, as evidenced by his warm descriptions of her as the woman chosen by God to bear the Saviour.[117] Although the Marian devotion of the Roman Catholic Church was one factor that kept him from converting sooner than he did, there was a consistency in his adult views of Mary, especially once he had abandoned the evangelicalism of his youth. After 1845, he elaborated on the meaning of Mary's virtues, but his basic appreciation of her as a model of faith remained. His sermons and other writings, first as an Anglican and then as a Roman Catholic, are evidence of this. Newman described the Virgin Mary as the embodiment of Christian virtues, including 'purity and innocence of heart', and a 'confiding trust in her God',[118] leavened by humility. At the Annunciation, he assured an Anglican congregation, 'She of course would feel her own inexpressible unworthiness; and again, her humble lot, her ignorance, her weakness in the eyes of the world.'[119] For Newman, as for all Catholics, the double facts that Mary was chosen to and herself chose to bear the Saviour were her key characteristics, as well as affording the justification for praising her. Thus, as noted in chapter 2, Newman happily acknowledged Mary's pregnancy and her care of the infant Jesus. He further described Mary as enjoying a privileged intimacy with her son throughout his early years: 'She was the witness of His growth, of His joys, of His sorrows, of His prayers; she was blest with His smile, with the touch of His hand, with the whisper of His affection, with the expression of His thoughts and feelings.'[120] Her uniquely intimate relationship with Jesus both testified to and increased her virtues. As much as he praised her motherhood, he did not consider that she had authority over Jesus into adulthood. There is nothing in Newman's language to suggest that Mary expected this childhood intimacy to continue: the Mary described by Newman accepted the limits of her maternal power.

Newman praised Mary as a role model for all Christians, and thus he believed that Marian devotion would bring people closer to God, rather than make Mary an object of worship in her own right. Rejecting Protestant concerns that Marian devotion would distract one from God, Newman argued that

> her glories and the devotion paid her proclaim and define the right faith concerning Him as God and man. Every Church which is dedicated to her, every altar which is raised under her invocation, every image which represents her, every Litany in her praise, every Hail Mary for her

continual memory, does but remind us that there was One who, though He was all-blessed from all eternity, yet for the sake of sinners, 'did not shrink from the Virgin's womb'.[121]

Yet, having confessed that Marian devotion had been a stumbling-block to his own conversion, Newman readily acknowledged that Marian devotion was an acquired taste: 'the prerogatives with which the Church invests the Blessed Mother of God … are startling and difficult to those whose imagination is not accustomed to them'.[122] It was typical of Newman to assert a position forcefully but not stridently, and to acknowledge when appropriate the good faith of those who disagreed with him.

Newman's self-confident esteem for Mary as an admirable woman who could bring him closer to God was consistent with his attitude to women whom he knew. Although he had determined at an early age that he would not marry, Newman enjoyed warm relationships with women throughout his life. Though no believer in the equality of the sexes, he took issue with the double standard that restricted admission in the Tamworth Reading Room to 'virtuous women', when no such restriction on men's characters were enforced.[123] Nor did he believe that women still bore special culpability for the fall: 'Thus has the Blessed Virgin, in bearing our Lord, taken off or lightened the peculiar disgrace which the woman inherited for seducing Adam.'[124] He advocated convents as an option for women who preferred not to marry.[125] Near the end of his life, he commented to his niece Jane Mozley: 'It is one of the best points of this unhappy age, that it has made so many openings for the activity of women.'[126]

Newman's sympathetic stance towards women was learned at home. At two significant points in his life – when he was ordained as an Anglican priest and shortly before he converted to Roman Catholicism – he credited his aunt Elizabeth and his grandmother with nourishing his religious faith.[127] He especially loved his sister Mary, whom he described as being so 'gifted with that singular sweetness and affectionateness of temper that she lived in an ideal world of happiness, the very sight of which made others happy'.[128] Her sudden death in 1828 at the age of 19 was a tragedy from which he never entirely recovered.[129] Although Newman spent his life in the homosocial environments of the university and thereafter the religious order, he was not hostile to women. In fact, he had close friendships with women throughout his life. Newman was no indiscriminate idealiser of women, however. He was not particularly close to his mother, whom he suspected of not understanding his religious views and of not supporting the Oxford Movement. When she and his sisters moved to Oxford after his father's death, he found their presence a demand on his time. His sister Harriet Mozley broke off relations with him prior to his conversion, blaming him for her husband's interest in converting to Roman Catholicism; brother and sister were not reconciled until the late 1860s. Newman, then, neither idealised women nor distrusted them; he saw them as individuals and related to them as such. Thus Newman's view of Mary was a piece of his attitude towards women and the feminine: he esteemed women and enjoyed warm relationships with some of them, but he was neither slavishly adoring of the feminine nor reflexively distrustful of women in general.

Describing the Virgin Mary as a role model for Christians while never seeing her as a competitor to Jesus enabled Newman to define a masculine identity that appreciated the feminine as complementary rather than as potentially challenging. Newman's masculine identity was never a mainstream one. In his person as well as his personality, Newman was the antithesis of aristocratic values: he was the son of a bankrupted businessman. Newman's belief in clerical celibacy, even when he was an Anglican, put him at odds not just with the aristocratic models of manliness, but with Victorian values more generally. Newman was an emotional man who could be prone to despair, particularly when he was attacked publicly.[130] He was often contrasted unfavourably with the athletic Manning, his fellow convert and frequent rival, who made a more successful transition to the Roman Catholic Church. Newman was also subject to the standard charges of effeminacy and dishonesty: for example, when Kingsley attributed priestly dishonesty to celibacy in his attack on Newman, he defined him as doubly unmanly. Although Newman is now one of the most famous representatives of Victorian religion, at many points in his life he seems to have been less than successful. Neither the Anglican Church of his birth nor the Roman Catholic Church he chose as a middle-aged man ever was comfortable enough with him to make full use of his gifts. He did not begin to win widespread acclaim until the mid-1860s, and it was not until 1879 that he was made a cardinal.

Newman's masculine identity was not merely a pallid rejection of prevailing norms, however. He consciously created a model of masculinity that drew on central elements of English culture, including Christianity, with roots in the homosocial world of the university. Most significantly, Newman frequently described himself as a gentleman addressing other gentlemen, rather than as a priest communicating divine law. 'Gentleman' had no precise meaning in his era, partly because men like Newman sought to disassociate the term from the landed classes who had previously claimed it. Certainly, however, part of its meaning for Newman was honesty and forthrightness. When he wrote to the publishers of *Macmil-*

lan's magazine to complain about Kingsley's original attack on his honesty, his biographer Ian Ker explains, his 'letter was not the complaint of an aggrieved Roman priest, but the protest of an affronted English gentleman to other English gentlemen.'[131] His satire on Kingsley's proposed 'apology' also referenced the idea that both were 'gentlemen'. In the 1840s, when he delivered in Dublin the lectures that became *The idea of a university*, Newman identified himself as a gentleman speaking to gentlemen. A full subsection of Discourse 8, 'Knowledge viewed in relation to religion', was devoted to describing the qualities of the gentleman, whom Newman likened to 'an easy chair or a good fire':[132] that is, the gentleman's role was to bring out the best in others without drawing attention to himself. Thanks to a 'disciplined intellect', the gentleman would neither provoke arguments nor remember insults, and he certainly never spread gossip. He was almost ennervated: 'He is patient, forbearing, and resigned, on philosophical principles; he submits to pain, because it is inevitable, to bereavement, because it is irreparable, and to death, because it is his destiny.'[133] The ideal described in Newman's writings is often restrained to the point that it has been called feminine. However, one should not overestimate the passivity of the ideal he described, for the gentleman was also forceful: 'He may be right or wrong in his opinion, but he is too clear-headed to be unjust; he is as simple as he is forcible, and as brief as he is decisive.'[134] Newman displayed the same qualities in his own life, for he responded strongly and directly when challenged by adversaries such as Faber, Kingsley, Manning, and Giovanni Giacinto Achilli (the Italian apostate priest who successful suit against Newman for libel was justly overturned on appeal). Newman did value qualities, such as humility, more often associated with the feminine in a culture that worked rigorously to categorise the sexes. But to categorise humility as feminine is to forget that it was also a Christian virtue. Furthermore, as Newman articulated the role of humility in his life and work, it was a strength, not a weakness: he was so sure of what he was doing that he did not need to seek external approval.

Newman described the Virgin Mary as a woman who complemented his masculine self-identity as a humble, principled, Christian gentleman, able to engage in worldly contests without having his pride dependent on them. This Virgin Mary confirmed Newman's identity as a man who was not threatened by women but who saw men and women as complementary. While he was no feminist in the modern sense, his masculine self-identity was secure enough to acknowledge a role for women. Although he defined a masculine self-identity that worked cooperatively with women, he did not do it in the manner of the ideology of separate spheres, which was designed to limit the woman's sphere of influence, but in a way that genuinely saw the possibility of men and women cooperating together. Newman was not servile before the Virgin Mary, as Faber was, or somewhat aloof, as Pusey was. He admired her and did not presume to be her equal, but he did not abase himself. Newman, whose concept of masculinity was perhaps the most complex of the four men considered here, could describe an ideal of manliness that did not depend on fearing or subordinating women.

Protestant women and the Virgin Mary

The debate over the role and nature of the Virgin Mary was dominated by men, especially by clerics. This was so partly because they had the training and the access to the venues – pulpits, periodicals, platforms – to engage in the disputes. The absence of similar opportunities helped to ensure that few women wrote publicly and extensively on the Virgin Mary.[135] A more significant reason for women's lack of public contributions was that the Virgin Mary was not a viable role model for Protestant women. As Julie Melnyk notes, the Protestant Mary is 'meek and mild' and the Roman Catholic

> Virgin Mary is ... defined as a 'relative creature'; motherhood is essential to her power, making her useless as a model for the growing numbers of single, or childless, women. Partly because of these symbolic inadequacies, and partly because of Protestant suspicion, few female religious writers invoke the Madonna to reinforce women's spiritual power.[136]

The unsuitability of the Virgin Mary as a role model is underscored by Josephine Butler's biography of Catharine of Sienna, published in 1879. Butler, although married to a clergyman, praises the saint as a Christian woman who confronts and reforms the corrupt male hierarchy. The Virgin Mary offered no such possibilities to reform-minded women like Butler.

Another reason for the lack of participation by Protestant women was that anti-Catholic discourse reinforced the negative designation of Catholicism as a feminine religion. Even to associate themselves with the Virgin in opposition would link them too closely with a negative image of woman, and it would be impossible for them to use her as a positive symbol of feminine identity. Thus, some women who dared to discuss religion went out of their way to avoid mentioning the Virgin Mary even when it would have been logical for them to do so. 'Lydia', author of the series '(Female) Biography of Scripture' that ran from 1839 to 1843 in the *Christian lady's magazine*, confined her examples of virtuous women who were to be models for her readers to women of the Old Testament, including minor figures such as Abigail, Manoah's wife, and the widow of Zarephath, rather than discussing better-known New Testament figures, including the Virgin. Those Victorians who worked for women's advancement did not find her a viable role model because of the persistent prejudice against her and against Catholicism generally, which they may have shared. They therefore devoted their energies elsewhere: to opening schools for young women, to urging Parliament to pass legislation that would expand women's legal rights, to fighting for female suffrage.

Women's inability to use the Virgin Mary as a feminist icon is underscored by Kimberly van Esveld Adams's admission that the three subjects of her work – George Eliot, Anna Jameson, and the American feminist Margaret Fuller – 'were quite unusual among their English-speaking and Protestant contemporaries in seeing feminist possibilities in the Madonna.'[137] Even her qualified statement is unduly optimistic, for the two English women were at best ambivalent about the feminist possibilities of the Virgin Mary. While Jameson describes the Virgin Mary depicted in Luke's Gospel as 'the most perfect moral type of the intellectual, tender, simple and heroic woman that was ever placed before us for our edification and example,'[138] her discussion of artistic representations in Legends of the Madonna often assumes that Roman Catholics 'worship' Mary or consider her to be 'divine'. Jameson's use of such words signalled her anti-Catholicism and reinforced the conviction of her Protestant readers that the Virgin Mary was a pagan goddess who was certainly not a viable role model. Adams acknowledges that Eliot's use of the Madonna as an empowering symbol is limited to Romola, although she describes Adam Bede's Dinah Morris as a partial Madonna-figure.[139] Nevertheless, both Romola and Dinah are immured in the home by the end of the novels in which they figure, as Adams concedes. Adams further admits: 'In Eliot's subsequent works, though, the Madonna starts to function negatively and in more limited ways in the author's feminist arguments even as she becomes central to the meditation on religious differences and religious inheritance.'[140] In this case, the dog that did not bark is significant: in general, the Virgin Mary had little appeal for Victorian Protestant women.

The overall lack of female participation is unfortunate, because the occasional contributions of women offered tantalisingly different readings from those of their male counterparts. In 1852 Charlotte Yonge's Monthly packet suggested that the Annunciation raised the status of all women, who would then be able to approach God on the same terms as men did.[141] Three years later, and from the other end of the denominational spectrum,

Catherine Booth argued that the honour conferred on the Virgin Mary in becoming the mother of Jesus supported her claim that women should be allowed to preach, and longed for the day when 'many Marys may yet *tell* of His wonderful salvation'.[142] The Anglo-Catholic reformer Ellice Hopkins hoped that awareness of the honour given to the Virgin Mary at the Incarnation would encourage Christians to save women from prostitution:

> Surely the Church, which believes in the Incarnation, that God sent forth His own Son, made of a woman, will cease to look supinely on her desecration, or to combat it only by the most inadequate and desultory means, but by the most powerful organization she can command will endeavour to arrest and stamp out this deadliest of evil, and realise something of the divine ideal of womanhood, what the fact of the Incarnation has made it, consecrating it as the Divine Mother, to be the fountain of life, and love, and purity to the world.[143]

Hopkins's invocation of the Virgin Mary to support her argument that women should be given assistance was unusual, but her argument was quite conservative: she was not asking for political or economic rights but for an end to prostitution. Sally Cunneen was, unfortunately, overly optimistic when she concluded, on the basis of a few examples, that in the nineteenth century 'a growing number of Protestant women in England and the United States, though not attracted by Catholic Marian dogma, recognised the absence of a strong feminine presence in Protestant life and devotion and turned to Mary as a compelling and unifying symbol'.[144] It was not until later in the twentieth century that feminist theology began to describe the Virgin Mary as an empowering figure for women.

If the Virgin Mary did not offer most Victorian women a model of female behaviour, the same was not true for men. Whether Catholic or Protestant, clergymen could shape a masculine self-identity by responding to the Catholic Mary. The timing as well as the content of the Marian debates suggest the soundness of this conclusion. English clerics, who had both the training and the venues to debate the role and nature of the Virgin Mary, did not engage in this question publicly or to a significant extent until the nineteenth century, a time during which masculinity became, like femininity, a more publicly contested issue. I do not mean to suggest that masculine identity had been fixed in earlier periods, but only that it became a more obviously contested issue from the 1830s as a result of the convergence of a variety of factors, including challenges to the traditional ways middle- and working-class men had defined their masculinity through ownership and labour relationships . The evangelical and Oxford movements, which raised the standards of personal holiness for clergymen, made it harder for them to conform to the dominant models of masculinity that were realised through physical prowess, worldly glory or earnings capability. An added burden for Catholic men was the identification of Roman Catholicism and advanced Anglicanism as the religion of women and effeminate men. This is not to dismiss the reality of the theological concerns that motivated many participants, but only to note additional factors that had not previously been significant in English public life. When these factors did emerge, and when Catholicism re-emerged at home as an apparent threat to Protestantism, debating the role and nature of the Virgin Mary became one way in which to address the new variety of religious and secular concerns.

Conclusion

Two-and-a-half decades after John Keble's friends advised him not to publish 'Mother out of sight', the ritualist cleric and future Roman Catholic convert Orby Shipley praised the poem for exemplifying 'the position which we should seek to occupy towards the Mother of God of all Saints.'[145] Shipley was somewhat in advance of Victorian culture, but by the 1880s the Marian controversies began to subside. This was partly in response to changing realities: as women gained access to higher education, the polling place, and governing bodies it was no longer possible to define them as innocent domestic creatures. Furthermore, the appearance of alternative models of womanhood somewhat alleviated the tensions engendered by the feminine ideal. The 'Angel out of the house' had begun, starting in the 1860s, to resolve the anxiety about how to restrict women to the home: admitting that women could not be confined to the home, this model of feminine behaviour urged women to apply their domestic virtues to improving the public sphere. Emerging in the 1880s and flourishing in the 1890s and beyond, the New Woman radically rejected not only the confines of the domestic sphere, but also the constraints of traditional behaviour, clothing, and occupation. Both models of womanhood recognised the impossibility of restricting women to the home and thus rejected the domestic ideal. Furthermore, the New Woman gave traditionalists a more pressing cause for concern: although widely lampooned and perhaps even more distant from real women's lives than were her idealised predecessors, in her various manifestations she rode a bicycle, smoked, wore men's clothing, campaigned for the vote, and even practised free love, all to the consternation of traditionalists. These new models of female behaviour as well as the new educational and professional opportunities available to women helped to effect the demise of the feminine ideal associated with the early and middle Victorian years. When the ideal of womanhood as maternal, non-sexual, and morally superior no longer wielded the cultural power it had possessed earlier in the century, there was less reason to attack the Virgin Mary as a way of limiting the power this ideal offered women.

Another factor in the decline of those controversies was the increasing acceptance of Roman Catholicism. This trend was observable as early as 1864, with the Victorian reading public's sympathetic reception of Newman's *Apologia pro vitâ suâ*. By 1874 the trend had become more marked: Joseph Altholz concludes that the lack of response to the publication of William Ewart Gladstone's *The Vatican Decrees* in that year marked the end of anti-Roman Catholicism in England,[146] while John Shelton Reed sees the failure of the Public Worship Regulation Act, which was passed that same year, as leading to greater acceptance, or at least tolerance, of Anglo-Catholics.[147] Certainly vestiges of the old feelings remained – as late as 1887, Charles Hastings Collette could pose the question *Is Dr Manning, who claims to be a cardinal and Archbishop of Westminster, a loyal Englishman?*[148] as a pamphlet title – but anti-Catholicism was clearly waning by the 1880s. With a diminishing need to describe Roman Catholics as semi-pagan foreigners, and Anglo-Catholics as secret Roman Catholics, there was less need to indict them by defining the Virgin Mary as a pagan goddess. Finally, the rise of the 'New Imperialism' in the 1880s provided an alternative means of defining a national identity, for religious differences could be subsumed under a shared Christianity as imperialism posited a more obviously different other. The decline of organised Christianity generally may also have prompted ecumenical stirrings. Those developments made the English reluctant to be reminded of the theological differences that divided them and thus further explains why the Marian controversies declined significantly at the end of the century. However, while the Virgin Mary remained a prominent and controversial figure in the middle decades of the nineteenth century, she illuminated some of the tensions that defined Victorian culture. Keble's poem lamented the 'Mother out of sight', but in fact the problem was that the Virgin Mary was not out of sight. She was controversial in the Victorian era in a way that she had never been in English history because, by describing her, Victorians described themselves.

Notes

1 Roper and Tosh, 'Historians and the politics of masculinity', p. 2, emphasis in original.

2 Brian Heeney, *A different kind of gentleman: parish clergy as professional men in early and mid-Victorian England* (Hamden, CT: Archon Books for the Conference on British Studies and Wittenberg University, 1976).

3 Anthony Russell, *The clerical profession* (London: SPCK, 1980).

4 John Tosh, 'Domesticity and manliness in the Victorian middle class: the family of Edward White Benson', in Roper and Tosh (eds), *Manful assertions*, pp. 44–73.

5 Philip Healy, 'Man apart: priesthood and homosexuality at the end of the nineteenth century'; Lori M. Miller, 'The (re)gendering of high Anglicanism'; Frederick S. Roden, 'Aelred of Rievaulx, same-sex desire and the Victorian monastery', all in Bradstock et al. (eds), *Masculinity and spirituality in Victorian culture*.

6 These numbers are not absolutely reliable: some chapelgoers attended more than one service a day and so were counted more than once; some clergy opted out of the census. More recently, Hugh McLeod and Callum Brown have disputed the contemporary interpretation of the census as indicating a connection between urbanisation and secularisation. Even with these caveats, however, the census is useful for giving a rough idea about church attendance patterns.

7 Florence Nightingale, *Suggestions for thought*, ed. Michael Calabria and Janet A. Macrae (Philadelphia: University of Pennsylvania Press, 1994), p. xv.

8 See Julie Melnyk (ed.), *Women's theology in nineteenth-century Britain: transfiguring the faith of their fathers* (New York: Garland, 1998), especially the essays by Robert M. Kachur, Frederick S. Roden, David Goslee, Julie Melnyk, and Virginia Bemis.

9 Paz, *Popular anti-Catholicism in mid-Victorian England*, p. 103.

10 Tosh, 'Domesticity and manliness in the Victorian middle class', p. 49.

11 John Tosh, *A man's place: masculinity and the middle-class home in Victorian England* (New Haven, CT, and London: Yale University Press, 1999).

12 Trollope, *Framley parsonage*, p. 413.

13 David Forrester, *Young Doctor Pusey: a study in development* (London: Mowbray, 1989), p. 113.

14 Adams, *Dandies and desert saints*, p. 7.

15 A Lady, *The contented widow: a narrative illustrative of the importance and necessity of church extension* (Bristol: John Wright, 1849), p. 3.

16 British Library, London, Add. MS 41298, letter from Charles Kingsley to an unnamed person, 1 May 1849, fol. 46.

17 Hampson, *Religious deceptions of the Church of Rome*, p. 25, emphasis in original.

18 Maudson, 'The dogma of the Virgin Mary's Immaculate Conception', 238.

19 Adams, *Dandies and desert saints*, p. 101.

20 Gay, 'The manliness of Christ', p. 102.

21 Thomas Hughes, *The manliness of Christ* (London: Macmillan, 1879), p. 61.

22 Hughes, *The manliness of Christ*, p. 25.

23 Hughes, *The manliness of Christ*, p. 101.

24 Gay, 'The manliness of Christ', p. 108.

25 Hughes, *The manliness of Christ*, p. 70.

26 F. W. Robertson, *The loneliness of Christ* (London: H. R. Allenson, n.d.), pp. 22–3.

27 Frederick Croly, 'Biographical sketch', in George Croly, *The Book of Job, with a biographical sketch of the author by his son* (Edinburgh and London: William Blackwood and Sons, 1863), p. xxv.

28 George Croly, *The Church of England, founded on Scripture, and essential to the constitution: a sermon preached at the visitation of the Venerable the Archdeacon of London, William Hale Hale, A.M., May 3, 1853* (London: Seeleys, 1853), p. 31.

29 Hughes, *The manliness of Christ*, p. 6.

30 Hughes, *The manliness of Christ*, p. 36.

31 This tactic is especially apparent in children's literature, particularly in the latter decades of the nineteenth century: Nelson, *Boys will be girls*; Veldman, 'Dutiful daughter versus all-boy'.

32 For a discussion of Victorian painters' attempts to depict a Jesus who would serve as a model of masculinity, see Sean Gill, '*Ecce homo*: representations of Christ as the model of masculinity in Victorian art and lives of Jesus', in Bradstock et al. (eds), *Masculinity and spirituality in Victorian culture*, pp. 164–78.

33 Sarah Ellis, *The daughters of England* (New York: Appleton, 1843), pp. 6, 8, and quoted in Nelson, *Boys will be girls*, p. 10.

34 Dobney, *The Virgin Mary*, p. 49.

35 Dobney, *The Virgin Mary*, p. 55.

36 (Edouart) *An address to the parishioners of Leominster*, p. 12.

37 (Eduoart) *An address to the parishioners of Leominster*, p. 17.

38 Hughes, *The manliness of Christ*, p. 3; Colloms, *Charles Kingsley*, p. 240.

39 Kingsley, *Yeast*, p. 56.

40 Kingsley, *Yeast*, p. 56.

41 Newman, *Apologia pro vitâ suâ*, p. 38.

42 Charles Kingsley, *Westward Ho!*, 2 vols (New York: Fred DeFau & Co., 1889 [1855]), vol. 2, p. 78.

43 Kingsley, *Yeast*, p. iii.

44 Kingsley, *Yeast*, pp. iii–iv.

45 David J. Delaura identifies Luke as a 'cleverly malicious caricature' of Newman: David J. Delaura, '"O unforgotten voice": the memory of Newman in the nineteenth century', *Renascence*, 43 (1990–91), 90.

46 Kingsley, *Yeast*, p. 86.

47 Kingsley, *Yeast*, p. 282.

48 Charles Kingsley, *Charles Kingsley: his letters and memories of his life*, ed. by his wife (2 vols.; London: Macmillan, 1890), vol. 1, p. 100, emphasis in original.

49 Kingsley, *Charles Kingsley*, vol. 1, pp. 104–5, emphasis in original.

50 The pattern was repeated when, some years later, Fanny's sister Charlotte met her future husband, James Anthony Froude, at the Kingsleys' home when she was on the verge of entering a Roman Catholic convent.

51 British Library, London, Add. MS 41298, Kingsley Papers, vol. 2, letter from Charles Kingsley to an unnamed correspondent, 1 May 1849, fol. 42; reprinted in Margaret Farrand Thorp, *Charles Kingsley 1819–1875* (NY: Octagon Books, 1969 [1937]), p. 20.

52 Colloms, *Charles Kingsley*, p. 270.

53 Susan Chitty, *The beast and the monk: a life of Charles Kingsley* (London: Hodder & Stoughton, 1974), p. 239.

54 Adams, *Dandies and desert saints*, p. 132.

55 Chitty, *The beast and the monk*, p. 24.
56 Kingsley, *Westward Ho!*, vol. 1, p. 32.
57 Kingsley, *Westward Ho!*, vol. 1, p. 31.
58 Kingsley, *Westward Ho!*, vol. 1, p. 75.
59 Pusey, *First letter to Newman*, p. 24.
60 Pusey, *First letter to Newman*, p. 23, emphasis in original.
61 Pusey, *First letter to Newman*, p. 33; see also Pusey House, Oxford, LBV 121/14, letter from E. B. Pusey to J. H. Newman, 2 November 1865.
62 Pusey, *Eirenicon*, p. 108.
63 Pusey, *The presence of Christ in the Holy Eucharist*, p. 23; Pusey, *The doctrine of the Real Presence*, pp. 58–9.
64 Pusey House, Oxford, LBV 121/25, letter from E. B. Pusey to Newman, undated (?21 January 1866).
65 Pusey, *First letter to Newman*, p. 23.
66 Pusey, *First letter to Newman*, p. 23.
67 Pusey, *First letter to Newman*, p. 36.
68 Pusey, *First letter to Newman*, p. 45; see also p. 49.
69 Pusey, *Eirenicon*, p. 117.
70 Pusey, *Eirenicon*, p. 119, emphasis in original.
71 Pusey, *Eirenicon*, p. 111.
72 Forrester, *Young Doctor Pusey*, p. 11.
73 Liddon, *Life of Pusey*, vol. 1, p. 2.
74 Liddon, *Life of Pusey*, vol. 1, p. 5.
75 Liddon, *Life of Pusey*, vol. 1, p. 6.
76 Liddon, *Life of Pusey*, vol. 1, p. 7.
77 Liddon, *Life of Pusey*, vol. 1, p. 7.
78 Liddon, *Life of Pusey*, vol. 1, p. 5.
79 Liddon, *Life of Pusey*, vol. 1, pp. 23, 29, 141–3.
80 Liddon, *Life of Pusey*, vol. 1, pp. 124–5, 131.
81 Forrester, *Young Doctor Pusey*, pp. 66–8, 70–1.
82 Liddon, *Life of Pusey*, vol. 2, pp. 83–6.
83 See Forrester, *Young Doctor Pusey*, chapter 3; Forrester makes essentially the same argument in 'Dr Pusey's marriage', in Perry Butler (ed.), *Pusey rediscovered* (London: SPCK, 1983), pp. 119–38.
84 Hill, *The religious order*, pp. 232–3; Mumm, *Stolen daughters, virgin mothers*, p. 155.
85 Michael Chandler, *The life and work of John Mason Neale* (Leominster: Gracewing, 1995), p. 77.
86 Mumm, *Stolen daughters, virgin mothers*, pp. 157–8.
87 Faber, 'Jesus crucified', *Jesus and Mary*, p. 26, lines 29–31.
88 Faber, 'The apparition of Jesus to our Blessed Lady', *Jesus and Mary*, pp. 40–5.
89 (F. W. Faber) *Our Lady and the Eucharist: selections from Father Faber*, by the compiler of *Father Faber's May book* (London: R. & T. Washbourne, 1898), p. 66.
90 F. W. Faber, *The foot of the cross: or, the sorrows of Mary* (London: Thomas Richardson & Son, 1858), p. 11.
91 Faber, *The foot of the cross*, p. 15.
92 Frederick Faber, 'The Most Holy Trinity', *Jesus and Mary*, p. 3, stanza 7.
93 Faber, *The foot of the cross*, p. 2.

94   Faber, *Faber: poet and priest*, p. 105.
95   Chapman, *Father Faber*, pp. 101, 108.
96   Quoted in Chapman, *Father Faber*, p. 146.
97   (F. W. Faber) *Father Faber's May book*, compiled by an Oblate of Mary Immaculate (London: Burns & Oates; New York, Cincinnati, and Chicago: Benziger Brothers, n.d. [?1894]), p. 11.
98   Faber, Preface, in Louis-Marie Grignon de Montfort, *A treatise on the true devotion to the Blessed Virgin*, trans. Frederick William Faber (London: Burns & Lambert, 1863), p. ix.
99   Chapman, *Father Faber*, p. 148.
100 Chapman, *Father Faber*, p. 230.
101 Chapman, *Father Faber*, p. 305.
102 Chapman, *Father Faber*, p. 149.
103 Faber, *The precious blood*, pp. 29–30.
104 Pusey, *Eirenicon*, p. 174.
105 Newman, 'Letter to Pusey', p. 433.
106 Newman, 'Letter to Pusey', p. 454.
107 See Pusey, *Eirenicon*, pp. 169–71.
108 Chapman, *Father Faber*, p. 4.
109 *All for Jesus* (n.p.; Thomas Richardson, 1853) went through nine editions in under twenty years, *The foot of the cross: or, the sorrows of Mary* went through ten editions in under thirty years, and *Jesus and Mary: or, Catholic hymns* went through at least four editions in thirteen years.
110 Chapman, *Father Faber*, pp. 299–300.
111 Chapman *Father Faber*, p. 291.
112 Chapman *Father Faber*, p. 301.
113 Chapman *Father Faber*, p. 291.
114 Faber, *The precious blood*, p. 1.
115 Chapman, *Father Faber*, p. 98.
116 Chapman, *Father Faber*, p. 48.
117 Newman denied, however, in a handwritten note on the cover of his unpublished sermon 'On the faith of Mary', his brother Francis' accusation, originally made in 1879, that he had defended the invocation of Mary while still an Anglican.
118 Newman, 'The reverence due to the Virgin Mary', *Parochial and plain sermons*, 8 vols (New York and London: Longmans, Green, & Co., 1924), vol. 2, p. 128.
119 Newman, 'The reverence due to the Virgin Mary', 128.
120 Newman, 'On the fitness of the glories of Mary', p. 362.
121 Newman, 'The glories of Mary for the sake of her son', p. 349.
122 Newman, 'The glories of Mary for the sake of her son', p. 344.
123 Ker, *John Henry Newman*, p. 210.
124 Newman, 'The reverence due to the Virgin Mary', p. 131.
125 Ker, *John Henry Newman*, p. 190.
126 John Henry Newman, *The letters and diaries of John Henry Newman*, vol. 30, ed. Charles Stephen Dessain and Thomas Gornall (Oxford: Clarendon, 1976), p. 316.
127 Ker, *John Henry Newman*, pp. 3, 25.
128 John Henry Newman, *The letters and diaries of John Henry Newman*, vol. 2, ed. Ian Ker and Thomas Gornall (Oxford: Clarendon, 1979), pp. 49–50.

129 Ker, *John Henry Newman*, pp. 76, 714.
130 Ker, *John Henry Newman*, pp. 502, 508.
131 Ker, *John Henry Newman*, p. 533.
132 John Henry Newman, *The idea of a university*, ed. Frank M. Turner (New Haven, CT: Yale University Press, 1996), p. 145.
133 Newman, *The idea of a university*, p. 146.
134 Newman, *The idea of a university*, p. 146.
135 While private diaries might reveal the ways in which women shaped their gender identities in response to the Virgin Mary, these would likely be diaries of Catholic women, and so there would be no opportunity to contrast Catholic and Protestant women's responses. Furthermore, examining private devotions would be an entirely different project than my analysis of the public debate, albeit one that would be instructive of private devotions.
136 Melnyk, '"Mighty victims"', p. 135.
137 Adams, *Our Lady of Victorian feminism*, p. 2.
138 Jameson, *Legends of the Madonna*, p. 49.
139 Adams, *Our Lady of Victorian feminism*, p. 159.
140 Adams, *Our Lady of Victorian feminism*, pp. 149–50.
141 'Conversations on the Catechism', 87.
142 Harold Begbie, *The life of General William Booth* (London: Macmillan, 1920), p. 249, emphasis in original; quoted in Helsinger et al., *The woman question*, vol. 2, p. 182.
143 Ellice Hopkins, *A plea for the wider action of the Church of England in the prevention of the degradation of women, as submitted to a committee of Convocation on July 3, 1879* (London: Hatchards, 1879), p. iv.
144 Cunneen, *In search of Mary*, p. 227.
145 Shipley (ed.), *Invocation of saints and angels*, p. xxxviii.
146 Josef Altholz, 'The Vatican Decrees controversy, 1874–1875', *Catholic historical review*, 57 (1972), 593.
147 Reed, *Glorious battle*, chapter 13.
148 London: privately printed, 1887.

Bibliography

Primary sources

Archived papers

Records of the Anglo-Catholic Society, Lambeth Palace Library, London
Bristol Church Union Papers, Lambeth Palace Library, London
Broughton Papers, British Library, London
English Church Union Papers, Lambeth Palace Library, London
Gladstone Papers, British Library, London
Golightly Papers, Lambeth Palace Library, London
Home Office Papers, Public Record Office, London
Layard Papers, British Library, London
Newman Papers, Birmingham Oratory, Birmingham
Pusey Papers (Liddon Bound Volumes), Pusey House, Oxford
Wilberforce Papers, Bodleian Library, Oxford

Periodicals

Anthill's monthly chronicle and illustrated advertiser
Baptist magazine
British banner
British mothers' magazine
British Protestant; or, journal of the Special Mission to Roman Catholics in Great Britain
Church and state gazette: the churchman's family newspaper
Dublin review
Englishwoman's magazine and Christian mothers' miscellany
London investigator: a monthly journal of secularism
Monthly letter of the Protestant Alliance
Monthly messenger
Monthly packet of evening readings for younger members of the English Church
Nonconformist
Quarterly review
Watchman and Wesleyan advertiser
Wesleyan–Methodist magazine
Wesleyan times

Printed sources

'A.B.' 'Mariolatry'. *Church and state gazette* 12: 606 (23 September 1853), 614.
Acton, William. *The functions and disorders of the reproductive organs*. Philadelphia, PA: Lindsay & Blakiston, 1867.

(Adams, W. H. D.) *The catacombs of Rome: historical and descriptive, with a chapter on the symbolism of early Christian art.* London: T. Nelson & Sons, n.d. (1877).

Aitken, W. Hay M. H. *Mission Sermons.* 3rd edn. London: John F. Shaw & Co., n.d. (?1880).

A.M. *A brief review of the Rev. Hobart Seymour's Pilgrimage to Rome.* London: Longman and Co., London: Whitaker & Co.; Bath: Collings; Bath: Godwin, 1849.

Anglicans of the day. By the author of 'My clerical friends'. Reprinted from the *Dublin review.* London: Burns & Oates, 1875.

Animadversions by distinguished divines & others, on the false position of the ritualistic clergy in the Church of England. London: Hamilton, Adams, & Co.; Bristol: I. E. Chillcott, 1882.

The apparition of the Blessed Virgin at Petigny, in Belgium; and sudden cure of Madame Jalhay. London: Burns, Lambert, & Oates, n.d. (1866).

An appeal to the associates of the Apostleship of Prayer in Great Britain and Ireland. Reprinted from 'The Messenger of the sacred heart,' July 1878, n.p.: n.p., n.d.

Armstrong, John E. *Armstrong's reply to Wiseman's pastoral letter on the Immaculate Conception.* London: Wertheim & Macintosh, 1855.

Arnold, Thomas. 'The Oxford malignants and Dr Hampden'. *Edinburgh review* 63 (April 1836), 225–39.

Arthur, William. 'The church in the catacombs'. Reprinted in *Twelve lectures delivered before the Young Men's Christian Association, in Exeter Hall, from November 1849, to February 1850.* London: James Nisbet & Co., 1850, pp. 161–210.

Bagehot, Walter. *The English constitution.* 1867; Ithaca, NY: Cornell University Press, 1966.

Baillie, John. *The revival: or, what I saw in Ireland; with thoughts suggested by the same: the result of two personal visits.* London: James Nisbet & Co., 1860.

Baillie, Marianne. *First impressions on a tour upon the Continent in the summer of 1818, through parts of France, Italy, Switzerland, the borders of Germany, and a part of French Flanders.* London: John Murray, 1819.

Baines, P. A. 'A history of the pastoral addressed to the faithful of the western district, on occasion of the Fast of Lent 1840'. Unpublished. British Library, London; shelfmark 4499.m.15.

Beavan, W. F. *A brief account of the miraculous movement of the eyes of the sacred image of the Most Holy Virgin Mary Della Pietà, venerated in the parochial church of the Minor Conventual Fathers of St Francis, at Civita Vecchia, with the critical examination and opinion of Prof. Seraf Belli, M.D., physician at Civita Vecchia, inserted in the proces-verbal.* London: Thomas Richardson & Son, 1861.

Benham, William. *The Lambeth Conference, 1867.* Reprinted from the *Guardian* (June 1878), n.p.: n.p., 1878.

Biber, G. E. *Fiat justitia: a letter to the Reverend E. B. Pusey, D.D., in reply to his speech at the meeting of the London Union on church matters, at St Martin's Hall, on Tuesday, the 15th of October, since published with a postscript.* London: Francis & John Rivington, 1850.

Biber, G. E. *The evidence for popish miracles not to be heard: a sermon, preached in the district chapel of the Holy Trinity, Roehampton, on the nineteenth Sunday after Trinity, October 26th, 1851.* London: F. & J. Rivington: 1851.

Bickersteth, Edward. *Come out of Rome; the voice from Heaven to the people of God: a sermon preached before the Protestant Association, on Wednesday Evening, April 22, 1840, at St Clement Danes Church.* London: Protestant Association, 1840.

Birks, T. R. *Memoir of the Rev. Edward Bickersteth, late rector of Watton, Herts.* 2 vols. London: Seeleys, 1851.

Birks, T. R. *Modern popery: its strength and its weakness, as an aggressive power. A lecture, delivered at the request of the Bristol Protestant Alliance, at the Victoria Rooms, Clifton, on September 13, 1852.* Bristol: Wheceat, 1852.

Blunt, J. J. *Sketch of the Reformation in England.* London: John Murray, 1832.

Boase, J. J. A. 'A ramble on the Continent in 1824'. 3 vols. Hand-written books, with illustrations. British Library, London. Add. MSS 35045 (Vol. 1), 35046 (Vol. 2), 35047 (Vol. 3).

Boase, J. J. A. 'A ramble on the Continent in 1850'. Vol. 4, Part First. Handwritten book. British Library, London. Add. MS 35048.

Boase, J. J. A. 'A ramble on the Continent in 1851'. Vol. 4, Part Second. Handwritten book. British Library, London. Add. MS 35049.

Boase, J. J. A. 'A ramble on the Continent in 1855'. Vol. 4, Part Third. Handwritten book. British Library, London. Add. MS 35050.

Bradlaugh, Charles. *George, Prince of Wales, with recent contrasts and coincidences.* London: C. Bradlaugh, n.d.

Bradley, Charles. *Practical and parochial sermons.* New York: Appleton, 1849.

(Bridgett, T. E.) *The faith of the ancient English Church concerning the Blessed Virgin Mary.* n.p.: n.p., n.d.

A brief account of the indulgences, privileges, and favours, conferred on the order, confraternities, and churches, of the Most Glorious Mother of God, the Virgin Mary of Mount Carmel: with distinct instructions for the Brothers and Sisters of the Sacred Scapular, and for all the faithful, who visit the churches of the said order. Trans. the Very Rev. Thomas Coleman, Provincial of the Cal. Carmelites in Ireland. Dublin: Confraternity of the Holy Scapular, 1826.

Browne, Edward Harold. *The Old Catholic movement on the Continent of Europe.* London: William Wells Gardner, 1875.

Browning, Elizabeth Barrett. 'The Virgin Mary to the child Jesus'. *The complete poems of Elizabeth Barrett Browning.* Ed. Charlotte Porter and Helen A. Clarke. New York: Thomas Y. Crowell & Co., 1990, pp. 72–7.

Browning, Elizabeth Barrett. *The letters of Elizabeth Barrett Browning to her sister Arabella.* 2 vols. Ed. Scott Lewis. Waco, TX: Wedgestone Press, 2002.

Bunbury, Selina. *A visit to the Catacombs, or first centuries at Rome: and a midnight visit to Mount Vesuvius.* London: W. W. Robinson, 1849.

(Burgess, Thomas) Bishop of Salisbury *A letter to the Right Honourable Lord Viscount Melbourne, on the idolatry and apostasy of the Church of Rome: in proof that the doctrines of the Church of Rome are not fundamentally the same with those of the Church of England.* Salisbury: J. Hearn; London: Rivingtons, 1835.

Burgon, John W. *Letters from Rome to friends in England.* London: John Murray, 1862.

Burgon, John W. *Woman's place: a sermon preached at S. Mary-the-Virgin's, Oxford, on Sexagesima Sunday, Feb. 12, 1871.* Oxford and London: James Parker, 1871.

Butler, Alban. *The lives of the Fathers, martyrs, and other principal saints, compiled from original documents and other authentic records.* 2 vols. Ed. F. C. Husenbeth. 1756–59; London and Dublin: Henry & Co., n.d. (1857–60).

Butler, Josephine E. *Catherine of Sienna: a biography.* 2nd edn. London: Dyer Brothers, 1879.

Calthrop, Annette. 'Jael and Mary: a contrast'. *Christian world magazine and family visitor* 20: 9 (September 1884), 713–16.

Calthrop, Gordon. *The secret of Rome's strength: a sermon preached at the parish church, Islington, on Sunday morning, November 20th, 1864, on behalf of the Islington Protestant Institute.* London: William Hunt, n.d. (?1864).

'Cardinal Wiseman on the worship of the Virgin'. *Church and state gazette* 12: 606 (23 September 1853), 596.

Carre, Thomas (Miles Pinkney). *Sweet thoughts of Jesus and Mary: meditations for the Feasts of Our Saviour and of his Blessed Mother.* Ed. Orby Shipley (1658, 1665). London: Burns & Oates; New York: Catholic Publication Society Co., 1889.

Carter, T. T. *Mercy for the fallen: two sermons in aid of the House of Mercy, Clewer.* London: Joseph Masters, 1856.

Carter, T. T. *Fellowship with the saints: a sermon preached at All Saints', Margaret Street, on the Festival of All Saints, 1868.* London: Joseph Masters, 1868.

'Catholics and Roman Catholics'. *Longhurst's church tracts*, No. 6. London: E. Longhurst; London: Mowbray, n.d. (?1871).

'Celebrated sanctuaries of the Madonna'. *Littell's living age* (4th series) 98: 10 (July–September 1868), 413–20.

Challoner, Richard. *The garden of the soul, or a manual of spiritual exercises and instructions for Christians who (living in the world) aspire to devotion.* Philadelphia, PA: Matthew Carry, 1792.

Challoner, Richard. *The garden of the soul, or a manual of spiritual exercises and devotions, for Christians, who, living in the world, aspire to devotion: a new and amended edition.* Birmingham: W. Stone, 1844.

Challoner, Richard. *The garden of the soul, or a manual of spiritual exercises and devotions, for Christians, who, living in the world, aspire to devotion: a new edition, containing: Devotions to the Blessed Sacrament, to the Sacred Heart, to St Joseph, and a collection of indulgenced prayers.* London and Derby: Thomas Richardson & Sons, 1877.

Chambers, Mary Catharine Elizabeth. *The life of Mary Ward*. Ed. Henry James Coleridge, SJ. 2 vols. London: Burns & Oates, 1882, 1885.

Christianus. *An address to the plenipotentiaries on the affairs of Italy, proposed by Napoleon III, Emperor of the French, to assemble at Paris, for conciliation and peace*. n.p.: n.p., n.d. (?1868).

(Church, R. W.) *Life and letters of Dean Church* (1894). Ed. Mary C. Church. London and New York: Macmillan, 1895.

Church, R. W. *Village sermons preached at Whatley* (1892). London: Macmillan, 1897.

Church, R. W. *The Oxford Movement* (1892). Reprinted London: Macmillan, 1922.

Close, Francis. 'The Catholic revival', or ritualism and Romanism in the Church of England: illustrated from 'The Church and the world': a paper read at the annual meeting of the Evangelical Union for the Diocese of Carlisle. London: Hatchard & Co.; Carlisle: C. Thurnam & Sons, 1866.

Coleridge, Henry James. *The mother of the Church: Mary during the first apostolic age*. London: Burns & Oates, 1887.

Coleridge, Henry James. *The seven words of Mary: derived from St Bernardine of Siena*. London: Burns & Oates, 1889.

Coleridge, J. T. *A memoir of the Rev. John Keble, M.A., late vicar of Hursley*. 2nd edn. Oxford and London: James Parker & Co., 1869.

Collette, Charles Hastings. *Invocation of saints: the doctrine and practice of the Church of Rome. A lecture, delivered at the Literary Institution, Gravesend*. London: Wertheim & Macintosh, 1857.

Collette, Charles Hastings. *Is Dr Manning, who claims to be a cardinal and archbishop of Westminster, a loyal Englishman?* London: privately printed, 1887.

Conference of Bishops of the Anglican Communion, holden at Lambeth Palace, September 24–27, 1867. London: Rivingtons, 1867.

Conference of Bishops of the Anglican Communion, holden at Lambeth Palace, July 1878: letter from the bishops, including the reports adopted by the Conference. London, Paris, and New York: Cassell, Petter, & Galpin, 1878.

The conspirators' schemes: homes, convents, confession, and education. n.p. (London): Protestant Evangelical Mission and Electoral Union, n.d. (1871).

'Continental Romanism'. *The Christian remembrancer* 6 (July–December 1843), 507–17.

'Conversations on the Catechism'. *The monthly packet* 3: 14 (February 1852), 81–95.

Croly, Frederick. 'Biographical sketch'. In George Croly, *The Book of Job, with a biographical sketch of the author by his son*. Edinburgh and London: William Blackwood & Sons, 1863.

Croly, George. *The divine origin, appointment, and obligation of marriage: a sermon, preached on Sunday, March 20, 1836, in the Church of St Stephen's, Walbrook*. London: James Duncan, 1836.

Croly, George. *The Church of England, founded on Scripture, and essential to the constitution: a sermon preached at the visitation of the Venerable the Archdeacon of London, William Hale Hale, A.M., May 3, 1853.* London: Seeleys, 1853.

(Croly, George.) 'The new article of "faith".' *The Wesleyan-Methodist magazine* (5th series) 1:1 (January 1855), 79–83.

Croly, George. *The Book of Job, with a biographical sketch of the author by his son.* Edinburgh and London: William Blackwood & Sons, 1863.

Crouch, William. *On the invocation of saints: a paper read before the September Synod of the Society of the Holy Cross, 1885.* n.p.: privately printed for the Society, n.d.

C.S.G. *Is it right for a woman to preach in the public congregation? And what says the Bible?* Taunton: J. F. Hammond, 1884.

Cullen, Paul. *Pastoral letter of His Grace the Most Rev. Dr Cullen, Archbishop, etc., Primate of Ireland, to the Catholic clergy and laity of the diocese of Dublin, on the Festival of the Purification of the Blessed Virgin Mary.* Dublin: James Duffy, 1856.

(Cumming, John) *Dr Cumming's lecture on the Papal Aggression.* London: Charles Westerton, 1850.

Cumming, John. *Romish miracles: a lecture delivered in the Town Hall, Birmingham, on Tuesday, December 16, 1851.* London: Arthur Hall, Virtue, & Co., 1852.

Cumming, John. Letter to the editor of *The Times*, reprinted in *Church and state gazette* 12: 606 (23 September 1853), 593.

Cumming, John. 'Our Lady of Salette'. *Church and state gazette* 12: 606 (23 September 1853), 593.

(Cumming, John) *The Romish oath: being the correspondence of Cardinal Wiseman and the Rev. Dr Cumming on the episcopal oath, and its persecuting clauses.* London: British Society for Promoting the Religious Principles of the Reformation, n.d.

Cumming, John. *The Immaculate Conception: its antecedents and consequences; taken from the 'Times', and corrected by the author.* London: published for the Protestant Reformation Society by James Miller, n.d.

(Cumming, John and Daniel French.) *The Hammersmith Protestant discussion; being an authenticated report of the controversial discussion between the Rev. John Cumming, D.D., of the Scottish National Church, Crown Court, Covent Garden, and Daniel French, Esq., barrister-at-law, on the differences between Protestantism and popery; held at Hammersmith, during the months of April and May, MDCCCXXXIX.* From the short-hand notes of Charles Maybury Archer, Esq. New edn. London: Arthur Hall & Co., 1851.

Daniel, C. *Exposure of 'The vindication of the Church of England', by the Rev. H. Townsend Powell, vicar of Stretton-on-Dunsmore, addressed to the Protestants of the said parish.* London: P. & M. Andrews, 1840.

Darwin, Charles. *The descent of man, and selection in relation to sex.* 2 vols. London: John Murray, 1871.

Davey, George. *The Established Church the ancient Catholic Church of England: a refutation of certain assertions in 'A letter to his late parishioners, by H. W. Wilberforce, M.A., late vicar of East Farleigh'.* Maidstone: Hall & Son; London: F. & J. Rivington, 1851.

Declaration of the Catholic bishops, the vicars apostolic and their coadjutors in Great Britain. New edn. London: Catholic Institute of Great Britain, 1838.

(De Q) 'The conception of the Blessed Virgin Mary'. *Union review: a magazine of Catholic literature and art* 6 (1868), 513–27.

De Vio, Thomas, Cardinal Cajetan. *The judgment of Thomas de Vio, Cardinal Cajetan, against the Immaculate Conception of the Blessed Virgin Mary.* Trans. Robert C. Jenkins. Canterbury: Thomas Ashenden, 1858.

'Devotion to the Most Holy Virgin'. *Dublin review* 21: 41 (September 1846), 37–65.

Dickens, Charles. *The life of Our Lord.* London: Associated Newspapers, 1934.

Dickens, Charles. *David Copperfield* (1849–50). New York: Signet, 1962.

Dickens, Charles. *Hard times* (1854). London: Penguin, 1995.

Dobney, H. H. *The Virgin Mary.* London: Ward & Co.; Maidstone: J. Brown, 1859.

Dobney, H. H. *Free churches: a tract for my own congregation.* London: Strahan & Co., 1871.

'Dr Pusey on Marian devotion'. *Dublin review* (new series) 7: 13 (July 1866), 142–99.

'Dr Pusey on Marian doctrine: peace through the truth'. *Dublin review* (new series) 7: 14 (October 1866), 455–514.

'Dr Pusey's apology for Anglicanism'. *Dublin review* (new series) 6: 11 (January 1866), 188–239.

Dziewicki, Michael Henry. *Legend of the Blessed Virgin Mary, mother of Christ Our Lord.* London and Derby: Thomas Richardson & Son, 1882.

'Ecclesiastical rambles at Leeds: Puseyism – popery – Puritanism'. *British banner* 2: 66 (4 April 1849), 213.

(Edouart, Augustin Gaspard) *An address to the parishioners of Leominster upon the worship of the Virgin Mary.* London: John F. Shaw & Co., 1866.

Edwards, John. 'The purification of the Virgin–Mother'. In Frederick George Lee (ed.), *Miscellaneous sermons by clergymen of the Church of England.* London: Joseph Masters; Aberdeen: A. Brown & Co., 1860, pp. 51–9.

Eliot, George. *The mill on the Floss* (1860). London: Penguin, 1979.

Eliot, George. *Adam Bede* (1859). New York: Penguin, 1980.

Eliot, George. *Romola* (1862–63). London: Penguin, 1996.

Ellis, Mrs (Sarah). *The women of England: their social duties, and domestic habits.* London: Fisher, Son, & Co., 1839.

Ellis, Mrs (Sarah). *The mothers of England: their influence and responsibility.* New York: D. Appleton & Co.; Philadelphia, PA: George S. Appelton, 1844.

An English Catholic. *Monsignore Capel and the ritualists: a review of a recent controversy by an English Catholic.* London: Basil Montagu Pickering, 1875.

E.T. 'Mariolatry'. *Wesleyan–Methodist magazine* (3rd series) 20 (September 1841), 736–42.

Evans, John. *The origin and progress of Mariolatry; being intended as a companion to the Rev. T. H. Horne's 'Mariolatry'.* London: William Edward Painter, 1852.

Evans, Thomas Edward. *The glories of Jesus or the glories of Mary?* London: James Nisbet & Co., 1865.

Exposition of the beatitudes, as applied to those about to embrace the religious life. Ed. Mission Priests of S. John the Evangelist. London: J. T. Hayes, n.d.

Extracts from the Tracts for the times, the Lyra apostolica, and other publications; showing that to oppose ultra-Protestantism is not to favour popery. London: Gilbert & Rivington, n.d.

Faber, Frederick W. *Jesus and Mary: or, Catholic hymns.* London: James Burns, 1849.

Faber, Frederick W. *The devout child of Mary, the Immaculate Mother of Jesus Christ.* Baltimore, MD: John Murphy & Co., London: C. Dolman, 1855.

Faber, Frederick W. 'The doctrine and definition of the Immaculate Conception'. In *The devout child of Mary, the Immaculate Mother of Jesus Christ.* Baltimore, MD: John Murphy & Co., London: C. Dolman, 1855, pp. 269–84.

Faber, Frederick W. *The foot of the cross: or, the sorrows of Mary.* London: Thomas Richardson & Son, 1858.

Faber, Frederick W. *The precious blood: or, the price of our salvation.* London: Thomas Richardson & Son, 1860.

Faber, Frederick W. Preface. In Louis-Marie Grignon de Montfort, *A treatise on the true devotion to the Blessed Virgin.* Trans. F. W. Faber. London: Burns & Lamber, 1863.

(Faber, Frederick W.) *Our Lady and the Eucharist: selections from Father Faber.* By the compiler of *Father Faber's May book.* London: R. & T. Washbourne, 1898.

Faber, Frederick W. *Faber: poet and priest.* Ed. Raleigh Addington. Glamorgan, Wales: D. Brown & Sons, 1974.

(Faber, Frederick W.) *Father Faber's May book.* Compiled by an oblate of Mary Immaculate. London: Burns & Oates; New York, Cincinnati, OH, and Chicago, IL: Benziger Brothers, n.d. (?1894)

Farrar, Frederic W. *Eternal hope: five sermons preached in Westminster Abbey, November and December, 1877.* New York: E. P. Dutton & Co., 1878.

'The Feast of the Conception'. *Quarterly review* 97 (June 1855), 153.

'The Feast of the Conception'. *Quarterly review* 98 (1856), 144–77.

Forbes, A. P. *The sanctity of Christian art: a sermon preached at the reopening of the chapel at Roslin, on Easter Tuesday, 1862.* Edinburgh: Edmonston & Douglas, 1862.

Forbes, A. P. *An explanation of the thirty-nine articles.* 2 vols. Oxford and London: James Parker, 1868.

Forbes, A. P. *The invocation of saints: a reprint from an explanation of the thirty-nine articles* (1867). London: English Church Union, 1903.

(Former rector) *Cautions for the times: addressed to the parishioners of a parish in England.* London: John W. Parker & Son, 1851.

'France'. *Baptist magazine* 45: 201 (September 1854), 557–9.

Frith, W. *Why worship the Virgin Mary? An unanswerable challenge.* 3rd edn. London: John Kensit, n.d. (1892).

Gaskell, Mrs (Elizabeth). *North and south* (1854). New York: G. P. Putnam's Sons; London: Smith, Elder, & Co., 1906.

Gibbings, Richard. *The diptychs: a prelection, delivered in the Divinity School, Trinity College, Dublin, in Michaelmas term, 1864.* Dublin: William McGee; London: Simpkin, Marshall, & Co., 1864.

Gillis, James. *Pastoral charge, by the Right Rev. Bishop Gillis, on the recent dogmatical definition of the Immaculate Conception of the Most Blessed Virgin Mary.* Edinburgh: Marsh & Beattie, 1855.

Gladstone, W. E. 'The Vatican Decrees in their bearing on civil allegiance: a political expostulation'. In *Rome and the newest fashions in religion: three tracts.* London: John Murray, 1875.

The golden manual: being a guide to Catholic devotion, public and private, compiled from approved sources. London: Burns & Lambert, 1850.

Golightly, C. P. *Look at home, or, short and easy method with the Roman Catholics.* Oxford: J. H. Parker; London: J. G. & F. Rivington, 1837.

Goulburn, Edward Meyrick. *John William Burgon, late dean of Chichester: a biography, with extracts from his letters and early journals.* 2 vols. London: John Murray, 1892.

Goulburn, Edward Meyrick. *Reminiscences of Charles Pourtales Golightly: a letter reprinted, with additions, and a preface, from 'The Guardian' newspaper of Jan. 13, 1886.* Oxford and London: Parker & Co., Norwich: Stacey, n.d.

Grahame, Maria. *Three months passed in the mountains east of Rome, during the year 1819.* 2nd edn. London: Longman, Hurst, Rees, Orme, & Brown; Edinburgh: A. Constable & Co., 1821.

'The great fallacy'. *Church and state gazette* 13: 665 (10 November 1854), 710.

Gresley, W. *Four letters on the Rev. J. Spencer Northcote's pamphlet, entitled 'The four-fold difficulty of Anglicanism'.* Reprinted, with additions and corrections, from *The English Churchman.* London: Henry Batty, 1846.

Gresley, W. *A word of remonstrance with the evangelicals: addressed to the Rev. Francis Wilson, M.A., in reply to his pamphlet called 'No peace with Tractarianism'.* London: Joseph Masters; Lichfield: Thomas George Lomax, 1850.

Gresley, W. *A second word of remonstrance with the evangelicals: addressed to the Rev. Francis Wilson, M.A., incumbent of Armitage, in consequence of his pamphlet called 'No peace with Tractarianism'.* London: Joseph Masters; Lichfield: Thomas George Lomax, 1851.

Hamilton, Otto W. H. 'Recollections of a tour, 1822'. 3 vols. Volume 2: 'Milan, Venice, Bologna, Florence'; Volume 3: 'Rome and Naples'. Hand-written, unpublished book. British Library, London. Add. MSS 44837, 44838.

Hampson, R. T. *Religious deceptions of the Church of Rome exposed.* London: C. Mitchell, n.d.

Historical notices concerning some of the peculiar tenets of the Church of Rome. London: J. G. & F. Rivington, 1836.

H.N.T. *May we ask the saints to pray for us?* London: Charles Taylor, n.d.

Hook, Walter Farquhar. *The novelties of Romanism; or, popery refuted by tradition:*

a sermon, preached in St Andrew's Church, Manchester. London: F. C. & J. Rivington; London: J. Burns, 1840.

Hook, Walter Farquhar. *Take heed what ye hear: a sermon, with a preface on some of the existing controversies in the Church.* London: F. & J. Rivington, 1844.

Hopkins, Ellice. *A plea for the wider action of the Church of England in the prevention of the degradation of women, as submitted to a committee of Convocation on July 3, 1879.* London: Hatchards, 1879.

Hopkins, Gerard Manley. 'The Blessed Virgin compared to the air we breathe'. In *Poems and prose.* Ed. W. H. Gardner. New York: Penguin Viking, 1985, pp. 54–8.

(Horne, Thomas Hartwell.) *Mariolatry: or, facts and evidences demonstrating the worship of the Blessed Virgin Mary by the Church of Rome, derived from the testimonies of her reputed saints and doctors, from her Breviary, and other authorized Romish formularies of devotion, confirmed by the attestations of travellers.* 2nd edn. London: William Edward Painter, 1841.

(Horne, Thomas Hartwell.) *Reminiscences personal and bibliographical of Thomas Hartwell Horne, B.D., F.S.A., with notes by his daughter, Sarah Anne Cheyne, and a short Introduction by the Rev. Joseph B. M'Caul.* London: Longman, Green, Longman, & Roberts, 1862.

Hughes, Thomas. *The manliness of Christ.* London: Macmillan, 1879.

Husband, Edward. *Family prayers for Catholic households.* London: G. J. Palmer, 1868.

Husband, Edward. *What will Dr Newman do? A letter to the Very Reverend J. H. Newman, D.D.* London: G. J. Palmer, 1870.

Husenbeth, F. C. *The chain of fathers, witnesses for the doctrine of the Immaculate Conception of the Blessed Virgin Mary, Mother of God.* London: Thomas Richardson & Son, 1860.

Husenbeth, F. C. *Our Blessed Lady of Lourdes: a faithful narrative of the apparitions of the Blessed Virgin Mary, at the rocks of Massabielle, near Lourdes, in the year 1858.* London: Robert Washbourne, 1870.

Hutton, Arthur Wollaston. *Our position as Catholics in the Church of England: a letter to a friend.* London: Rivingtons, 1872.

Hutton, Arthur Wollaston (comp.) *Some account of the family of Hutton of Gate Burton, Lincolnshire, their ancestors and descendants.* n.p.: privately printed, 1898.

Hutton, Arthur Wollaston. *A supplementary chapter and index to the account of the family of Hutton, of Gate Burton, Lincolnshire (written in 1898) bringing the record down to the end of the year 1902.* London: Kenny & Co., n.d.

Hymns ancient and modern, for use in the services of the Church. London: Novello & Co., n.d. (1865).

Ignatius, Fr (Joseph Leycester Lyne). *The Catholic Church of England and what she teaches: a lecture by Father Ignatius (monk of the Order of Saint Benedict), delivered in the Corn Exchange, Manchester, Tuesday, September 27th, 1864.* Manchester: John Heywood, n.d.

Ignatius, Fr (Joseph Leycester Lyne). *Outlines of two sermons preached at S. John*

Baptist's Church, Frome Selwood, on All Hallows' Eve and the Feast of All Hallows, 1871. London: John Hodges, n.d.

'Ignotus'. *Letters from Oxford, in 1843.* Dublin: Andrew Milliken; London: J. Hatchard & Son, 1843.

'Illustrations of the invocation and worship of the Blessed Virgin Mary, in the churches of Belgium'. *Congregational magazine* 26: 7 (September 1843), 622–6.

'The Immaculate Conception'. *Church and state gazette* 14: 673 (5 January 1855), 4–5.

'The Immaculate Conception'. *Wesleyan–Methodist magazine* 1: 6 (June 1855), 523–41.

'The Immaculate Conception'. *Wesleyan times* 7: 335 (12 February 1855), 108–9.

'Interesting cases of conversion from Romanism'. *British Protestant; or, journal of the Special Mission to Roman Catholics in Great Britain* 104 (August 1854), 196–206.

Jackson, Thomas. *A warning against popery: being an exposure of a stealthy attempt to promote the worship of the Virgin Mary, by the erection of her effigy beside the church and school of my native village.* London: Wesleyan Conference Office, 1867.

Jackson, Thomas. *The works of the Reverend, learned, and pious divine, Thomas Jackson, D.D.* Vol. 3. London: John Martin, Richard Chiswell, & Joseph Clark, 1673.

Jameson, Anna Brownell. *Legends of the Madonna as represented in the fine arts* (1852). London: Unit Library, 1904.

J.D.D. 'The miraculous conception'. *London investigator: a monthly journal of secularism* 1: 9 (December 1854), 129–30.

Jerome, John. *Cuddesden versus Vatican, or, a lawyer's demurrer to the Oxford theology concerning the Immaculate Conception and worship of the Blessed Virgin Mary.* Paris: J. Lerous & Jouby; Tours: Jules Bouserez; London: Burns & Lambert; London: Richardson & Son, 1855.

Keble, John. *On eucharistic adoration.* Oxford and London: John Henry & James Parker, 1857.

Keble, John. *Pentecostal fear: a sermon preached in the parish church, Cuddesden, on Tuesday, May 24, 1864, on the anniversary of the Theological College.* Oxford and London: John Henry & James Parker, 1864.

Keble, John. 'Mother out of sight'. In J. T. Coleridge, *A memoir of the Rev. John Keble, M.A., late vicar of Hursley.* 2nd edn. Oxford and London: James Parker, 1869, pp. 314–16.

Keble, John. *Studia sacra: commentaries on the introductory verses of St John's Gospel, and on a portion of Paul's Epistle to the Romans; with other theological papers.* Oxford and London: James Parker & Co., 1877.

Keble, John. 'The Annunciation of the Blessed Virgin Mary'. In *The Christian year* (1827). New York: Thomas Y. Cromwell, 1890, pp. 231–2.

Keble, John. *The Christian year, Lyra innocentium and other poems.* London: Oxford University Press, 1914.

Keenan, Stephen. *Controversial Catechism: or, Protestantism refuted, and Catholicism established, by an appeal to the Holy Scriptures, the testimony of the Holy Fathers, and the dictates of reason; in which such portions of Scheffmacher's Catechism as suit modern controversy are embodied.* 3rd edn. Edinburgh: Marsh & Beattie; London and Manchester: Charles Dolman, 1854.

Ken, Thomas. *The works of the Right Reverend, learned and pious Thomas Ken, D.D.* 4 vols. London: John Wyat, 1721.

Kerr, Walter. *A charge to the clergy and churchwardens of the diocese of Salisbury, at his triennial visitation, in May, 1867.* Salisbury: Brown & Co.; London: Rivingtons; Oxford: Parker, 1867.

The key of heaven; or, a posey of prayers, selected from Catholic authors: to which are added, Gother's instructions and devotions for confession and communion. 14th edn. London: Keating, Brown, & Co., 1819

The key of heaven; or, a posey of prayers, selected from Catholic authors: to which are added, Gother's instructions and devotions for confession and communion. 17th edn. London: Keating, Brown, & Co., 1834.

King, Robert. *The Psalter of the Blessed Virgin Mary illustrated: or a critical disquisition and enquiry concerning the genuineness of the parody on the Psalms of David, commonly ascribed to St Bonaventure; comprehending the first fifty psalms of the Psalter of the B.V.M., with selections from the remainder.* Dublin: Grant & Bolton, 1840.

Kingsley, Charles. *Yeast: a problem.* London: John W. Parker, 1851.

Kingsley, Charles. *Hypatia* (1853) New York: Macmillan, 1880.

Kingsley, Charles. *Westward Ho!* (1855) 2 vols. New York: Fred DeFau & Co., 1889.

Kingsley, Charles. *Charles Kingsley: his letters and memories of his life.* Edited by his wife (Frances Eliza Kingsley). 2 vols. London: Macmillan, 1890.

(Laborde, Jean Joseph). *The Abbé Laborde in Rome; his protest and persecution: being a narrative of the opponents of the novel dogma of the Immaculate Conception.* Trans. and with an introductory essay by Rev. Robert Maguire, M.A. London: Seeley, Jackson, & Halliday, 1855.

A lady. *The contented widow: a narrative illustrative of the importance and necessity of church extension.* Bristol: John Wright, 1849.

A late member of the University of Oxford. *Four years' experience of the Catholic religion, with observations on its effects, intellectual, moral and spiritual; and on the thraldom of Protestantism.* London: James Burns, 1849.

Latimer, Hugh. *Sermons on various subjects.* 2 vols. London: T. Pitcher, 1788.

Latimer, Hugh. 'A sermon preached in the first Sunday after Epiphany, 1552'. In *The fathers of the English Church: a selection of the reformers and early Protestant divines, of the Church of England.* Vol. 2. London: John Hatchard, 1808, pp. 446–66.

Law, William Towry. *Attempted usurpation of authority over the Church in England, by the Bishop of Rome.* London: F. & J. Rivington; Birmingham: Henry C. Langbridge, 1850.

Law, William Towry. *Unity, and faithful adherence to the Word of God, are only* to be found in the Catholic Church: a letter to his late parishioners. London: Burns & Lambert, 1852.

A layman. *Popery in the Church of England: a letter to the Lord Bishop of London*. London: n.p., 1864.

A layman. *The solemnity of our Anglo-Catholic ritualism defended: a letter to the Lord Bishop of London in reply to certain censures in his recent charge to the clergy*. London: W. J. Cleaver, 1850.

A layman. *Stray thoughts on London, religious or irreligious, at Eastertide*. London: Elliott Stock, 1875.

A layman. *Vox Dei aut vox populi: a review of the primary charge of the Bishop of Huron, and of a correspondence between sundry laymen of Toronto, and the Lord Bishop of that diocese, on the teaching of the Church of England as to the doctrines of the adorable sacrifice of the Mass, the invocation of saints and angels, and prayers for the faithful departed*. Dominion of Canada: n.p., 1874.

'Lecky's "History of rationalism"'. *Dublin review* (new series) 7: 13 (July 1866), 188–239.

'Lectures on the non-divinity of Jesus Christ: at the Religious Discussion Hall, George Street, Euston Road, St Pancras'. *Anthill's monthly chronicle and illustrated advertiser* 6 (1 May 1863), 4–5.

Lee, Frederick George (ed.). *Miscellaneous sermons by clergymen of the Church of England*. London: Joseph Masters; Aberdeen: A. Brown & Co., 1860.

Lee, Frederick George. *Mary, the Mother of God*. London: Chiswick Press, 1868.

Lee, Frederick George. *The truth as it is in Jesus: a sermon preached at the Church of S. Martin, Leicester, on Monday, March 2, 1868, at the opening of the Lent Assizes*. London: Joseph Masters, 1868.

Lee, Frederick George (ed.). *Memorials of the late Rev. Robert Stephen Hawker, M.A., sometime vicar of Morwenstow, in the diocese of Exeter*. London: Chatto & Windus, 1876.

(Leeson, Jane Eliza) *The wreath of lilies: a gift for the young*. London: James Burns, 1847.

Lefroy, William. 'A plea for the old Catholic movement': the old Catholic and Roman Catholic faiths compared; being two sermons, preached in St Andrew's Church, on Sunday, September 27th, 1874*. London: Rivingtons; Liverpool: A. Holden, 1874.

Legeyt, C. J. *Incense at the 'Magnificat' not 'Mariolatry': a letter, to the Very Rev. the Dean of Chester*. London: G. J. Palmer, 1867.

Le Mesurier, Thomas. *The invocation of the Virgin Mary and of the saints, as now practised in the Church of Rome, shewn to be superstitious and idolatrous: a sermon preached before the archdeacon of Durham, at his visitation held at South-Church on Wednesday the 5th day of July, 1815*. Durham: G. Walker, 1815.

Liguori, Alphonsus. *The glories of Mary*. Trans. by 'A father of the same congregation'. New York: Edward Dunigan & Brother, 1852.

Liguori, Alphonsus. *Visits to the Most Holy Sacrament and the Blessed Virgin Mary*. Trans. and ed. R. A. Coffin. London: Burns & Lambert, 1855.

Lingard, John. *Catechetical instructions on the doctrines and worship of the Catholic Church*. Rev. edn. London: Charles Dolman, 1844.

Lingwood, Thomas J. *Was the Virgin Mary immaculate, and born without sin? A sermon, preached in the Chapel of St Andrew and St Mary, Maidenhead, on Sunday, October the 15th, 1871*. London: William Hunt & Co., 1872.

Littledale, Richard Frederick. *Ritualists not Romanists*. n.p.: n.p., n.d.

Littledale, Richard Frederick. *Why ritualists do not become Roman Catholics: a reply to the Abbé Martin*. London: Strahan & Co., Ltd, n.d.

Lockhart, J. G. *Charles Lindley, Viscount Halifax*. Part 1: *1830–1885*. London: Geoffrey Bles–Centenary Press, 1935.

(Lockhart, William). *The Rosary of the Most Blessed Virgin Mary: with the Litany of Loretto, and other devotions*. London: James Burns, n.d. (1849).

(Lockhart, William) *Biography of Father Lockhart: reprinted, with additions, from the autumn number of 'The Ratcliffian'*. Leicester: Ratcliffe College; Market Weighton: St William's Press, 1893.

Lockhart, William. *The communion of saints; or the Catholic doctrine concerning our relation to the Blessed Virgin, the angels, and the saints*. 2nd edn. London: Burns, Oates, & Co., n.d.

(Longley), Charles Thomas. *Christ's dying hours: a sermon preached on the occasion of the re-opening of St Margaret's Church, Hilston, Holderness, on Thursday, July 31, 1862*. London: for private circulation, 1862.

Lord Bishop of Down and Connor, and Dromore. *The laws of the Church, the churchman's guard against Romanism and Puritanism*. Reprinted from the *Irish ecclesiastical journal*. Dublin: Grant & Bolton; London: J. G. F. & J. Rivington, 1842.

Lowder, C. F. *To the parishioners & congregation of S. Peter's, London Docks*. n.p. (London): n.p., n.d. (1872).

Luscombe, Bishop. *The Church of Rome, compared with the Bible, the Fathers of the Church and the Church of England*. Trans. Henry Press Wright. London: J. Nisbet & Co., 1841.

Lush, Alfred. *A sermon, preached in the Church of Saint Mary, Greywell, on Good-Friday, 1853: being also the Festival of the Annunciation of the Blessed Virgin Mary*. London: John & Charles Mozley, 1853.

'Lydia'. 'Female biography of Scripture: Rebekah', part 1. *Christian lady's magazine* 14 (July–December 1840), 542.

Mackeson, H. B., FGS. *The Fraternity of the Assumption of the Blessed Virgin Mary at Hythe*. London: John Russell Smith, 1873.

Manning, Henry Edward. 'Dogmatic authority: supernatural and infallible'. In *Sermons on ecclesiastical subjects*. Vol. 1. Dublin: James Duffy, 1863, pp. 117–45.

Manning, Henry Edward. *The workings of the Holy Spirit in the Church of England: a letter to the Rev. E. B. Pusey, D.D.* London: Longman, Green, Longman, Roberts, & Green, 1864.

Manning, Henry Edward. Preface. *Meditations on the life of the Blessed Virgin, for every day in the month; suitable for all seasons, and especially for the month of May*. London: Derby, 1870.

'Mariolatry'. *North British review* 8: 16 (February 1848), 339–65.

Marshall, W. *Mary or Madonna?* 2nd edn London: Chas. J. Thynne, 1896.

'Mary in the gospels'. *Dublin review* (new series) 8: 16 (April 1867), 435–55.

Maskell, William. *A second letter on the present position of the high church party in the Church of England: the want of dogmatic teaching in the reformed English Church*. London: William Pickering, 1850.

(Maskell, William) *Some remarks upon two recent memoirs of R. S. Hawker, late vicar of Morwen-Stowe*. Reprinted from the *Athenaeum* (26 March 1876), with additions. n.p.: 30 copies printed for private circulation, 1876.

Maton, William George. 'Journal of a tour to France, Flanders, Germany, Italy, and Switzerland, 1822'. British Library, London. Add. MS 32442.

M'Caul, Joseph B. *The Rev. Thomas Hartwell Horne, B.D.: a sketch*. London: privately printed, 1862.

Maudson, W. T. 'The dogma of the Virgin Mary's Immaculate Conception: a sermon'. *Pulpit* 67: 1,784 (8 March 1855), 233–40.

A member of the Church of England. *A few remarks upon the letter of Lord John Russell to the Bishop of Durham*. London: Francis & John Rivington, 1850.

A member of the Sodality of the Living Rosary. *The Rosary of the Blessed Virgin Mary: a selection of poetry arranged in accordance with the prayers and meditations of the Rosary*. London: Thomas Richardson & Son, n.d. (1848).

Merewether, Francis. *Popery a new religion, compared with that of Christ and his apostles: a sermon*. 3rd edn. Loughborough and Ashby Protestant Tract Society, 1836.

Meyrick, Frederick (ed.). *Correspondence between members of the Anglo-Continental Society and (1) Old Catholic (2) Oriental churchmen*. London: Rivingtons, 1874.

Miller, George. *A letter to the Rev. E. B. Pusey, D.D., in reference to his letter to the Lord Bishop of Oxford*. London: Duncan & Malcolm, 1840.

Miller, John C. 'The Immaculate Conception: a sermon'. *Pulpit* 67: 1,793 (10 May 1855), 423–32.

Miller, John C. 'Subjection; no, not for an hour'; a warning to Protestant Christians, in behalf of the 'truth of the Gospel', as now imperiled by the Romish doctrines and practices of the Tractarian heresy: being the substance of a sermon preached in St Martin's Church, Birmingham, on Sunday evening, September 8, 1850. 3rd edn. London: T. Hatchard; Seeleys; Hamilton, Adams, & Co., n.d.

'Missionary operations: Broadway, Worcestershire'. *British Protestant; or, journal of the Special Mission to Roman Catholics in Great Britain* 108 (December 1854), 261–5.

'Missionary operations: Hull'. *British Protestant; or, journal of the Special Mission to Roman Catholics in Great Britain* 108 (December 1854), 265–72.

'Mr Murphy at Bacup'. *Bacup times* (25 April), 1868, 6.

Moore, Daniel. 'Lectures on the life of Christ. No. IV: The Nativity'. Delivered in Camden Church, Camberwell, Sunday evening, 5 February 1854. Reprinted in *Pulpit* 65 (1854), 173–8.

Morris, John Brande. *Talectha koomee: or the gospel prophecy of Our Blessed Lady's Assumption: a drama in four acts*. London: Burns & Lambert, 1858.

'Mother's words'. *Monthly messenger* 168 (?December 1863), 1–4.

Mozley, Thomas. *Reminiscences chiefly of Oriel College and the Oxford Movement*. 2 vols. Boston, MA: Houghton Mifflin, 1882.

Mulholland, J. Shaw. *The world's Madonna: a history of the Blessed Virgin Mary*. London: Burns & Oates; New York, Cincinnati, OH, Chicago, IL: Benziger Brothers, 1909.

Neale, John Mason. *Annals of virgin saints*. London: Masters, 1846.

Neale, John Mason. *Secession: A sermon preached in the Oratory of S. Margaret's, East Grinstead, November 18, 1859*. London: Joseph Masters, 1868.

Neale, John Mason. *Sermons for some feast days in the Christian year, as preached in the Oratory of S. Margaret's, East Grinstead*. London: J. T. Hayes, n.d.

Neale, John Mason *Sermons on the blessed sacrament: preached in the Oratory of S. Margaret's, East Grinstead* (1870). 7th edn. London: J. T. Hayes, n.d. (1871).

Nevins, Willis Probyn. *'May canonized saints be in hell?' A letter to His Eminence Cardinal Manning*. London: Williams & Norgate, n.d. (1880).

Newman, F. W. *Contributions chiefly to the early history of the late Cardinal Newman*. London: Kegan, Paul, Trench, Trubner, & Co., 1891.

Newman, John Henry. 'On the faith of Mary'. No. 137, Lecture 3. Preached at St Clements, 19 February 1826. Birmingham Oratory, Newman Papers.

Newman, John Henry. 'The Annunciation of the Blessed Virgin Mary – on the honour due to her'. In 'Course of sermons and lectures on Saints days & holidays', No. 291. Preached at St Mary the Virgin (Oxford), Friday March 25, 1831, and Wednesday March 25, 1835; preached at St Mary's, Littlemore, Wednesday March 25, 1840 and Saturday March 25, 1842. Birmingham Oratory, Newman Papers.

Newman, John Henry. *A letter to the Right Reverend Father in God, Richard, Lord Bishop of Oxford, on occasion of No. 90, in the series called the Tracts for the times*. Oxford: John Henry Parker; London: J. G. F. & J. Rivington, 1841.

(Newman, John Henry) *Tract 1: Thoughts on the Ministerial Commission*. London: Gilbert & Rivington, 1843.

Newman, John Henry. 'A letter addressed to the Rev. E. B. Pusey, D.D., on occasion of his Eirenicon'. In *Certain difficulties felt by Anglicans in Catholic teaching considered* (1865). London: Burns, Oates, & Co., 1875, pp. 355–496.

Newman, John Henry. 'On the fitness of the glories of Mary'. In *Discourses addressed to mixed congregations* (1849). London: Longmans, Green, & Co., 1897, pp. 360–76.

Newman, John Henry. 'The glories of Mary for the sake of her son'. In *Discourses addressed to mixed congregations* (1849). London: Longmans, Green, & Co., 1897, pp. 342–59.

Newman, John Henry. *Apologia pro vitâ suâ*. Introduction by Philip Hughes (1864). New York: Doubleday, 1956.

Newman, John Henry. 'The Blessed Mary'. In *Selected treatises of St Athanasius in controversy with the Arians*. Vol. 2. London: Longmans, Green, & Co., 1903.

Newman, John Henry. *Selected treatises of St Athanasius in controversy with the Arians.* Vol. 2. London: Longmans, Green, & Co., 1903.

Newman, John Henry. *Sermon notes of John Henry Cardinal Newman.* Ed. Fathers of the Birmingham Oratory. London: Longmans, Green, and Co., 1913.

Newman, John Henry. 'The reverence due to the Virgin Mary'. In *Parochial and plain sermons.* New York and London: Longmans, Green, & Co., 1924, Vol. 2, pp. 127–38.

Newman, John Henry. 'Our Lady in the gospel'. In *Faith and prejudice, and other unpublished sermons of Cardinal Newman.* Ed. Birmingham Oratory. New York: Sheed & Ward, 1956, pp. 85–96.

Newman, John Henry. *The parting of friends: a sermon preached on the anniversary of the consecration of a chapel.* Westminster, MD: Newman Press, 1961.

Newman, John Henry. *The letters and diaries of John Henry Newman.* 31 vols. Ed. Charles Stephen Dessain et al. London: Thomas Nelson & Sons, 1961–72; Oxford: Clarendon Press, 1973–77 and 1978–99.

Newman, John Henry. *Mary: the second Eve.* Comp. Eileen Breen. Rockford, IL: TAN Books & Publishers, 1982.

Newman, John Henry. *Sermons 1824–1843.* Ed. Vincent Ferrer Blehl. Vol. 2: *Sermons on biblical history, sin and justification, the Christian way of life, and biblical theology.* Oxford: Clarendon Press, 1993.

Newman, John Henry. *The idea of a university.* Ed. Frank M. Turner. New Haven, CT: Yale University Press, 1996.

Newman, John Henry. *The stations of the cross.* London: Catholic Truth Society, n.d.

(Newman, John Henry) *Tract 75: On the Roman Breviary as embodying the substance of the devotional services of the Church Catholic.* 2nd edn. London: J. G. & F. Rivington, n.d. (1837).

Newton, Thomas. *Beware of popery: read, mark and understand the following testimony of Holy Scripture, against the antichristian Church of Rome.* Birmingham: Charles Hammond, 1835.

Nicolas. *The Virgin Mary according to the gospel.* Trans. Vicomtesse de L.S.J. and Sister M. Christopher, OSF. Ed. Rev. H. Collins. London: Thomas Richardson & Sons, 1876.

Nightingale, Florence. *Suggestions for thought.* Ed. Michael Calabria and Janet A. Macrae. Philadelphia: University of Pennsylvania Press, 1994.

Noel, M. H. *Do Roman Catholics worship the Blessed Virgin Mary? A sermon preached at S. Barnabas', Oxford, on the twelfth Sunday after Trinity, 1872.* Oxford: A. R. Mowbray & Co.; London: Simpkin, Marshall, & Co., n.d.

A nonconformist. *Two tracts for the times: I. The duty of the ritualists to quit the Established Church. II. The duty of the State in relation to religion.* London: John Bale & Sons, 1872.

Northcote, J. Spencer. *The Roman catacombs; or, some account of the burial-places of the early Christians in Rome.* London: Charles Dolman, 1857.

Northcote, J. Spencer. *A visit to the Roman catacombs.* London: Burns and Oates, 1877.

Northcote, J. Spencer and W. R. Brownlow. *Roma sotterranea, or account of the Roman catacombs, especially of the cemetery of St Callixtus, compiled from the works of Commendatore de Rossi with the consent of the author.* 2 vols (1869). 2nd edn. London: Longmans, Green, & Co., 1879.

'North-west London Mission'. *British Protestant; or, journal of the Special Mission to Roman Catholics in Great Britain* 113 (May 1855), 70–2.

Norton, Caroline. *English laws for women in the nineteenth century.* London, 1854; reprinted as *Caroline Norton's defense.* Chicago, IL: Academy Chicago, 1982.

'A novel importation'. *British banner* 3: 151 (20 November 1850), 787.

A Novena in honour of the Most Blessed Virgin Mary of Mount Carmel, Mother of God, and Our Dear Lady: together with a devout manner of reciting the Holy Rosary, as used in some of the noviciates of the Order of Mount Carmel. Trans. from the Spanish. London: Burns & Lambert, 1852.

Oldknow, Joseph. *A letter to the Rev. John Cale Miller, M.A., rector of St Martin's, Birmingham, on the comparative relations of the Church of England to the Church of Rome and the Protestant bodies.* London: F. & J. Rivington and J. Masters; Birmingham: H. C. Langbridge & Alfred Hodgetts, 1848.

Oldknow, Joseph. *The evil of forsaking the Church of England for the communion of Rome.* London: F. & J. Rivington; Birmingham: Hodgetts & Langbridge, 1850.

Oliphant, Mrs (Margaret). 'Madonna Mary'. *Good words* 7 (1866).

One of themselves. *The Pope, the premier, and the people: plain words to plain churchfolk on the late Papal Aggression.* London: Joseph Masters, 1851.

Orsini, Abbé. *The history of the Blessed Virgin Mary, Mother of God: completed by the traditions of the East, the writings of the Holy Fathers, and the private history of the Hebrews.* Trans. F. C. Husenbeth. In Alban Butler, *The lives of the Fathers, martyrs, and other principal saints, compiled from original documents and other authentic records.* Ed. F. C. Husenbeth. Vol. 2. London and Dublin: Henry & Co., n.d. (1857–60), pp. v–cxliv.

'Outrages on missionaries'. *Baptist magazine* (4th series) 47: 211 (July 1855), 445.

Owen, Robert. *An essay on the communion of saints, together with an examination of the cultus sanctorum, being an appendix to a work intituled 'Santorale Catholicum'.* London: C. Kegan Paul & Co., 1881.

Oxenham, Henry Nutcombe. *Dr Pusey's Eirenicon considered in relation to Catholic unity: a letter to the Rev. Father Lockhart of the Institute of Charity.* London: Longmans, Green, & Co., 1866.

Palmer, William. *A letter to N. Wiseman, D.D. (calling himself Bishop of Melipotamus), containing remarks on his Letter to Mr Newman.* Oxford: John Henry Parker, 1841.

Palmer, William. *A fifth letter to N. Wiseman, D.D., containing a reply to his remarks on Letter I: with additional proofs of the idolatry and superstition of Romanism.* Oxford: John Henry Parker; London: J. G. F. & J. Rivington, 1841.

Palmer, William. *A narrative of events connected with the publication of the Tracts for the times, with reflections on existing tendencies to Romanism, and on the present duties and prospects of members of the Church.* Oxford: John Henry Parker, 1843.

Palmer, William. *A statement of circumstances connected with the proposal of resolutions at a special general meeting of the Bristol Church Union, October 1, 1850.* London: Francis & John Rivington, 1850.

'Papal infallibility'. *English Church defence tracts*, No. 3. London: Rivingtons, 1872.

A parish priest. *Concerning the honour due to Our Lady.* Holborn: W. Knott, 1885.

'Passaglia on the prerogatives of Mary'. *Dublin review* 41 (September 1856), 117–71.

Patmore, Coventry. *The angel in the house.* London and Cambridge: Macmillan & Co., 1863.

Pennington, Arthur Robert. *The worship of the Virgin Mary: its origin and progress.* Tract No. 234. London: Religious Tract Society, n.d.

(Perceval, Arthur Philip) *The churchman's manual; or, questions and answers on the Church; on Protestant and Romish dissenters; and Socinians.* Oxford: S. Collingwood, 1834.

Phillips, Ambrose Lisle. *Manual of devotion for the use of the brethren and sisters of the Confraternity of the Living Rosary of the Blessed Virgin Mary, established in the parishes of Grace Dieu and Whitwick.* Derby: Richardson & Son for the Catholic Book Society, 1843.

Phillips, Ambrose Lisle. *Some remarks on a letter addressed to the Reverend R. W. Jelf, D.D., in explanation of No. 90 in the series called the Tracts for the times.* London: Charles Dolman, 1841.

(Phillpotts, Henry), Henry, Lord Bishop of Exeter. *Charge delivered to the clergy of the diocese of Exeter.* London: John Murray, 1839.

Pius IX. *Ineffabilis Deus: official documents connected with the definition of the dogma of the Immaculate Conception of the Blessed Virgin Mary.* Baltimore, MD: John Murray & Co.; London: Charles Dolman, 1855.

'The Pope and the Romans'. *British banner* 2: 53 (3 January 1849), 9.

'Popery: Pope Pius IX'. *British banner* 7: 351 (20 September 1854), 659.

'The Pope's encyclical letter'. *British banner* 2: 69 (25 April 1849), 266.

(Powell, Henry Townsend) *Roman fallacies and Catholic truths*, No. 7: *Worship of the Virgin Mary.* London: William Edward Painter, n.d. (1840).

(Powell, Henry Townsend) *Roman fallacies and Catholic truths*, No. 8: *Canonization of saints.* London: William Edward Painter, n.d. (1840).

(Powell, Henry Townsend) *Stretton tracts*, No. 6: *Saint worship.* Coventry: C. A. N. Rollason, n.d. (1840).

Poynder, John. *Popery in alliance with heathenism: letters proving that where the Bible is wholly unknown, as in the heathen world, or only partially known, as in the Romish Church, idolatry and superstition are inevitable.* 2nd edn. London: J. Hatchard & Son, 1835.

Poynder, John. *Extracts from three speeches delivered by the late John Poynder, Esq., at the East India House, in the years 1830, 1836, and 1839: demonstrating the direct support and encouragement given by the company to idolatry; together with extracts from other sources on the subject of idolatry, and the Indian mutinies, with remarks by the editor.* Ed. G. Poynder. London: Wertheim & Macintosh, 1857.

Prayers for the conversion of England. London: Catholic Truth Society, 1895.

Prayers for the conversion of the people of England; and of all others separated from the faith and unity of the Church, set forth by the authority of the bishops of England, and recommended for the use of the faithful in their several dioceses. New edn. London: Burns, Oates, & Co., n.d.

The present treatment of Protestants by the Church of Rome where dominant, and its intentions here. N.p.: n.p., n.d. (1862).

A priest of the diocese. *Pictorial crucifixes: a letter to the Lord Bishop of Chichester.* London: Joseph Masters, 1852.

Prynne, George Rundle. *Emmanuel, God with us, in the sacraments of the Church: a sermon preached in S. Peter's Church, Plymouth, on the Sunday within the octave of Christmas, 1868.* London: Joseph Masters, 1869.

The Psalter of the Blessed Virgin, written by St Bonaventure. Ed. John Cumming. London: British Reformation Society, 1852.

Pusey, E. B. *Letter to the Right Rev. Father in God, Richard Lord Bishop of Oxford, on the tendency to Romanism imputed to doctrines held of old, as now, in the English Church.* Oxford: J. H. Parker; London: J. G. & F. Rivington, 1839.

Pusey, E. B. *A letter to His Grace the Archbishop of Canterbury, on some circumstances connected with the present crisis in the English Church.* Oxford: John Henry Parker; London: J. G. F. & J. Rivington, 1842.

Pusey, E. B. *The Presence of Christ in the Holy Eucharist: a sermon, preached before the University, in the Cathedral Church of Christ, in Oxford, on the second Sunday after Epiphany, 1853.* Oxford: John Henry Parker; London: Francis & John Rivington, 1853.

Pusey, E. B. *The doctrine of the Real Presence, as contained in the fathers from the death of S. John the Evangelist to the fourth General Council, vindicated, in notes on a sermon, 'The Presence of Christ in the Holy Eucharist', preached A.D. 1853, before the University of Oxford.* Oxford: John Henry Parker; London: F. & J. Rivington, 1855.

Pusey, E. B. *The Real Presence of the body and blood of Our Lord Jesus Christ the doctrine of the English Church, with a vindication of the reception by the wicked and of the adoration of Our Lord Jesus Christ truly present.* Oxford: John Henry Parker, 1857.

Pusey, E. B. *The Church of England a portion of Christ's one Holy Catholic Church, and a means of restoring visible unity: an Eirenicon in a letter to the author of The Christian year.* Oxford: John Henry & James Parker; London: Rivingtons, 1865.

Pusey, E. B. *First letter to the Very Rev. J. H. Newman, D.D., in explanation chiefly in regard to the reverential love due to the ever-blessed Theotokos, and the doctrine of her Immaculate Conception.* Oxford: James Parker; London: Rivingtons, 1869.

Pusey, E. B. 'Eve: the course of temptation'. In *Lenten sermons, preached chiefly to young men at the universities, between A.D. 1858–1874*. Oxford: James Parker; London: Rivingtons, 1874.

The Raccolta; or, collection of indulgenced prayers. Trans. Ambrose St John. London: Burns & Lambert, 1857.

Redesdale, Lord. *Reasonings on some disputed points of doctrine*. 2nd edn. London: Rivingtons, 1874.

Redesdale, Lord and Charles L. Wood. *The doctrine of the Real Presence: correspondence between the Earl of Redesdale and the Honourable Charles L. Wood*. London: John Murray, 1879.

'The religion of the Oratorians'. *Church and state gazette* 12: 617 (9 December 1853), 765–7.

Remarks on the Churches of Rome and England, respectfully addressed to the Right Rev. Dr Wiseman and the Rev. William Palmer. London: J. Hatchard & Son, 1841.

Report of the inquiry instituted by the Right Reverend the Lord Bishop of Exeter, as Visitor of the Orphans' Home, established by the Sisters of Mercy, at Morice Town, Devonport, into the truth of certain statements published in the 'Devonport Telegraph', February 10th, 1849. Plymouth: Roger Lidstone; London: J. Masters; Exeter: H. J. Wallis, 1849.

'The retrospect of 1849'. *British banner* 3: 105 (2 January 1850), 3.

A review of Dr Pusey's Eirenicon, reprinted from the 'Weekly register', with two letters to the editor from Dr Pusey on his hopes of the reunion of the Church of England with the Catholic Church: also, letters from Dr Newman and Canon Oakley. London: George Cheek, n.d.

'Review of Edward Jewitt Robinson's *The mother of Jesus not the papal Mary*'. *London Quarterly Review* 45 (October 1875 and January 1876), 436–75.

Richards, Richard R. *The birth, life, and death of the Blessed Virgin Mary: also, the birth, life, sufferings, and death of Our Lord and Saviour Jesus Christ; to which are added retaliations of divine providence*. St Day: Richard Skinner, 1861.

Ridley, W. H. *Intercession a Christian duty*. London: G. J. Palmer for the Association for Intercessory Prayer, 1864.

'The rise and progress of Mariolatry'. *Contemporary review* 4 (January–April 1867), 473–87.

Robertson, Frederick W. *Sermons on Christian doctrine*. London and Toronto: J. M. Dent & Sons; New York: E. P. Dutton, 1921.

Robertson, Frederick W. *The loneliness of Christ*. London: H. R. Allenson, n.d.

Robinson, Edward Jewitt. *The mother of Jesus not the papal Mary*. London: Wesleyan Conference Office, 1875.

'Roman Catholic London'. *The Christian world magazine and family visitor* 11: 2 (February 1875), 154–60.

'Roman misquotations'. *English Church defence tracts*, No. 1. London: Rivingtons, 1872.

'Romish ritualism: an ecclesiastical death-bed'. *Wesleyan–Methodist magazine* (5th series) 11: 11 (November 1865), 994–1000.

Rossetti, Christina. 'A Christmas carol'. *The complete poems of Christina Rossetti*. Ed. R. W. Crump. Baton Rouge and London: Louisiana State University Press, 1979, pp. 216–18.

Rouvier, Dom Louis-Marie. *A complete Novena in preparation for the festivals of the Blessed Virgin Mary; together with a collection of extracts from the Holy Fathers suitable for the month of Mary*. Trans. Agnes M. Stewart. Ed. Carthusian Fathers of Saint Hugh's, Parkminster. London: Burns & Oates; New York: Catholic Publication Society, 1888.

Ruskin, John. 'Of Queens' Gardens'. In *Sesame and lilies* (1865). London and New York: Everyman, 1965, pp. 48–79.

'S. Alfonso de Liguori's *Glories of Mary'*. *Christian remembrancer* 30 (July–December 1855), 417–67.

St Leger, William N. *Gorham v. the Bishop of Exeter: Protestant v. Catholic: heresy v. truth: 'a tract for the times'*. London: William Pickering, 1850.

Sarnelli, Januarius Mary. *The Holy Rosary*. Trans. Albert Barry. London and New York: Burns & Oates; Dublin: M. H. Gill, n.d.

'S.B.H.' 'A British mother's address to Queen Victoria'. *Christian lady's magazine* 15 (January–June 1841), 128.

Scally, M. *A sermon on the most ancient and venerable order of the Ever Blessed Virgin Mary of Mount Carmel: in which is clearly explained, the devotion peculiar to that same; the duties to be performed by the members of the confraternity correctly expounded; the errors of many uninformed on these duties corrected; and by which all who desire in sincerity the conversion of England are invited to become the advocates of devotion to Mary*. London: Henry Lucas, 1849.

Sebastian, Fr, of the Blessed Sacrament (Sebastian Keens). *Manual of devotions in honour of the seven dolours of the Blessed Virgin Mary*. 2nd edn. London: Denis Lane, 1868.

Selections from a work entitled 'The ideal of a Christian church, &c. &c. &c.', illustrative of its tendency to promote dutifulness to the English Church, unity among her members, and charity towards dissentients. London: James Toovey, 1844.

(Sellon, P. Lydia) Superior of the Society. *Reply to a tract by the Rev. J. Spurrell, vicar of Great Shelford, containing certain charges concerning the Society of the Sisters of Mercy of Devonport and Plymouth*. London: Joseph Masters, 1852.

Senior, Jam. *Religio modesta: or, a sigh for peace*. London: Simpkin, Marshall, & Co.; Salisbury: Brown & Co., 1874.

Sewell, Mrs S. A. *Woman and the times we live in*. 2nd edn. Manchester: Tubbs & Brook; London: Simpkin, Marshall & Co., 1869.

Seymour, M. Hobart. *A pilgrimage to Rome*. London: Seeleys, 1848.

Seymour, M. Hobart. *Mornings among the Jesuits at Rome: being notes of conversations held with certain Jesuits on the subject of religion in the city of Rome*. London: Seeleys, 1849.

Seymour, M. Hobart. *A lecture, delivered at the Guildhall, Bath, on Monday, Dec. 2, 1850, on the recent papal aggression*. Bath: M. A. Pocock, n.d.

Shipley, Orby (ed.). *Lyra Mystica: hymns and verses on sacred subjects, ancient and modern*. London: Longman, Green, Longman, Roberts, & Green, 1865.

Shipley, Orby. *The Saturday review and Lyra Mystica: a letter to the editor of the Saturday review*. London: Longman, Green, Longman, Roberts, & Green, 1865.

Shipley, Orby. 'On the cultus of the Blessed Virgin Mary'. In Anthony Stafford, *Life of the Blessed Virgin, together with the apology of the author, and an essay on the cultus of the Blessed Virgin Mary*. 4th edn. Ed. Orby Shipley. London: Longmans, Green, Reader, & Dyer, 1869, pp. xxv–lxxiii.

Shipley, Orby (ed.). *Invocation of saints and angels: compiled from Greek, English, and Latin sources, for the use of members of the Church of England*. London: Longmans, Green, Reader, & Dyer, 1869.

Shipley, Orby. *Truthfulness and ritualism: Dr Littledale's reply to the Abbé Martin; 'why ritualists do not become Roman Catholics'* (1st series). London: Burns & Oates, 1879.

Shipley, Orby (ed.). *Carmina Mariana: an English anthology in verse in honour of or in relation to the Blessed Virgin Mary*. London: Spottiswoode & Co., 1893.

Sinclair, Catherine. *Popish legends, or Bible truths*. London: Longman, Brown, Green, & Longmans, 1852.

Sinclair, Catherine. *Beatrice; or, the unknown relatives* (1852). London: Ward, Lock, & Tyler, 1890.

Sinclair, Hannah. *A letter on the principles of Christian faith*. Ed. Catherine Sinclair. Edinburgh: William Whyte; London: Hamilton, Adams, 1852.

Sisterhood of St Margaret's, East Grinstead. *Breviary offices from Lauds to Compline inclusive, translated and arranged for use from the Sarum Book*. 2nd edn. London: J. T. Hayes, 1880.

(Sitwell, Francis). *The recent decree on the Immaculate Conception of the Blessed Virgin Mary: a sign of the present time. A sermon preached at Albury, on the twenty-fifth of December, 1854*. London: Thomas Bosworth, 1855.

Skilton, W. J. *Neither inconsistency, nor unfaithfulness to the word of God, justly chargeable upon the authorised teaching of the Church of England: a letter to the parishioners of Harbone, from the Rev. W. J. Skilton, M.A., late curate of that parish, with reference to some statements contained in a recently-published letter of the Hon. and Rev. W. T. Law, M.A*. London: F. & J. Rivington; Birmingham: H. C. Langbridge, 1852.

'S.M.' 'Christmas Day'. *Christian lady's magazine* 12 (July–December 1839), 525–31.

'Southwark mission: missionary report'. *British Protestant; or, journal of the Special Mission to Roman Catholics in Great Britain* 116 (August 1855), 214–19.

Stafford, Anthony. *Life of the Blessed Virgin, together with the apology of the author, and an essay on the cultus of the Blessed Virgin Mary*. Ed. Orby Shipley. 4th edn. London: Longmans, Green, Reader, & Dyer, 1869.

Starke, Mariana. *Travels in Europe, for the use of travellers on the Continent, and likewise in the island of Sicily; to which is added an account of the remains of ancient Italy, and also of the roads leading to those remains*. 8th edn. Paris: A. & W. Galignani, 1833.

Talbot, Edward Stuart. *Memories of early life*. London: A. R. Mowbray, 1924.

Taylor, Catharine. *Letters from Italy to a younger sister*. 2 vols. London: John

Murray, 1840 (vol. 1), 1841 (vol. 2).

Thirlwall, Connop. *A charge delivered to the clergy of the diocese of St David's.* London: Rivingtons, 1857.

'Thoughts on the Assumption'. *Irish monthly* (1877), 501–11.

Trollope, Anthony. *Framley parsonage* (1861). Ware, Hertfordshire: Wordsworth, 1994.

(Turpin, G. M.) *The Rev. Thomas Hartwell Horne, B.D.: A memoir.* n.p.: n.p., n.d.

Tyler, J. Endell. *Primitive Christian worship: or, the evidence of Holy Scripture and the Church, concerning the invocation of saints and angels, and the Blessed Virgin Mary.* London: J. G. F. & J. Rivington, 1840.

Tyler, J. Endell. *The worship of the Blessed Virgin Mary in the Church of Rome contrary to Holy Scripture, and to the faith and practice of the Church of Christ through the first five centuries.* London: Richard Bentley, 1844.

Ullathorne, William. *The Immaculate Conception of the Mother of God: an exposition.* Baltimore, MD: John Murphy & Co.; Pittsburgh, PA: George Quigley, 1855.

Ullathorne, William. *The Devil is a jackass.* Ed. Leo Madigan. Leominster: Gracewing; Bath: Downside Abbey, 1995.

Vance, William Ford. *On the invocation of angels, saints, and the Virgin Mary: two sermons preached at Tavistock chapel, Drury Lane, in the course of lectures on the points in controversy between Roman Catholics and Protestants.* London: James Nisbet, 1828.

Van Volckxsom, J. *A month of pious thoughts under the special patronage of the Blessed Virgin Mary.* Trans. Mrs. E. Harting. Liège: H. Dessain, London: Burns & Oates; Dublin: Gill & Son, 1887.

'Vicesimus' (John Oakley). *H. N. Oxenham: recollections of an old friend.* Manchester: Guardian Printing Works, 1888.

The views of Bishop Pearson and the fathers of the English Reformation on the subject of the ever-virginity of Saint Mary the Virgin. London: J. H. Parker & Co.; Brighton: H. & C. Treacher, 1889.

'The Virgin Mary'. *Littell's living age* 98: 1269 (26 September 1868), 793–95.

The Virgin Mary, a married woman. London: William Macintosh, n.d. (1869).

A voice from Rome. London: James Burns, 1843.

Walker, J. Edgar. *Notes on the Church Catechism.* London: Church Printing Co., 1885.

Ward, Wilfrid. *The life and times of Cardinal Wiseman.* 2 vols. London, New York and Bombay: Longmans, Green, & Co., 1897.

Was the British Church Roman Catholic? London: Catholic Truth Society, n.d.

Waterton, Edward. *Pietas Mariana Britannica: a history of English devotion to the Most Blessed Virgin Mary, Mother of God.* London: St Joseph's Catholic Library, 1879.

Watson, Alexander. *The Church's own action the safeguard of the Church and realm of England from Romish aggression.* London: Joseph Masters, 1850.

Wesley, John. *The letters of John Welsey.* Ed. John Telford. Vol. 3. London: Epworth, 1931.

What is Romanism? No. 10: *On the worship of the Virgin Mary: evidence of Holy Scripture against it.* London: SPCK, 1846.

Who is your patron saint? London: Catholic Truth Society, n.d.

'Why working men mean to stand by the ritualistic clergy'. St. Alban's, Holborn: Working Men's Committee, 1875.

Wilberforce, Samuel. 'The character of the Virgin Mary'. In *Four sermons preached before her Most Gracious Majesty, Queen Victoria in 1841 and 1842.* London: James Burns, 1842.

Wilberforce, Samuel. 'Diary of a holiday in Europe', 1851. Bodleian Library, Oxford. MSS Wilberforce e. 9.

(Wilberforce) Samuel, Lord Bishop of Oxford. *Rome – her new dogma and our duties: a sermon, preached before the university, at St Mary's Church, Oxford, on the Feast of the Annunciation of the Blessed Virgin Mary, 1855.* Oxford and London: John Henry Parker, n.d.

Wild, J. W. Notebook from his journey to Rome, 1848. Bodleian Library, Oxford. MSS Eng. Misc., fo. 15.

Williams, Isaac. *Devotional commentary on the Gospel narratives.* 8 vols. New edn. London, Oxford, Cambridge: Rivingtons, 1869.

Williams, Isaac. *Female characters of Holy Scripture.* New edn. London, Oxford, Cambridge: Rivingtons, 1869.

Williams, Isaac. *The autobiography of Isaac Williams, B.D.* London and New York: Longmans, Green, & Co., 1892.

Wills, Freeman. *Seven last words from the cross.* London: R. Clay, Sons, & Taylor, 1876.

Wilson, Edward. *Prayer for the dead; and the 'Mater Dei': a letter respectfully addressed to His Grace the Archbishop of Canterbury.* London: Longmans, Green, & Co.; Norwich: Samuel Miller, 1870.

Wilson, Edward. *Our Church calls on ritualists.* Norwich: Stevenson & Co.; London: Longman & Co., n.d. (?1871).

Wilson, Edward. *Our relation to the saints: some notes gathered from English divines.* Privately printed: n.d. (?1874).

Wilson, R. J. *A letter to the Archbishop of Canterbury, on his statements made in the House of Lords, May 8th, with reference to altar cards.* Oxford: A. R. Mowbray & Co., 1874.

Wirgman, A. Theodore. 'The perpetual virginity of the Blessed Virgin Mary'. *The Church eclectic: a monthly magazine* 33: 3 (December 1903), 197–206.

Wiseman, Nicholas. *Lectures on the doctrines and practices of the Roman Catholic Church.* London: J. S. Hodson, 1836.

Wiseman, Nicholas. *Letters to John Poynder, Esq., upon his work entitled 'Popery in alliance with heathenism'.* London: Joseph Booker, 1836.

Wiseman, Nicholas. *A letter respectfully addressed to the Rev. J. H. Newman, upon some passages in his Letter to the Rev. Dr Jelf.* London: Charles Dolman, 1841.

Wiseman, Nicholas. *Remarks on a letter from the Rev. W. Palmer.* London: Charles Dolman, 1841.

Wiseman, Nicholas. *Pastoral letter of His Eminence Cardinal Wiseman, Archbishop of Westminster, announcing the definition of the Immaculate Conception of the Blessed Virgin Mary.* London: T. Jones, 1855.

Wiseman, Nicholas. 'Extracts from a lecture by Cardinal Wiseman'. Ed. J. Shaw Mulholland. In *The world's Madonna: a history of the Blessed Virgin Mary.* London: Burns & Oates; New York, Cincinnati, OH, and Chicago, IL: Benziger Brothers, 1909, pp. 1–11.

W.J.S. 'Fragments on the "Immaculate Conception"'. *Wesleyan–Methodist magazine* (5th series) 1: 2 (February 1855), 150.

(Wood, Charles Lindley) Viscount Halifax. *Proposed legislation on the Prayer Book.* London: English Church Union Office, 1872.

(Wood, Charles Lindley) Viscount Halifax and Lord Redesdale. *The doctrine of the Real Presence: correspondence between the Earl of Redesdale and the Honourable Charles L. Wood.* London: John Murray, 1879.

(Wood, Charles Lindley) Viscount Halifax. *The agitation against the Oxford Movement: an address of Viscount Halifax, President of E.C.U., read at the annual meeting at the Church House on June 15, 1899.* London: Office of the English Church Union, n.d.

(Wood, Charles Lindley) Viscount Halifax. *Proposals for mutual explanation: eucharistic doctrine. An address delivered by Viscount Halifax, President of E.C.U., at the annual meeting at the Church House, on June 21st, 1900.* London: Office of the English Church Union, n.d.

(Wood, Charles Lindley) Halifax, Viscount and George W. E. Russell. *The present position and the common creed of Catholics and evangelicals: addresses by Viscount Halifax and George W. E. Russell delivered at a meeting of the E.C.U. held at the Church House, Westminster, on December 14th, 1898, together with letters written by Lord Halifax to the 'Record' on the proposed conference.* London: English Church Union Office, n.d.

Woodard, N. *A plea for the middle classes.* London: Joseph Masters, n.d. (?1848).

The words of the antiphons to the Magnificat; with a few simple rules for their use. London: J. T. Hayes, 1870.

On the worship of the Virgin Mary by the Church of Rome. n.p.: n.p., n.d. (1862).

The worship of Mary in the Church of Rome: (extracted from Dr. Pusey's 'Eirenicon'), with a few words to ritualists and Protestants. London: William Macintosh, 1868.

Secondary sources

Acton-Wilson, Rosemary. 'Catherine Sinclair (1800–1864) and her books for children'. M.A. dissertation, Loughborough University of Technology, 1983.

Adams, James Eli. *Dandies and desert saints: styles of Victorian masculinity.* Ithaca, NY, and London: Cornell University Press, 1995.

Adams, Kimberley van Esveld. *Our Lady of Victorian feminism: the Madonna in the work of Anna Jameson, Margaret Fuller, and George Eliot.* Athens: Ohio University Press, 2001.

Allchin, A. M. *The silent rebellion: Anglican religious communities 1845–1900*. London: SCM Press, 1958.

Allchin, A. M. *The joy of all creation: an Anglican meditation on the place of Mary*. Rev. edn. London: New City, 1993.

Altholz, Josef L. *The liberal Catholic movement in England: the 'Rambler' and its contributors, 1848–1864*. London: Burns & Oates, 1962.

Altholz, Josef L. 'The Vatican Decrees controversy, 1874–1875'. *Catholic historical review* 57 (1972), 593–605.

Anderson, Janice Capel. 'Mary's difference: gender and patriarchy in the birth narratives'. *Journal of religion* 67 (1987), 183–202.

Arnstein, Walter. *The Bradlaugh case: a study in late Victorian opinion and politics*. Oxford: Clarendon Press, 1965; Columbia: University of Missouri Press, 1984.

Arnstein, Walter. *Protestant versus Catholic in mid-Victorian England: Mr Newdegate and the nuns*. Columbia and London: University of Missouri Press, 1982.

Banks, J. A. and Olive Banks. *Feminism and family planning in Victorian England*. New York: Schocken Books, 1972.

Battiscombe, Georgina. *John Keble: a study in limitations*. London: Constable, 1963.

Battiscombe, Georgina. *Christina Rossetti: a divided life*. London: Constable, 1981.

Bellamy, Joan. 'Barriers of silence: women in Victorian fiction'. In Eric Sigsworth (ed.), *In search of Victorian values: aspects of nineteenth-century thought and society*. Manchester: Manchester University Press, 1988.

Benko, Stephen. *The Virgin Goddess: studies in the pagan and Christian roots of Mariology*. Leiden, New York; Köln: E. J. Brill, 1993.

Bicknell, E. J. *A theological introduction to the Thirty-Nine Articles of the Church of England*. 2nd edn. London: Longmans, Green, and Co., 1925.

Blackbourn, David. *Marpingen: apparitions of the Virgin Mary in nineteenth-century Germany*. New York: Alfred Knopf, 1994.

Blehl, Vincent Ferrer. *The white stone: the spiritual theology of John Henry Newman*. Petersham, MA: St Bede's Publications, 1994.

Bloch, Ruth. 'Untangling the roots of modern sex roles: a survey of four centuries of change'. *Signs* 4 (1978), 237–52.

Bossy, John. *The English Catholic community 1570–1850*. New York: Oxford University Press, 1976.

Bradley, Ian. *Abide with me: the world of Victorian hymns*. London: SCM Press, 1997.

Bradstock, Andrew, Sean Gill, Anne Hogan, and Sue Morgan (eds). *Masculinity and spirituality in Victorian culture*. New York: St. Martin's Press, 2000.

Brandreth, Henry R. T. *Dr Lee of Lambeth: a chapter in parenthesis in the history of the Oxford Movement*. London: SPCK, 1951.

Brendon, Piers. *Hawker of Morwenstow: portrait of a Victorian eccentric*. London: Jonathan Cape, 1975.

Brown, Peter. *The body and society: men, women, and sexual renunciation in early Christianity*. New York: Columbia University Press, 1988.

Brown, Raymond, Karl P. Donfried, Joseph A. Fitzmyer, and John Reumann (eds). *Mary in the New Testament*. New York and Mahwah: Paulist Press, 1978.

Burrow, John. 'Images of time: from Carlylean vulcanism to sedimentary gradualism.' In Stefan Collini, Richard Whatmore, and Brian Young (eds), *History, religion and culture: British intellectual history 1750–1950*. Cambridge: Cambridge University Press, 2000, pp. 198–223.

Butler, Perry (ed.). *Pusey rediscovered*. London: SPCK, 1983.

Carroll, Michael P. *The cult of the Virgin Mary*. Princeton, NJ: Princeton University Press, 1986.

Casteras, Susan P. 'Virgin vows: the early Victorian artists' portrayal of nuns and novices'. *Victorian studies* 24 (1981), 157–84.

Ceraldi, Gabrielle. "Popish legends and Bible truths': English Protestant identity in Catherine Sinclair's *Beatrice*'. *Victorian literature and culture* 31 (2003), 359–72.

Chadwick, Owen. *The Victorian Church*. 2 vols. New York: Oxford University Press, 1966.

Chadwick, Owen. *The spirit of the Oxford Movement*. Cambridge: Cambridge University Press, 1990.

Chandler, Michael. *The life and work of John Mason Neale*. Leominster, Herefordshire: Gracewing, 1995.

Chapman, Ronald. *Father Faber*. Westminster, MD: Newman Press, 1961.

Chinnici, Joseph P. *The English Catholic Enlightenment: John Lingard and the Cisalpine Movement, 1780–1850*. Shepherdstown, WV: Patmos Press, 1980.

Chitty, Susan. *The beast and the monk: a life of Charles Kingsley*. London: Hodder & Stoughton, 1974.

Clark, Anna. *The struggle for the breeches: gender and the making of the British working class*. Berkeley: University of California Press, 1995.

Colley, Linda. *Britons: forging the nation 1707–1837*. New Haven, CT, and London: Yale University Press, 1992.

Colloms, Brenda. *Charles Kingsley: the lion of Eversley*. London: Constable; New York: Barnes & Noble, 1975.

Cott, Nancy F. 'Passionlessness: an interpretation of Victorian sexual ideology, 1790–1850'. *Signs* 4 (1978), 219–36.

Cressy, David. *Birth, marriage and death: ritual, religion and the life-cycle in Tudor and Stuart England*. Oxford: Oxford University Press, 1997.

Cruise, Colin. 'Versions of the Annunciation: Wilde's aestheticism and the message of beauty'. In Elizabeth Prettejohn (ed.), *After the Pre-Raphaelites: art and aestheticism in Victorian England*. Manchester: Manchester University Press, 1999, pp. 167–87.

Cunneen, Sally. *In search of Mary: the woman and the symbol*. New York: Ballantine, 1996.

Curtis, L. P., Jr. *Anglo-Saxons and Celts: a study of anti-Irish prejudice in Victorian England*. Bridgeport, CT: Conference on British Studies, 1968.

Davidoff, Leonore and Catherine Hall. *Family fortunes: men and women of the English middle class, 1780–1850*. Chicago: University of Chicago Press, 1987.

Degler, Carl. 'What ought to be and what was: women's sexuality in the nineteenth century'. *American historical review* 79 (1974), 1467–90.

Delaura, David J. '"O unforgotten voice": the memory of Newman in the nineteenth century'. *Renascence* 43 (1990–91), 81–104.

Dever, Carolyn. *Death and the mother from Dickens to Freud: Victorian fiction and the anxiety of origins*. Cambridge: Cambridge University Press, 1998.

Doherty, Dennis. *The sexual doctrine of Cardinal Cahetan*. Regensburg: Verlag Friedrich Pustet, 1966.

Duggan, Paul E. *The Assumption dogma: some reactions and ecumenical implications in the thought of English-speaking theologians*. Dayton, OH.: International Marian Research Institute, University of Dayton, 1989.

Elliott, Dyan. *Spiritual marriage: sexual abstinence in medieval wedlock*. Princeton, NJ: Princeton University Press, 1993.

Engelhardt, Carol Marie. 'The paradigmatic angel in the house: Victorian Anglicans and the Virgin Mary'. In Anne Hogan and Andrew Bradstock (eds), *Women of faith in Victorian culture: reassessing 'The angel in the house'*. London: Macmillan, 1998, pp. 159–71.

Engelhardt, Carol Marie. 'The Virgin Mary and Victorian masculinity'. In Andrew Bradstock, Sean Gill, and Anne Hogan (eds), *Masculinity and spirituality in Victorian culture*. London: Macmillan, 2000, pp. 44–57.

Engelhardt, Carol Marie. 'Mother Mary and Victorian Protestants'. *Studies in church history* 39 (2002), 298–307.

Forrester, David. 'Dr. Pusey's marriage'. In Perry Butler (ed.), *Pusey rediscovered*. London: SPCK, 1983, pp. 119–38.

Forrester, David. *Young Doctor Pusey: a study in development*. London: Mowbray, 1989.

Franchot, Jenny. *Roads to Rome: the antebellum Protestant encounter with Catholicism*. Berkeley: University of California Press, 1994.

Gay, Peter. *The bourgeois experience: Victoria to Freud*. 5 vols. New York: Oxford University Press, 1984–98.

Gay, Peter. 'The manliness of Christ'. In R. W. Davis and R. J. Helmstader (eds), *Religion and irreligion in Victorian society*. London and New York: Routledge, 1992, pp. 102–16.

Gill, Sean. *Women and the Church of England: From the eighteenth century to the present*. London: SPCK, 1994.

Gill, Sean. 'How muscular was Victorian Christianity? Thomas Hughes and the cult of Christian manliness reconsidered'. *Studies in Church history* 34 (1998), 421–30.

Gill, Sean. '*Ecce homo*: representations of Christ as the model of masculinity in Victorian art and lives of Jesus'. In Andrew Bradstock, Sean Gill, Anne Hogan, and Sue Morgan (eds), *Masculinity and spirituality in Victorian culture*. New York: St. Martin's, 2000, pp. 164–78.

Gilley, Sheridan. *Newman and his age*. London: Danton, Longman, & Todd, 1990.

Golby, J. M. and A. W. Purdue. *The making of the modern Christmas*. Athens: University of Georgia Press, 1986.

Gorham, Deborah. *The Victorian girl and the feminine ideal*. Bloomington: Indiana University Press, 1982.

Gray, Robert. *Cardinal Manning*. New York: St. Martin's Press, 1985.

Graef, Hilda. *Mary: a history of doctrine and devotion*. 2 vols. London and New York: Sheed & Ward, 1965.

Hackett, Helen. *Virgin mother, maiden queen: Elizabeth I and the cult of the Virgin Mary*. London: Macmillan, 1995.

Haskins, Susan. *Mary Magdalene: myth and metaphor*. New York: Harcourt Brace, 1993.

Healy, Philip. 'Man apart: priesthood and homosexuality at the end of the nineteenth century'. In Andrew Bradstock, Sean Gill, Anne Hogan, and Sue Morgan (eds), *Masculinity and spirituality in Victorian culture*. New York: St. Martin's Press, 2000, pp. 100–15.

Heeney, Brian. *A different kind of gentleman: parish clergy as professional men in early and mid-Victorian England*. Hamden, CT: Archon Books for the Conference on British Studies and Wittenberg University, 1976.

Heimann, Mary. *Catholic devotion in Victorian England*. Oxford: Clarendon Press, 1995.

Helsinger, Elizabeth, Robin Lauder Sheets, and William Veeder. *The woman question: society and literature in Britain and America, 1837–1883*. 3 vols. New York: Garland, 1983.

Hill, Michael. *The religious order: a study of virtuoso religion and its legitimation in the nineteenth-century Church of England*. London: Heinemann Educational Books, 1973.

Hinchliff, Peter. *God and history: aspects of British theology, 1875–1914*. Oxford: Clarendon Press; Oxford and New York: Oxford University Press, 1992.

Hogan, Anne and Andrew Bradstock (eds). *Women of faith in Victorian culture: reassessing 'The angel in the house'*. London: Macmillan, 1998.

Homans, Margaret. *Royal representations: Queen Victoria and British culture, 1837–1876*. Chicago and London: University of Chicago Press, 1998.

Homans, Margaret. "To the Queen's private apartments': royal family portraiture and the construction of Victoria's sovereign obedience'. *Victorian studies* 37 (1993), 1–41.

Hudson, Pat. 'Women and industrialization'. In June Purvis (ed.), *Women's history: Britain, 1850–1945. An introduction*. New York: St. Martin's Press, 1995, pp. 23–49.

Hughes, T. Cann. *John Lingard: a learned Lancashire priest*. Lancaster: E. & J. L. Milner, 1907.

Hutchings, W. H. (ed.). *Life and letters of Thomas Thelluson Carter: Warden of the House of Mercy, Clewer; honorary canon of Christ Church, Oxford; and for thirty-six years rector of Clewer*. London: Longmans, Green, & Co., 1903.

......

Hutton, Ronald. *Charles II*. Oxford: Clarendon Press, 1989.

Hylson-Smith, Kenneth. *Evangelicals in the Church of England 1734–1984*. Edinburgh: T. & T. Clark, 1988.

Jankowski, Theodora. *Pure resistance: queer virginity in early modern English drama*. Philadelphia: University of Pennsylvania Press, 2000.

Jenkins, Roy. *Gladstone*. London: Macmillan, 1995.

Johansson, Sheila Ryan. 'Demographic contributions to the history of Victorian women'. In Barbara Kanner (ed.), *The women of England: from Anglo-Saxon times to the present*. Hamden, CT: Archon Books, 1979, pp. 259–95.

Johnson, Elizabeth. 'The symbolic character of theological statements about Mary'. *Journal of ecumenical studies* 22 (1985), 312–335.

Jones, Frederick M., CSSR. *Alphonsus de Liguori: the saint of Bourbon Naples 1696–1787*. Dublin: Gill & Macmillan, 1992.

Jones, O. W. *Isaac Williams and his circle*. London: SPCK, 1971.

Kelly, J. N. D. *Early Church doctrines*. 5th edn. London: A. & C. Black, 1977.

Ker, Ian. *John Henry Newman: a biography*. Oxford: Clarendon Press, 1988.

Ker, Ian. *Newman on being a Christian*. Notre Dame, IN: University of Notre Dame Press, 1990.

Kristeva, Julia. 'Stabat Mater'. *Poetics today* 6 (1985), 133–52.

Krueger, Christine L. *The reader's repentance: women preachers, women writers, and nineteenth-century social discourse*. Chicago and London: University of Chicago Press, 1992.

Kruppa, Patricia. '"More sweet and liquid than any other": Victorian images of Mary Magdalene'. In Richard W. Davis and Richard J. Helmstadter (eds), *Religion and irreligion in Victorian society: essays in honour of R. K. Webb*. London and New York: Routledge, 1992, pp. 117–32.

Laurentin, René. 'The role of the papal magisterium in the development of the dogma of the Immaculate Conception'. Trans. and abr. Charles E. Sheedy and Edward S. Shea. In Edward Dennis O'Connor (ed.), *The dogma of the Immaculate Conception*. Notre Dame, IN: University of Notre Dame Press, 1958, pp. 271–324.

Levine, Philippa. *Victorian feminism 1850–1900*. Gainesville: University Press of Florida, 1994.

Lewis, Judith Schneid. *In the family way: childbearing in the British aristocracy, 1760–1860*. New Brunswick, NJ: Rutgers University Press, 1986.

Lewis, Judith S. *Sacred to female patriotism: gender, class, and politics in late Georgian Britain*. New York and London: Routledge, 2003.

Liddon, Henry Parry. *Life of Edward Bouverie Pusey: Doctor of Divinity; Canon of Christ Church; Regius Professor of Hebrew in the University of Oxford*. 4 vols. 3rd edn. London: Longmans, 1893.

Lockhart, J. G. *Charles Lindley, Viscount Halifax*. Part I: *1830–1885*. London: Geoffrey Bles– Centenary Press, 1935.

Marks, Lara V. *Model mothers: Jewish mothers and maternity provision in East London, 1870–1939*. Oxford: Clarendon Press, 1994.

Magray, Mary Peckham. *The transforming power of the nuns: women, religion, and cultural change in Ireland, 1750-1900*. New York: Oxford University Press, 1998.

Martin, Brian W. *John Keble: priest, professor and poet*. London: Croom Helm, 1976.

Martin, Robert Bernard. *Gerard Manley Hopkins: a very private life*. London: Harper Collins, 1991.

Mason, Michael. *The making of Victorian sexual attitudes*. Oxford and New York: Oxford University Press, 1994.

Maynard, John. *Victorian discourses on sexuality and religion*. Cambridge: Cambridge University Press, 1993.

McDannell, Colleen. *Material Christianity: religion and popular culture in America*. New Haven, CT, and London: Yale University Press, 1995.

Melnyk, Julie (ed.). *Women's theology in nineteenth-century Britain: transfiguring the faith of their fathers*. New York: Garland, 1998.

Melnyk, Julie. "'Mighty victims": women writers and the feminization of Christ'. *Victorian literature and culture* (2003), 131-57.

Miller, Lori M. 'The (re)gendering of high Anglicanism'. In Andrew Bradstock, Sean Gill, Anne Hogan, and Sue Morgan (eds), *Masculinity and spirituality in Victorian Culture*. New York: St. Martin's Press, 2000, pp. 27-43.

Mole, David E. H. 'John Cale Miller: a Victorian rector of Birmingham'. *Journal of ecclesiastical history* 17 (1966), 95-103.

Moscucci, Ornella. *The science of woman: gynaecology and gender in England 1800-1929*. Cambridge: Cambridge University Press, 1990.

Mosse, George. *The image of man: the creation of modern masculinity*. New York and Oxford: Oxford University Press, 1996.

Mumm, Susan. *Stolen daughters, virgin mothers: Anglican sisterhoods in Victorian Britain*. London and New York: Leicester University Press, 1999.

Munich, Adrienne. *Queen Victoria's secrets*. New York: Columbia University Press, 1996.

Nelson, Claudia. *Boys will be girls: the feminine ethic and British children's fiction, 1857-1917*. New Brunswick, NJ: Rutgers University Press, 1991.

Nelson, Claudia and Ann Sumner Holmes (eds). *Maternal instincts: visions of motherhood and sexuality in Britain, 1875-1925*. Houndsmills and London: Macmillan; New York: St. Martin's, 1997.

Newsome, David. *The parting of friends: the Wilberforces and Henry Manning*. Grand Rapids, MI: William B. Eerdmans, 1993.

Nias, J. C. S. *Gorham and the Bishop of Exeter*. London: SPCK, 1951.

Nockles, Peter Benedict. *The Oxford Movement in context: Anglican high churchmanship, 1760-1857*. Cambridge: Cambridge University Press, 1994.

Norman, Edward. *The English Catholic Church in the nineteenth century*. Oxford: Clarendon Press, 1984.

O'Brien Susan. 'French nuns in nineteenth-century England'. *Past and Present* 154 (1997), 142-80.

O'Brien Susan. 'Religious life for women'. In V. Alan McClelland and Michael Hodgetts (eds), *From without the Flaminian Gate: 150 years of Roman*

Catholicism in England and Wales 1850–2000. London: Darton, Longman, & Todd, 1999, pp. 108–41.

O'Connor, Edward Dennis (ed). *The dogma of the Immaculate Conception: history and significance*. Notre Dame, IN: University of Notre Dame Press, 1958.

O'Connor, Maura. *The romance of Italy and the English political imagination*. New York: St. Martin's Press, 1998.

O'Meara, Thomas A. *Mary in Protestant and Catholic theology*. New York: Sheed & Ward, 1966.

O'Neil, Robert. *Cardinal Herbert Vaughan: Archbishop of Westminster, Bishop of Salford, founder of the Mill Hill Missionaries*. Tunbridge Wells, Kent: Burns & Oates, 1995.

Orsi, Robert. *The Madonna of 115th Street: faith and community in Italian Harlem, 1880–1950*. New Haven, CT: Yale University Press, 1985.

Pawley, Bernard and Margaret Pawley. *Rome and Canterbury through four centuries: a study of the relations between the Church of Rome and the Anglican Churches, 1530–1973*. New York: Seabury, 1975.

Pawley, Margaret. *Faith and family: the life and circle of Ambrose Phillips de Lisle*. Norwich: Canterbury Press, 1993.

Paz, D. G. *Popular anti-Catholicism in mid-Victorian England*. Stanford, CA: Stanford University Press, 1992.

Pelikan, Jaroslav. *Mary through the centuries: her place in the history of culture*. New Haven, CT, and London: Yale University Press, 1996.

Perkin, Joan. *Women and marriage in nineteenth-century England*. London: Routledge, 1989.

Peterson, M. Jeanne. *Family, love, and work in the lives of Victorian gentlewomen*. Bloomington and Indianapolis: Indiana University Press, 1989.

Poovey, Mary. *Uneven developments: The ideological work of gender in mid-Victorian England*. Chicago: University of Chicago Press, 1988.

Pope, Barbara Corrado. 'Immaculate and powerful: the Marian revival in the nineteenth century'. In Clarissa W. Atkinson, Constance H. Buchanan and Margaret R. Miles (eds), *Immaculate and powerful: the female in sacred image and social reality*. Boston, MA: Beacon Press, 1985. pp. 173–200.

Purvis, June (ed.). *Women's history: Britain, 1850–1945: an introduction*. New York: St. Martin's Press, 1995.

Reed, John Shelton. '"A female movement": the feminization of nineteenth-century Anglo-Catholicism'. *Anglican and episcopal history* 57 (1988), 199–238.

Reed, John Shelton. *Glorious battle: the cultural politics of Victorian Anglo-Catholicism*. Nashville, TN, and London: Vanderbilt University Press, 1996.

Reuther, Rosemary. 'The collision of history and doctrine: the brothers of Jesus and the virginity of Mary'. *Continuum* 7 (1969), 93–105.

Robson, Catherine. *Men in Wonderland: the lost girlhood of the Victorian gentleman*. Princeton, NJ, and Oxford: Princeton University Press, 2001.

Roden, Frederick S. 'Aelred of Rievaulx, same-sex desire and the Victorian monastery'. In Andrew Bradstock, Sean Gill, Anne Hogan, and Sue Morgan (eds), *Masculinity and spirituality in Victorian culture*. New York: St. Martin's

Press, 2000, pp. 85–99.

Roper, Michael and John Tosh (eds). *Manful assertions: masculinities in Britain since 1800*. London: Routledge, 1991.

Rowbotham, Judith. *Good girls make good wives: guidance for girls in Victorian fiction*. Oxford and New York: Blackwell, 1989.

Rowell, Geoffrey. *Hell and the Victorians: a study of the nineteenth-century theological controversies concerning eternal punishment and the future life*. Oxford: Clarendon Press, 1974.

Rowell, Geoffrey. *The vision glorious: themes and personalities of the Catholic revival in Anglicanism*. Oxford: Oxford University Press, 1983.

Russell, Anthony. *The clerical profession*. London: SPCK, 1980.

St Aubyn, Giles. *Edward VII: prince and king*. New York: Atheneum, 1979.

Schiefen, Richard J. *Nicholas Wiseman and the transformation of English Catholicism*. Shepherdstown, WV: Patmos Press, 1984.

Showalter, Elaine. 'Florence Nightingale's feminist complaint: women, religion, and *Suggestions for thought*'. *Signs* 6 (1981), 395–412.

Singleton, John. 'The Virgin Mary and religious conflict in Victorian Britain'. *Journal of ecclesiastical history* 43 (1992), 16–34.

Snead-Cox, J. G. *The life of Cardinal Vaughan*. 2 vols. London: Herbert & Daniel; St Louis: B. Herder, 1910.

Stearns, Carol Z. and Peter N. Stearns. 'Victorian sexuality: can historians do it better?' *Journal of social history* 18 (summer 1985), 625–34.

Stearns, Peter. *Be a man! Males in modern society*. 2nd edn. New York & London: Holmes & Meier, 1990.

Stephens, W. R. W. *The life and letters of Walter Farquhar Hook*. 6th edn. London: Richard Bentley & Son, 1881.

Stocking, George W., Jr. *Victorian anthropology*. New York: Free Press; London: Collier, Macmillan, 1987.

Strange, Roderick. 'Reflections on a controversy: Newman and Pusey's "Eirenicon"'. In Perry Butler (ed.), *Pusey rediscovered*. London: SPCK, 1983, pp. 332–48.

Thompson, Dorothy. *Queen Victoria: the woman, the monarchy, and the people*. New York: Pantheon, 1990.

Toon, Peter. *Evangelical theology 1833–1856: a response to Tractarianism*. Atlanta, GA: John Knox Press, 1979.

Tosh, John. 'Domesticity and manliness in the Victorian middle class: the family of Edward White Benson'. In Michael Roper and John Tosh (eds), *Manful assertions: masculinities in Britain since 1800*. London: Routledge, 1991, pp. 44–73.

Tosh, John. *A man's place: masculinity and the middle-class home in Victorian England*. New Haven, CT, and London: Yale University Press, 1999.

Twycross-Martin, Henrietta. 'Woman supportive or woman manipulative? The "Mrs Ellis" woman'. In Clarissa Campbell Orr (ed.), *Wollstonecraft's daughters: womanhood in England and France 1780–1920*. Manchester and New York: Manchester University Press, 1996. pp. 109–20.

Urban, Linwood. *A short history of Christian thought*. Rev. edn. New York and Oxford: Oxford University Press, 1995.

Vanden Bussche, Jozef. *Ignatius (George) Spencer, Passionist (1799–1864), crusader of prayer for England and pioneer of ecumenical prayer*. Leuven, Belgium: Leuven University Press, 1991.

Vandervelde, George. *Original sin: two major trends in contemporary Roman Catholic reinterpretation*. Washington, DC: University Press of America, 1975.

Vanita, Ruth. *Sappho and the Virgin Mary: same-sex love and the English literary imagination*. New York: Columbia University Press, 1996.

Vannete, Alfred. *The dogma of original sin*. Trans. Edward P. Callens. Louvain: Vander, 1975.

Veldman, Meredith. 'Dutiful daughter versus all-boy: Jesus, gender, and the secularization of Victorian society'. *Nineteenth-century studies* 11 (1997), 1–24.

Vickery, Amanda. *The gentleman's daughter: women's lives in Georgian England*. New Haven, CT, and London: Yale University Press, 1998.

Vickery, Amanda. 'Golden age to separate spheres? A review of the categories and chronology of English women's history'. In Pamela Sharpe (ed.), *Women's work: the English experience 1650–1914*. London: Arnold, 1998, pp. 294–332.

Walker, Pamela. *Pulling the Devil's kingdom down: the Salvation Army in Victorian Britain*. Berkeley and Los Angeles: University of California Press, 2001.

Warner, Marina. *Alone of all her sex: the myth and the cult of the Virgin Mary*. New York: Knopf, 1976.

Webb, R. K. 'The Victorian reading public'. In Boris Ford (ed.), *The new Pelikan guide to English literature*. Vol. 6: *From Dickens to Hardy*. New York: Penguin Books, 1982.

Weintraub, Stanley. *Four Rossettis: a Victorian biography*. London: W. H. Allen, 1978.

Weintraub, Stanley. *Victoria: an intimate biography*. New York: E. P. Dutton, 1987.

Wheeler, Michael. *Ruskin's God*. Cambridge: Cambridge University Press, 1999.

Wolfe, John. *The Protestant crusade in Great Britain, 1829–1860*. Oxford: Clarendon Press, 1991.

Woodham-Smith, Cecil. *Queen Victoria: from her birth to the death of the Prince Consort*. New York: Alfred A. Knopf, 1972.

Yarnold, Edward. *The theology of original sin*. Notre Dame, IN: Fides Publishers, 1971.

Yates, Nigel. *Anglican ritualism in Victorian Britain, 1830–1910*. Oxford and New York: Clarendon Press, 1999.

Zimdars-Swartz, Sandra L. *Encountering Mary: from LaSalette to Medjugorge*. Princeton, NJ: Princeton University Press, 1991.

Index

Note: 'n.' after a page number indicates the number of a note on that page.

Lightning Source UK Ltd.
Milton Keynes UK
UKOW04f1128300514

232595UK00015B/199/P